LIVING IN, LIVING OUT

LIVING IN, LIVING OUT

▼▼▼

AFRICAN AMERICAN DOMESTICS IN WASHINGTON, D.C., 1910–1940

ELIZABETH CLARK-LEWIS

SMITHSONIAN INSTITUTION PRESS

WASHINGTON AND LONDON

TO
LAWRENCE J. LEWIS
AND
ABENA M. S. LEWIS

© 1994 by the Smithsonian Institution
All rights reserved

Copy Editor: Karin Kaufman
Production Editor: Jenelle Walthour
Designer: Janice Wheeler

Library of Congress Cataloging-in-Publication Data
Clark-Lewis, Elizabeth.
   Living in, living out : African American domestics in Washington, D.C., 1910-1940 /
Elizabeth Clark-Lewis.
       p.   cm.
Includes bibliographical references.
ISBN 1-56098-362-0 (cloth)
   1. Women domestics—Washington (D.C.)—History—20th century. 2. Afro-Ameri-
can women—Employment—Washington (D.C.)—History—20th century. I. Title.
HD6072.2.U52W183   1994
331.4'8169046'09753—dc20   94-14415

British Library Cataloguing-in-Publication Data is available

Manufactured in the United States of America
01 00 99 98 97 96 95   5 4 3 2

♾ The paper used in this publication meets the minimum requirements of the
American National Standard for Permanence of Paper for Printed Library Materials
Z39.48-1984.

CONTENTS

PREFACE

The pictures of women in my family are portraits of persons who defiantly believed you worked "to survive." Their lives were full of family work, community work, church work, work-work, and more work. My mother spent four of her forty-five years of employment as a "dayworker." My grandmother, Katie Chivis, had been a live-in servant for eight years—until her marriage and migration to Pennsylvania in 1916. My great-grandmother, Eliza S. Johnson, was born a slave in Virginia in 1853. After the end of slavery, she worked sixteen years as a "servant" and an additional sixty as a washerwoman while bearing a child every twenty-three months, rearing seventeen children, and mothering her husband's other sixteen children. My great-great-grandmother, "Miss Winnie," was a slave in Fauquier County, Virginia, until 1865. She worked as a servant for twenty-two of the twenty-four years she lived after emancipation.

I knew all these women's names but only some of their stories. As a child I loved to sit and listen as my mother, aunts, and their friends talked about their daywork stories. Each story had an Anansee quality to it; the African American poor girl outwits "Miss Ann" in the end.

When my great-aunts visited Pennsylvania, however, they told stories far better than those of my mother and her sisters. They talked about "live-in service" and chided the women of my mother's generation for not knowing hard times and for never having to work day and night on a stay-in job for twenty-five cents a month. They made my mother's ten-to-twelve-hour work days and two dollars a day appear to be a great improvement. They openly lamented missing "the money and better daywork-work" era of the women of the Depression! Then they always ended with a prayer of thanks for not having been slaves. They talked for hours, comparing their mothers' and grandmothers' plight to that of women born after "slave times."

Writing a book about these women and the work they performed demanded extensive research. Using the existing histories, I learned about the great women—those with well-known names—and their contributions to history in spite of the double confinements of discrimination and oppression, but not about women like my ancestors, living relatives, and neighbors. Where were they in the books, where were their voices? This book tries to recover those voices.

ACKNOWLEDGMENTS

They came from Midnight, Mississippi, and Dawn, Virginia; they told about families left behind in Blackman, Florida, and Whitesville, Kentucky; they shared the secrets of African American culture learned in Faith, North Carolina, and Hope, Texas. First and foremost, it is to these women I extend my thanks. My debt is deep to all of the women who agreed to be interviewed for this book. They unselfishly gave their time, shared with me their history, and filled in the gaps of my history. Without the willingness of each of them to be interviewed, this book would not exist. They helped me travel to different places, explore new worlds, and understand life for women reared eighty to more than a hundred years ago. They enriched my understanding of the past and deepened my appreciation of the many ways young African Americans owe a debt of gratitude to them all.

Mrs. K. Elizabeth J. Campbell helped me to arrange my first family interviews. She also shared her insights on many sensitive local historical points during the project, and gave this manuscript its final review. Her seventy-six years of wisdom helped me, and I thank her. Betty Robertson and Kenneth Banks each introduced me to ten women, and the twenty interviews they made possible are the core of my research. These two friends have been essential to this book's development. My special thanks go to the following for their invaluable contacts and assistance: Elaine Blackwell, Delta Towers Senior Citizens Residence; Rosetta Bailey, Pendleton House Senior Citizens Residence; Ellen Killens, Portner Place Senior Center; LaShawn Bynum, Campbell Heights Senior Center; Carmen James Lane and Thelma Russell, Potomac Gardens

Senior Citizens Council; Gwendolyn Coleman, Columbia Heights Senior Citizens Center; Ruth DeBerry, Pentacle Senior Citizens Center; Brenda Tucker, First Baptist Senior Center; Carolyn Mills-Bowden, Washington, D.C., Office on Aging; Seniors Coalition, James Creek Public Housing Community Center; and the Senior Citizens Club, Shiloh Baptist Church.

Many scholars have kindly shared their research with me, always going beyond the ordinary requirements of scholarly pursuit: Drs. Phyllis Palmer, Faye Dudden, Robert Hall, Jacqueline Jones, Daphaney Harrison, Paul Phillips Cook, Debra Newman Ham, Thomas Battle, Walter Hill, and Pamela Ferrell; Artie Myers, Library of Congress; Karen Jefferson, Director of the Manuscript Division, Moorland Spingarn Research Center; Roxanna Deane, Director, and Mary Ternes, Photo Librarian, in the Washingtoniana Division, Martin Luther King Memorial Library, Washington, D.C.; and the staff of the Schomburg Center for Research in Black Culture.

Mark Hirsch of the Smithsonian Institution Press supported this project and made its completion possible. The cogent editing skills, suggestions, and directions of Jenelle Walthour, Judith Sacks, and Karin Kaufman immeasurably improved the final draft of the manuscript. The critical judgment and literary suggestions of Elizabeth F. Rankin and Carmen Lattimore shaped the early drafts of the manuscript. The keen eye and good judgment of Jeff Fearing assisted me in all aspects of my photograpic research work. I thank Tamas deKun for his photo-copying workmanship. Friends Yvette Murphy Aidara, Barbara Carter, Dureau Smith, and my niece, Kim Williams, each read, re-read, and re-reread drafts. For their support I am grateful.

Especially in connection with the beginning of the project, I thank Professor John Caughey and the late Gene Wise of the University of Maryland for their support. Drs. Olive Taylor, Roy Rosensweig, and Claire Moses were dissertation committee members who lovingly supported me in the last stages of graduate school and tirelessly helped me with this project. Drs. Mary Beth Norton, Elizabeth Higgenbotham, Bonnie Thorton Dill, Joseph Jordan, Darlene Clark-Hine, Katherine Kish Sklar, and Thomas Dublin are thanked for the comments they made on articles that I have written. Many of their thoughtful suggestions are incorporated here.

In 1986, the Smithsonian Institution awarded me a postdoctoral fellowship, and its many scholars made invaluable suggestions for my research. Among these, Dr. Spencer Crew has become a friend, counselor, and advocate. Drs. Bernice Reagon, James Horton, and Gwendolyn Keita Robinson also provided important support. As the 1987 Benjamin Banneker Professor of George Washington University, I benefited from the comments of Professors Howard Gillette, Dennis Gale, and John M. Vlach. In 1990, a Penn State University Visiting Professorship allowed me to examine the cross-regional dimensions of women's migration, and to Dr. William Mahar of Pennsylvania State-Capital Campus, I am grateful. In 1991, the Office of the Vice President for Academic Affairs at Howard University awarded me a research grant that allowed for the transcription of ten tapes and the reindexing of more than one hundred tapes made during this project. To Dr. Joyce Ladner I am especially grateful for this support. Dr. Emory J. Tolbert and Elizabeth Lambert Johns, my departmental chairpersons at Howard University and Northern Virginia Community College, provided unfailing encouragement. The Department of History at Howard University provided two things most scholars find in short supply, time and money. I thank the department for the two research-support grants. At both institutions, I have been inspired by the confidence of my colleagues in my ability to complete this book.

Many people helped me along by asking about my work and validating my ideas: Robyn Penn, Marsha Gundy, Garnett Stowe, Patricia Long, Doris Howard, Anita Byrd, Sonja Ray. Drs. Thomas Gay, Lorranine Gillian, and Shana Beatty provided essential care for the Lewis family, and each took time away from their busy schedules to talk to me and to encourage me in my work. The Shiloh Baptist Church (especially the John A. Miles Sunday school class) and the Bible study group of St. Mary's Baptist Church gave me essential support.

This project also owes much of its existence to those people who had a part in my Harrisburg, Pennsylvania, childhood. The Clark, Chivis, and Johnson families taught me my earliest and most important history lessons. I thank the Lewis, Mapoma, and Johnson families of Philadelphia for their patience and support.

My family is a constant source of inspiration and caring. My father, the late Edward T. Clark, Sr., and Jean Elizabeth Clark, my mother, always believed in me and encouraged my interest in "Negro History." Via lengthy long-distance calls, my sister, Dr. Carolyn Carter of Harrisburg, Pennsylvania, and, my brothers, William Dillon and Robert Dillon of California, gave me encouragement to complete this book. My sister, Kathryn Clark-Benjamin, and brother, Edward T. Clark, Jr., because they live closest to me, shouldered unfair burdens without complaint. From pulling weeds in my yard to preparing meals in my home, Kathryn did everything possible to help me stay focused on the completion of this book during my last months of work. From automobile emergencies to food shopping tasks, Edward was supportive in too many ways to list, but his willingness to "be there for me" must be acknowledged.

My daughter, Abena M. S. Lewis, is a Tuesday-born gift of God. As a preschooler, her loving smiles inspired me as I wrote my dissertation. She helped me research information for articles during her elementary school years and complete a television documentary while she was in middle school. As a high school student, she enthusiastically read and edited the manuscript of this book. Her insightful comments defied her youthful age. Abena, you are my inspiration for the book, and I pray you will be inspired by it.

My husband, Lawrence J. Lewis, must receive my deepest thanks. He has supported me in every project—from my thesis during our first year of marriage to this book in our twenty-second. His love gave me the courage I needed to succeed and the his willingness to juggle parental and professional responsibilities make each day truly easier than it would otherwise be. His careful attention to details—especially his computer expertise—moved my research along. There are not enough words to thank him for all of his support.

INTRODUCTION

My eighty-eight-year-old great-aunt Marie Stone[1] had long promised to take me to a "social" meeting of her "ladies' association," the Twelfth Street Bible Club in Washington, D.C. For me this was an eagerly anticipated event, not only because I was researching household workers and all the members of the group were former domestics, but also because this club has been in operation for more than sixty-seven years, and each member has acquired some modicum of social or civic prominence in her own right. Over the years these women have saved large sums of money together and assisted one another during hard times. Collectively, they have recognized the weddings, birth dates, and illnesses of fellow members and their families. And they faithfully attend and support all activities and programs honoring their members for church, "court," or community service.

The meeting was at one o'clock on a Saturday afternoon in October. It was a comfortable and blustery day, with the early autumn leaves falling all over the streets. I arrived at the home of my aunt and found her prepared to begin the long, slow walk out of her house. Each step was followed by a lengthy rest for the legs that had carried her for nearly nine decades. During our walk to the car, we talked about her club and why it was important for her to attend the monthly meetings. As I drove her to the meeting, held at a large house on New Jersey Avenue in northwest Washington, D.C., she explained the Bible club's history.

It was now warm in the sunlight, and as we approached the front of the house, we could see the Capitol (on our left and about one mile away) framed by red and gold leaves. The house had been converted into three small apartments. The doorbell for the first-floor apartment we wanted did not work, and we had to knock for several minutes before our hostess, a slim, demure, light brown woman, answered the door. She apologized for being slow but said she was "old now and don't move good no more."

The apartment was decorated with beautiful antique furniture, which the hostess said was still in style when her employer gave it to her in 1919. The other eight women laughed with me, and I felt less foreign in this group of elegantly clad, proper ladies. I wore a simple skirt, open-collar shirt, and blazer to the meeting. The club members were dressed in expensive, tailored suits and dress ensembles with matching hats and gloves. Although the women complained of age-associated physical ailments, their minds were sharp and their conversation crisp. They discussed current events, the presidency, and local politics with ease and accuracy. They were not at all what I had expected.

At eighty-eight, my Aunt Marie was the youngest member and served as secretary. After giving "sick" reports, assigning benevolences, and collecting dues (savings) in a small envelope, which my aunt tucked back into her "pocketbook," the meeting was adjourned, and the hostess summoned us to move into the dining room, where a large table laden with exquisite sterling silver, English bone china, and fine crystal awaited us. Trying to appear nonplussed, I scanned the pyramid of seven plates, five forks, four spoons, and three knives set before me. There were at least four different glasses, a cup and saucer, and a bread and salad plate. In addition, there were some odd-shaped, unfamiliar objects on top of the setting that I did not know what to do with—eat, wear, or what.

After the senior member, the vice-president, blessed the food, the hostess began serving our meal in courses. I lost count after the sixth course. The ladies were adroitly manipulating the pyramid of dishes and processing the proper utensils for each course. After about my third faux pas, my poor aunt openly apologized to the others for my obvious lack of manners. She smiled timidly, saying, "This girl just doesn't know nothing about these things. She didn't ever do service work." They all nodded politely, making it clear that they were fully aware of my embarrassing conduct.

With my humble admission of guilt, they collectively offered me some pointers on the proprieties of multicourse dining. And, most important, they felt free to divulge how they had learned about such meals. They described how the help served courses, noting that wealthy persons wrongly assumed that every servant was born knowing how to function at even the most formal occasions. Women served certain courses, they explained, but the butler was expected to serve others.

They giggled and winked as privileged allusions were drawn of some of Washington's most famous and wealthy families. The women were clever mimics, and it was clear that they knew intimately the mannerisms of these famous people. They talked about employers who had tried to "use" them and how they had always managed to use their employers just as much.

According to my great-aunt, in the more than sixty-seven years her Bible club has been meeting, wine had been served with every meal. She drolly confided that one member of the group had even kept the meetings supplied with "bathtub gin" during Prohibition. It was nearly dusk when we left the tea party (as I call it), and as I unlatched the wrought-iron fence that encompassed the house, Aunt Marie smiled at me and said how proud she was of me and all her young nieces and nephews. She had never had children herself, she said, but she tried to bring at least one of us to a meeting every year "to show us off."

On the drive back to her house she reminisced about having gone through "hell and high water" to get her driver's permit in the late twenties, recalling that her brother and other men had adamantly professed that women should never drive. She showed me where she lived when she first migrated north and where she had rented her first room after she had married. Both she and her husband were live-in servants at the time, and they paid rent on a room they slept in together maybe four times a month—if they were lucky! Most months they went there together just twice. But she said she slipped away to her apartment every opportunity she got, with or without him. She would cook on a tiny stove in the room, relax, and "have a few minutes of peace to myself." With a chuckle she admitted that she had enjoyed the room better when her husband had not been there.

When we reached her house she winked and said softly as she opened the car door that her only disappointment with younger women like myself was that we never wore hats and gloves. But again, she sighed, she was sure that it was because we had never been servants. To Aunt Marie, those of us who never had to "show or prove" that we were real women—ladies—seemed to "have forgotten the art altogether." There had been many gains "for colored girls," she admitted, nodding slowly, but she wondered if there had not been some losses too.

For a long time after she had gone inside, I sat in my car remembering the tea party and the lovely old ladies with their meticulously attended benevolences and their fashionable hats, gloves, and proper table manners. Staring blankly at my bare, untended hands on the steering wheel, I considered what my great-aunt had said. And I too wondered about my losses.

This book looks at the women, like my great-aunt Marie, who migrated to the urban North—Washington, D.C.—from the rural South to work as domestic servants in the first three decades of this century. The oral histories I collected from my own family members and other elderly women in the Washington area helped me recognize the subtle process of women's migration and provided me with insights into the impact of these African American migrants on United States history during an era of vast transformation.[2]

The story unfolds from the women's own words. I interviewed ninety-seven women who were a part of the Great Migration. Eighty-one were born in the rural South between 1882 and 1911. The majority of them came from the Atlantic coastal upper South—nineteen were born in Virginia, fifteen in North Carolina, and ten in South Carolina. Of the remaining women, eight were born in Georgia, seven in Mississippi, six in Alabama, five in Florida, four in Arkansas, three in Louisiana, and two each in Tennessee and Kentucky. For these African American women, their progression from South to North birthed a parallel progression to a world of expanded economic and social opportunity.[3]

These women brought to Washington, D.C., parcels of the South, both literal and figurative, in their "freedom bags"—the small suitcases they brought from the rural South. In time, however, their urban experiences caused them to modify many of their southern ideas and values. And they developed the determination to transform a master-servant relationship into an employer-employee relationship. This reformation of and by African American women at work is my subject.[4]

Chapter 1 traces the young women's roots from the post-Reconstruction South. Through a detailed account of African American family life in farming communities, the reader encounters a South in the throes of economic turmoil and racial oppression. In chapter 2, migration emerges as a complex response by African Americans to their limited economic and social prospects. We learn how families directed and timed the journeys of girls with an amazing degree of forethought and precision.

In chapter 3, the women recount how their families directed them through a critical transition: the adjustment to urban life in Washington, D.C. They experienced a radical reordering of their family life, worship, work, and leisure time. Like many of the stories migrants tell to establish their identities after they have settled in a new community, this chapter posits both who the migrants were and who they were not.[5]

Chapter 4 surveys the life of domestic workers—the world of the vast proportion of employed African American women in Washington, D.C., between 1900 and 1920.[6] These migrants to the nation's capitol shared the prevailing view of domestic work as the only work for poor, African American women born in the rural South; however, we discover that the white households of Washington proved to be environments of abuse and frustration for many domestic workers.

Chapter 5 presents a historic moment in the migrant women's social and occupational evolution: the awakening of a sense that they might determine their own work lives, independent of familial and social pressures. The women show how they overcame the limits placed on them and prepared to make the transition from live-in servant to daily paid worker. Chapter 6 paints a richly detailed portrait of these women after their change to daywork—a change so profound that it transformed their lives. They explain how live-out work granted them the ability to control their working hours and conditions, to have more privacy, and to participate more fully in African American community life. The women tell how small things, such as their desperate desire to attend Bible-study class or take in a show at the Howard Theater, prodded their quest for more independence and freedom.

Chapter 7 departs in format from the preceding narrative. In a series of vignettes, a select group of women flesh out their lives in detail, affording a more personal encounter with them as individuals. Pivoting around the theme of survival, chapter 7 opens the door to women who faced adversity in their own way, often armed with only their strong faith and their good will. Their testimonies speak clearly to the myths surrounding African American women's lives in America. Despite the constraints of their race, gender, and class, these women were never passive, powerless, one-dimensional workers. The barriers they encountered came to serve as impetuses for change; when courage collided with caution, they transformed work life not only for themselves but for all African American women.

My research has been guided by a scholarly interest in the migration experience of African American women in the beginning of this century. But beyond filling in the record for the sake of historians, I have worked to give voice to elderly African American women. In so doing, the women of *Living In, Living Out* refashion our knowledge of history, just as they remade the world of domestic work as young migrants so many decades ago. These women explain, as African American activist Anna J. Cooper stated in 1892, "when and where" they enter historical scholarship and tell their own story.[7] Herein lies the half that's never been told.

1
GOD AND
THEY PEOPLE:
THE RURAL SOUTH

Daddy worked the field and Ma always worked out by the week. All of us
childrens had chores to do day or night. But from little on up you knew you
had to help. Kids, everybody. You knew it was hard times and everybody was
expected to help the family.

—WEIDA EDWARDS, AGE EIGHTY-FOUR

Esther Lawson, a tall woman with soft eyes and a smooth, brown
complexion, was born "on a sharecrop in Bells Landing, Alabama. I
don't know how old I am or nothing. I go by a certificate that says
I'm ninety-one years old." Her family, like three out of four African
American families in the South, had worked for shares or wages.[1] "We
worked hard, moved every year, and never had two coins to rub together," said Mrs. Lawson. She described a life of picking cotton while
crawling on her knees. With clarity she recalled how the family would
plant, chop, and harvest cotton on the small plot of land they received
from white landowners. As a child, she also worked in the small garden
where the family grew vegetables. Mrs. Lawson knew the difficulties of
this life, and she said it was often compared to "slave times," a period
her family discussed a great deal.[2]

NOTHING IS WHAT

Velma Davis's family was unique as a tenant family. They had been
bound in a feudal relationship with the white Mitchell family of Nelson
County, Virginia, since slavery. The Davises were one of only two ten-

ant families that remained on the land of their former slave owner. With innocent pathos, this thin, light brown woman painstakingly described the patriarchal domination of her family by their rural southern employer prior to migration to Washington, D.C., in 1916:

I loved my fireside training. All of us, we'd be sitting around that open fireplace. We didn't have much else. So we'd be in the big room with Mr. Mitchell. We'd sit down there with him and do what you'd call hand work 'til he was ready to go to bed. We'd be picking beans, cleaning potatoes, or whatever we was told. And he'd look for us, too. If my uncle went out to deliver some furniture he'd made, or anything, Mr. Mitchell'd ask, "Where's Elliott? Somebody go see where he is." Then Mr. Mitchell would explain something he'd read in the Bible, and he'd help us understand what he'd read. He didn't have much education, but he taught us right there at the fireside. His father'd done the same with my grandmother and them way back too. . . . "If you wash dishes, do a good job; clean the best; farm the best," that's what he trained us. Mr. Mitchell liked us to sit with him. He'd talk about everything. Other than church, his words was the law. But even Mr. Mitchell didn't meddle with God and that church.

He didn't have an education. "So, I want you to get all you can," he said. But he seemed to get mad when my father and uncle cut wood for our school—but he never stayed that way. Now, during the war he'd fought to free niggers so he never stayed that way [angry]; not five minutes. Mr. Mitchell took care of us—the Wilsons. He never gave us money. When crops came in he took the money and put it all in the bank in Massies Mill [Virginia]. That's what he told my father and uncle for years. When the war come, though, the money was needed. My daddy and uncle went to the bank to get out the money Mr. Mitchell had been saving for us, and the bank manager laughed. [Mr. Mitchell] hadn't put in nothing. Not one dime. What could they do? *Nothing* is what! Two months later my daddy died of a stroke.

Only two women of the eighty-one interviewed remained on the land of their former masters[3] after slavery, but all recalled the nearly absolute power white landowners had over African American families.[4] In the post-Civil War South, nothing threatened whites more than the loss of control over African Americans. The federal government failed to institute a comprehensive land-confiscation and redistribution program, and southern whites refused to sell property or extend credit to former slaves. As a result, African Americans largely remained yoked economically to the people (if not the individual owners) whom they had served as slaves.[5]

African Americans confronted freedom well aware of rural white southerners' sensibilities and expectations. Segregation had shaped a world in which African American labor meant labor in the service of whites. In the words of ninety-year-old Fannie Sheffield, born in 1902 in Tennessee, "My granddaddy was a colored man. He used his back. My grandmama was colored, so she used her hands. We seen as the maid for somebody white—by every white. Period."

But survival was an active, not a reactive, process for African Americans. Emancipation was not seen as a gift bestowed on passive slaves by Union soldiers or presidential proclamation; it was seen as the opportunity for free people to cease to labor for masters and instead work to provide for one another. Gaining freedom did not change their view of work as a cardinal obligation of African American life, but for the first time African American women saw the possibility of setting their own work pace and shielding their families from the rancor of whites. Guided by the elders and leaders of the African American community—the grandfathers, grandmothers, granduncles, and grandaunts, as well as the heads of individual families[6]—the first generation of free women embarked on a journey toward self-determination.

WHO DIDN'T WORK?

For this generation of women, the constraints of race, gender, and class had defined household work as "their" work. They all knew women slaves and carried vivid memories of labor in the slave era. Contrary to the idea of some researchers of postemancipation African American life, none of the women of *Living In, Living Out* considered their family history "an unpleasant memory that they did not want to dwell upon."[7]

The Marrett family of Campbell County, Virginia, about 1920. Courtesy of the Marrett family.

Each spoke at length about her early life and the great influence of former slaves. Each was very willing to clarify historical myths, particularly the notion that African American women no longer worked outside the home after emancipation.[8] In fact, African American women provided much more than housework for their families; they also contributed financially to their households, enabling their families to enjoy the sweet fruits of emancipation.[9] Bernice Reeder's memory was as clean and uncluttered as her immaculate home, where she, at the age of ninety-seven, still clips her lawn down on her hands and knees with small hand shears. She articulated the realities of African American women's work life when she discovered that the 1900 census had recorded her mother's status as "keeping house." With one finger hiding a very rarely seen smile, she asked, "Is that what those papers says? Oh I guess that record said right. Keeping house. . . . 'tis true. But they didn't ask *whose* house she was keeping. I guess they needed to ask 'where do you keep house?' Then they'd heard 'for Miss Neill, Miss Campbell, the Ricks, or the Dickersons.'"

Freed women exercised considerable influence in their families and communities.[10] The mothers, not the fathers, decided which members of the family would work, and for whom. Speaking loudly to compensate for the shouts and giggles of the five preschoolers in her care, eighty-eight-year-old Beulah Nelson of Maytonsburg, South Carolina, stated:

All the womens—the ones what was under farming or off the farms, had to work in the fields, and then they had to work for these white people—domestic work. They had to work, baby . . . we children had to go in that field, pick that cotton. . . . We had to hoe that cotton, strip quarter, pick up the potatoes, pick peas—everything so she could work. My mother was the one who decided everything about housekeeping and us.

Darethia Handy, born in 1897 to an East Texas tenant farming family at the turn of the century, knew a world in which work was the only option for African American women. With one brow raised, she asked:

Who didn't work? From the time I knew anything about life as such, my grandmama, mama, and aunties worked. Period. I never heard them talking about a break for no time, to before even the end of slave days. Who could have lived without everybody working each day, every day just like Mama meant it to be? She had the last say on everything that had to do with work.

Darethia's mother, like Bernice Reeder's, also was recorded as "keeping house" in the censuses of 1900 and 1910. When asked to explain this error, Darethia shrugged: "Who'd tell them Cooks Mill [Titus County] people what anybody really did? Not us who'd know. Or maybe my daddy did, and he'd say that knowing different, I guess." Cordella May Lawson, a petite woman with very coarse brown skin, walked briskly with the aid of an ornate cane. The usually spirited woman, born in 1906, grew quiet as she considered the question. Perhaps, she suggested, a man's pride was at stake before the census taker:

A woman didn't talk out to anybody as I recall—it is just not like now for a woman. A man would talk on things like that to people. Then, you see, any man would try to talk hisself up—when he could—make his wife at home. I suppose to be like everybody else around, or maybe white people . . . but I know my Mama was always working, since she was two or so. No stopping.

In rejecting the forced pace of the slave regimen and embracing a new system of labor, freed women still maintained the values of traditional rural society, in which church, home, and family came before personal ambition.[11] Zelma Powell, a woman with very keen brown facial features and a clever mind, explained how her mother's work life had to adjust to the death of "Big Mom," her grandmother:

Mama did live-in work. She'd leave Sunday and be working at the Wills' 'til late Saturday. She did cooking, cleaning, and washing for them. My cousin was there to mind they childrens. Mama did everything for them people's house.

I was born in 1898, and Big Mom died when I was near seven, so I know she stopped then. We still needed money, but she had to come home to raise us up with Big Mom gone. From then she did wash, sewing, and working out just by the day. She could go when my sister was near ten and me seven. We could keep the five small ones by then—so she'd go all day Monday and Saturday and do wash and sewing nights.

Beulah Nelson recalled that her mother, more than forty years old when Beulah was born in 1893, worked as a live-in housekeeper until "my brother—he's three years behind me—was near five." Later, at forty-eight years of age,

Ma just did wash out. She'd go to one place for the day. She'd then stop another place and bring they wash home and do that at night. We'd help do the wash she'd bring home. The next day she'd drop that wash off as she went to another home.

She did this for years. Every day from Monday to Friday. She only dropped wash on Saturday so she was back home by noon. It seems a lot but she wasn't working out as much as most women as I remember. Most lived out by the week. She got home every night. Most didn't.

Sixty-nine of the eighty-one women interviewed remembered their father clearly as the head of their household. Of the other twelve women interviewed, ten said their mothers were "ground widows"—women whose husbands had died leaving the wife with a number of young children. Only two of the eighty-one women stated that their father had deserted the family. Of the sixty-nine women whose fathers lived with their family, fifty-two lived in families with grandfathers at the head of the extended-family household. The twelve women reared in families without the father present recalled that their families had been headed by a grandfather or an uncle. The two women who were "grass widows"—who had been deserted by the fathers of their children—lived in extended-family settings. Extended families provided a stable environment for the "ground" or "grass" widows, and each woman said it was easy for other relatives to take over the duties of an absent father. Bernice Reeder's scowl softened faintly as she explained how her father "worked right in there with all the family" in Amelia County, "but he made only a very little money." Beulah Nelson fondled the tip of her long braid and smiled broadly as she said: "My father didn't just farm. He was a fireman; he worked at the cotton mill, too. But it wasn't just Daddy or Momma when I think of people in my family—it was all of us, working along with everybody, on our land that Papa started each of us on."

"All of us" often included grandparents. Federal census data reveal that the "typical" African American household in the 1880–1900 period had an average of four to five members. In addition, at least one-third of all families lived near some of their relatives.[12] Beulah Nelson, speaking with distinctive "lowland Geechee Carolina" inflections, described her household, which had at its core parents and grandparents:

"Miss Winnie," the grandmother of Bernice Reeder,
pictured with her employers, the Ricks family.

My grandfather, who I got this picture of right downstairs now, was lucky
enough to own land. He was sharecropping first, then he got land. My grandfather, that's my mother's father now, when each one of his children got married, he would give them the land for them to build they house. Papa worked
our land and helped them get on they feet with that place in New Berkeley
Spring [South Carolina].

Weida Edwards recalled that each family member was assigned tasks in
the central Florida home where she was born in about 1895. Her sweet-
natured expression was framed by thick eyeglasses. Her stiff and slightly

puffy hands became agitated as she described her childhood: "Daddy worked the field and Ma always worked out by the week. All of us childrens had chores to do day or night. . . . But from little on up you knew you had to help. Kids, everybody. You knew it was hard times and everybody was expected to help the family up some." Thadella Crockett, a dark woman whose short legs are now bent and aided by a cane, remembers her farm home in Georgia and her father "working there all day—in the field. My mama worked out when I was young, but then she did work at home by day and did wash too. She did field work, but not much because she would often be having babies. We all helped on the farm at times. But mostly my daddy worked the field."

The women's households typically were extended families with no fewer than six persons: parents, siblings, and other relatives. The largest contained one grandparent, two parents, and a total of thirty-three children. Bernice Reeder recalled dolefully a large family and a short supply of beds:

We had three rooms and a back shed and I guess no more than sixteen at home at one time. Even when they came for Christmas or summer we had room for everybody! My grandmom was in an attic with us oldest girls. The boys was in the shed room. The babies was in with my parents—who had beds that fit under they big bed for the little ones to sleep in. Everybody visiting slept where they could! You didn't have no space nor bed for your own. But everybody round there lived that way. Who knew any better or different? Nobody, cause we all lived that way—lots of people in every room of every house.

Mrs. Madree Hershaw, a widow who lives alone in a small second-floor apartment in a senior citizens' building, spoke in a monotone about her early life. She explained why her "small" family[13]—with the least number of residents of the women surveyed—required more work for each member:

Down North Carolina we had just my dad, mama, my dad's aunt, my grandmom, and my sister and me. We had a small family. Now, we lived cross from my dad's people and next door to more. But there was only two kids in that house—so that meant more work for us, for sure! That's why people had big families—to help out with the work. But we had to work double hard cause we had so few in our place.

Family members were taught early in childhood that survival depended on the labor of all members, including the children. Ora Fisher, whose seventy-eight-year-old face is full and whose eyes were soft and dewy as she reflected on her home, grew up on

a small farm in North Carolina. We had just one room with a table and benches on one side of the room. The beds would be on the other side and down the other wall. There was a big fireplace on the other wall.

All ten of us were there; my father farmed and my mother worked and farmed too. I had an Aunt and two cousins that lived with us too. We was happy and learned to work but we had fun as we worked. We girls started early to work; my father was a great farmer but he never had his own land for his food and tobacco. So we all worked. It was hard, but you'd know no better so you loved it.

Information about survival was taught by the family's direct link to the past, the elderly. In the households of these women, those elderly teachers included at least one former slave. Each interviewee recalled being told stories of the former slaves' subjugation, and they emphatically asserted the belief that those former slaves had enabled their families to survive. Odessa Minnie Barnes, a South Carolinian with a rich, dark complexion, spoke with inflections that transformed her statements into questions: "My old Aunt brought us up. Mama lived out so she [my aunt] was there. Like milk she gave us the 'slave-days stories.' She'd tell you everything. They let you know they made it on prayer and each other. They had nothing. Day after day she'd tell it. Those times? No, they didn't forget; they didn't let you either."

Amy Kelly's gnarled[14] finger pointed to a picture of her tall, freckled grandmother, who, she proudly professed, had "walked to freedom":

I heard her say some people came early one morning and said they [the slaves] were free. Some cried, but my big mom just called her whole family together and walked away. My great-aunt said that by noon my grandmother had found work for herself and had a shed for everybody in the family to live in. She'd say, "Freedom never scared a colored person—that's one lie told."

These sage elders' oral testimonies provided a bridge of bent backs and laboring muscles that connected Africa, slavery, and the contemporary lives of the youth born after emancipation.[15] The women of this book stated that the former slaves specified the "opportunity screens" through which African Americans had to move if they were to go beyond survival to stability and social achievement. In every interview, three "screens" were explicitly mentioned: firm religious beliefs, strong kin or augmented family support networks, and education.[16] Bertha Jackson is a short, dark brown woman with prominent cheekbones and thick gray hair. Her light brown, deep-set eyes filled with sympathy as she shook her head and said:

Them people suffered all around Clarendon, Williamsburg, Calhoun, and Orangeburg [Counties]. They never let you forget. I was born ten miles from Fairmont, between Fair Buff and Cherry Grove [North Carolina]. We left to work in Zion, Rain, and settled in Johnsville [South Carolina]. Now every time they could tell it, you'd hear about the time when they was slaves. They had help from God, their family, and the other slaves. That's all. But they pulled together. They survived with only God and they people. . . . Every time they talked you'd hear that.

Mississippian Fannie King remembered the importance her grandparents and other former slaves accorded religious and family commitments:

They knew how far all them had come to get to Center Ridge, but they talked to us, still—growing up in Smith County back then—about how far we had to go. They said over and over, "Learn to read and then read that Bible, and try everyday to just help one of your people, your kin." Grandma said that day after day, and I know she was in her seventies when I was born.

Dorethia Handy, age eighty-nine in 1986, was one of the millions of African Americans who lived in the rural South and made their living as tenant farmers, sharecroppers, or contract laborers. Those African Americans bound to peonage as tenant farmers and sharecroppers rarely eked out enough in crops to pay for rent, food, and supplies. They not only did not own their own equipment but also could not even market their crops independent of the landlord. Each year landlords would sell the tenants seed and supplies on credit. The tenants would then pay back one-fourth to one-half of their harvested crop to the landlord. It was the life of all the African American people she knew:

I never knew a colored person who wasn't a farmer 'til I was near grown. Everybody—and I mean men, women, children—old or young, good or bad—they were all farmers. I know it was do that or die. That's just the way it was for any colored person. And I can only remember a very few—the Tillerys and the Persons—who could own they piece of land either!

Beulah Nelson, also from a tenant farming family, remembered the exorbitant prices, interest charges, and the reasons the sharecropping family's obligations devoured any remaining profit, so that year after year the tenant fell deeper in debt to the landlord.[17] With splendid clarity she revealed the annual cycle of sharecropping families, a slice of history shared by the majority of African Americans of that period. She also provided fresh insight into "the settle"—the predictable moment of bitterly dashed hope[18] all poor families could empathize with but only sharecropping families profoundly understood:

Now they had a place there, it was a big store they called the Commissary. Now I'm big enough to know what I'm saying—they would give you rice, some syrup, some fatback, grits, and them molasses. That's what you get. Now you better raise your own food, garden. They had to fix and raise they own vegetables. But now they, these farm people would be calling theyself giving you this rice and just junk, but they charged you for that and above that. And at the end of the year, they even charged you rent for the house, but they may pretend they wasn't charging you. But they would say they giving you a house

to stay in. You understand? And when they make [grew] enough cotton to get money back at the settle—they wouldn't give you but so much money. [The African American family was not paid fairly; they were cheated.] And that's how they was.

One time when Grandpappy was talking in the Commissary—a white charged him too much, just cheated him. I could cipher and told that man he added wrong, I mean he'd cheated Grandpappy. My daddy, standing right there, didn't say a word for his own father. So I said it louder and louder—two more times. Then my older brother said something, too. Nobody said nothing. But they looked at me; then Brother. What happened? I got my worst whipping—got beat for telling the truth! My brother was sent away that night. Then I had to go away to school. Just for telling how them people cheated Grandpappy at year's end.

I was born on a sharecrop. You know, we traveled, we worked on sharecrop. Picked cotton and the rest of my time I was taking care of children. It was hard working all year . . . for nothing.

Ophilia Simpson is a medium-tall, very light, and slender woman with wispy thin black hair. She has a weak voice with a marked southern accent. Her large home is filled with beautiful antiques she had been given in her seventy-one years of working "domestic jobs." Ophilia Simpson remembered the feeling of "owing your soul to the company store," to paraphrase Merle Travis: "My people worked for over thirty years in North Carolina growing tobacco and crops. There was never a year they made a dime or a difference. It was each of us working harder to get more behind. God knows how low croppings' people got as every new year came round."[19]

By comparison, Josephine Moss was fortunate. Her parents, Petty and Willa Gibson, were among the 187,000 African Americans who owned farms out of 6.5 million African Americans living on farms in the South.[20] According to Josephine Moss, her father was "proud to tell any colored person he owned land and owed nobody." But that was only half the story. As she put it:

But that's not to say how poor we were. I was born in 1906 and we worked that land. With God as my witness we never knew what it was to have a dress

Typical small home, owned by the Johnson family of Catalpa, Virginia. The section on the right was the original home, a log cabin built c. 1873. Working children sent money home to add a porch and picket fence (1909) and the tall section, left (1915-17). When the tall section was built, the log cabin was covered with the same wood siding so that the two sections would match.

from a new bolt or piece of cotton. My whole family was from right around there. We all pulled together, but they suffered just like we did.

To buffer themselves from the many harsh realities of life in the racist South, African Americans developed communal institutions. Foremost among these was the family network. Most newly freed slaves chose to live with their kin. Instead of depending on anonymous, often undependable sources of assistance from society at large, African Americans turned to an extended network of kin outside the immediate household. Dealing primarily with one's own people enabled African Americans to defend themselves from white hostility, intrusion, and domination. In this way African Americans gave high priority to the insulation of their family work and social life from white interference. They wanted a "true freedom," which encompassed land, higher education, security for their family, as well as protection from terrorism and poverty. They sought to eliminate the control that whites sought to retain.[21]

The postemancipation period was a time of economic crisis for African American families in the South. The adverse economic, political, and social climate naturally drove kin groups closer and made them more interdependent. At the turn of the century, African American sharecropping families became even more impoverished as landlords began to insist on a fixed amount of cash—rather than a share of the crop—as payment for rent in the faltering staple-crop economy. Conflict often resulted in violence, as this comment from a farm owner reveals: "When there's trouble I just go down with that [with a hickory wagon spoke] and lay one or two of 'em out."[22] A South Carolina planter emphasized that in the South the white man was the natural master. If there were ever difficulties or "a spirit of unruliness," he or one of his four armed riders "just go down . . . and lay one or two of 'em out. That ends the trouble . . . they're just like children and once in a while they simply have to be punished." Daily confrontations of this nature galvanized the development of the extended-kin community as a viable support network for African Americans.[23]

Self-sacrifice and family cooperation—critical strategies for survival—often meant that children played an important part in the household economy. Families turned to kin to assume child-care responsibilities when mothers worked outside the home. Many of the women remembered the role of kin[24] in their childhood, as Amy Kelly, born in North Carolina, noted:

I loved my grandmom like a mom 'til I left there. My mom worked all the time, so it was my grandmom who was with the childrens at home. She did everything for us. Same with my aunts' kids cross from us. She raised us all. Mama couldn't, and Daddy worked on crews from spring to late fall and did our farming. He couldn't do no more.

But Grandmom did. She was a big red woman who raised us. And some others stayed when people needed help. Them people raised everybody's childrens so the dad and mom could work. People had to pull together in them times.

Kin was a major aspect of identity from birth. Each child born into the community acquired initial recognition as part of a social group from his or her relationships with kin. These groups defined "your people" as all kin related by blood and marriage. What you did an as individual was seen in terms of how it reflected on your family, in its broadest sense. As Ora Fisher, wearing a gray housedress with white slippers, noted:

You was named a so-and-so first; whose child you was came after that. If you was bad they'd spank you and then tell your people. Any of your people they'd find. And it was like they'd told your mama, dad, or grandparents. Anyone would be on you 'cause you'd been a shame to the family—not just the peoples raising you up or just your mama and dad. Everybody in Rainbow Springs had it just the same.

Kin also provided moral and economic support in times of household crisis. Relatives helped with the care of the seriously ill, brought food to mourners when there was a death in the family, and assumed child-care responsibilities for other kin. Female kin assisted with shopping, cooking, and cleaning duties when live-in domestic work took the adult woman from the home. Men helped one another in the fields, which enabled cotton harvesting to be completed in a cooperative atmosphere.[25] Zelma Powell described the communal spirit of labor in her Albemarle County area of Virginia: "Like everybody around there, my people all lived right there together, we did everything for each other because that's all you had. People raised crops, animals, and houses year after year together. Whatever was needed one for the other was just done for everybody."

The household boundaries of the rural African American kin group were never static.[26] They shifted and expanded to meet the economic and social challenges of the community. Bernice Reeder said that in

Amelia County, Virginia, during the 1890s, "there wasn't another colored soul who could help a man like my daddy—he with his thirty-
odd children! Who else but his own people? For everything, they'd be
there to help him. I know it was hard for them too, but they'd be right
there helping us. As they could."

A WOMAN JUST WOULDN'T

African American women have always constituted an important labor
sector in the rural South. During slavery, white owners fully exploited
women who worked as field laborers, household laborers, breeders, and
objects of white male sexuality. This legacy of social and occupational
exploitation had a powerful impact on the societal perceptions of
African American women. Conveniently overlooking its instrumental
role in determining women slaves' lives, southern white society considered female slave agricultural workers debased, degraded, and mascu-
linized because they had entered a traditionally male labor environment.
This view resulted in the social judgment that women who worked in
the fields were unworthy of preferential treatment, or of the title
"lady."[27]

In the aftermath of slavery, African American women fought to de-
stroy the vestiges of slavery's denigration and devaluation of their own
labor and social status. They felt keenly the burden of the negative
stereotypes that they were sexually loose, masculine, dirty, and undigni-
fied. To combat the personal stigma of their purported masculinity,
women were careful to distinguish their labor from that of men. Eula
Montgomery remembered clear differences for women's work in her
Alabama hometown:

It was the same but different. Women could do anything. But generally they
didn't do some things. A woman wouldn't just pick up and hunt game. Or do
too much building on a house or trapping game—like that. They be the ones
to help in a home or field; maid work, I mean, for jobs out in places like

Nixburg and Cottage Grove [Alabama]. If they were alone, like a widow, a brother, cousin—some man'd do for them. If not, they made do or just try to do some things themselves.

Isetta Peters spoke about her difficult childhood as the eldest of ten children. Born north of Hickory, South Carolina, to a tenant farm family, she revealed that the women were busy

doing . . . mostly home things. Cooking, cleaning, caring for young or old in a house. Then they'd do field work and garden. Now when I was young you'd never see a woman hunt. After we moved to North Carolina, I never saw a woman do butchering. They'd never do fixing on a wagon or maybe smithing. Some did if they had to now. I once saw Miss Daisy Lucas's horse throw a shoe. Now she'd just delivered a baby. She went back and put the horseshoe on. Herself. But generally real heavy work would be done by a man or a boy with some size on him—fourteen, fifteen, like that.

On the Arkansas farm where Frances Pollard grew up, some jobs were handled by both sexes, but child care followed a particular pattern:

Anybody did what was to be done. Boys had to help wash; girls did field work and carried some of the wood for a fire. Everybody'd just put in and did in Back Gate [Arkansas].

If it was a young family this is what—down home—people would do. Your aunt, big cousin, somebody in the family would keep you while Ma worked. Now my Aunt Til kept us [and everybody around there so that the adults] could work. . . . No man would do that—just keeping children. If they was his or other people's—he'd not go place-to-place keeping people's childrens so they could work.

A blushing Velma Davis recalled only one job she was never allowed to perform in Virginia:

One thing would ruin a girl for life—having children and all [cause infertility]. So, I know a woman or girl never did only one thing. We never went into the ice house to get ice. My father, uncle, or brother went in to get ice. There you wouldn't go . . . not handling ice no matter when, and we had ice the whole year too. My uncle or father would get it off the pond below the house, put it in the ice house in blocks and it'd be there in July. But I never could touch or handle ice.

She also remembered an incident that clearly showed what jobs were women's and not to be performed by men or boys:

Now on the farm, about five minutes to or quarter to twelve, they say, Velma, go ring the bell. My aunt and mother was preparing the food and they told me to ring the bell. Now I was the oldest girl, and I had to go out there and take a piece of iron and bang on an old piece of railroad tie. Don't you know, wherever they was on the farm they'd hear that bell and they'd come first thing . . . water the horses, feed the horses, and come in an eat. Once my cousin did it and he was in trouble. He got told straight that was not a job a boy or man ever did.

If women rarely performed "men's work" at home, their hard labor both within and outside the home sometimes took a toll on their relationship with their children and with their family in general. All of the women proclaimed that whereas their fathers were often playful and attentive, their mothers were more austere and showed little or no affection toward them. From the time they could walk, life for their mothers had been synonymous with hard labor. Cassie Hackney, thoughtful and mentally clear in spite of a body weakened by a recent illness, has an angular, dark brown face. She remembered her mother as a stern woman who rarely smiled. Exchanges of tender feelings, words, or moments were not a part of her experience of the mother-child relationship. As she recalled her early years in Ashe County, North Carolina, her deeply wrinkled face registered pain: "My mother never played with her children like a mother is supposed to do. She never did. To her we were there to work and mind grown people. We said so little right to her. At most we said, 'Ma,' and better had said that carefully!"

Cassie Hackney's mother, Odella Ingraham, had worked on the nearby farm of a family as a live-in cook and nursemaid for a white lady named Miss Jennie. During the periods that she was separated from the

Eliza Jefferies, like many southern mothers, was reluctant to pose with female children in pictures. Eliza seriously reprimanded her daughter, Marie, for "sneaking" into this photograph without her knowledge or consent. Eliza considered this a ruined picture.

In contrast, Eliza Jefferies proudly posed for pictures with her male children.

home, her mother-in-law, Ida Jacobs, took care of the children and managed the family's small tenant farm. The birth of twins Mary Louise and Cassie had complicated Ida's life; and Cassie Hackney insisted that Odella particularly disliked the twins because, becoming too much for Ida to handle, she had to leave her live-in job and return home to help raise them.

Another twin, Marie Jefferies Stone (she and her twin brother were the twenty-third and twenty-fourth children of Peter and Eliza Jefferies), vividly recalled that her mother "never stopped working. She always had so many things to do, and even more things than that for you to do." Marie's mother, Eliza, had the primary responsibility for rearing the children, cleaning the farmhouse, cooking, doing laundry, sewing, and cultivating the family garden—while "being pregnant every year for twenty-three years, when you count the miscarriages and babies that died!" Eliza Jefferies was an industrious farm wife who sold eggs, fresh vegetables, and hand-sewn clothing and took in laundry to supplement her husband's small income. Marie recalled her mother working "when we got up and long after she'd put the children to bed." Her mother possessed a perpetually severe and uncompromising countenance. Marie Stone, always buoyant and sociable, laughed as she admitted knowing very little about her mother's employment outside the home before she was born. Marie was often told that her mother worked outside the home, "by the week until her fourth child was born." She was able to work as far away as Brightwood, Virginia, because her mother-in-law watched her young children. Eliza Jefferies believed in strict discipline for all her children, but she was hardest on her daughters: "My mother was strict, but with the girls she had no sympathy at all. To me she was a person who always felt nothing in life was worth looking at." Although Marie never stated that her mother was unduly harsh to her children, she did express a strong regret that she did not have a more intimate and caring relationship with her.[28]

Many women sounded a similar note of regret. Fannie King, for example, remarked that when mothers in rural Mississippi spoke, it was only "to give you directions: how to work, when to work, and what more to do when you did all that! That's the most she ever said to us. Period!" Despite her mother's consternation, however, Cassie Hackney remembered growing up surrounded by the laughter of her eight brothers and sisters on the farm of their caretaker, Miss Edith Moore. Miss Moore took special pride in the twins because they were born in the same month as her own youngest daughter's only surviving set of twins, and she personally prided herself on how well the Hackney twins "got on and grew up so nicely—from the first." Cassie Hackney described Miss Moore's home as "a place where I had real fun. When I think of good times down home—that's the place where I remember. We'd play around and have fun. We'd go behind the house or down near the spring and just laugh, tell jokes, and have a good time." But that ended quickly when "somebody'd miss you and call you to do what you come here for . . . work." As early as age four, Cassie "helped with the wash, picked the small plants in the garden, and helped to mind the babies." She carried clean wash and rinse water and fed the chickens.

By the age of seven, Marie Stone was considered "nearly trained up." Every morning, when she got up from the large bed she shared with her four sisters, she walked to the opposite side of the large living room/dining room/kitchen to "wash off in the tin pail of clean water." After washing off and eating a breakfast "of mostly molasses and cornmeal," she would begin to clear the table and wash the dishes. Then she would make the "girl's" bed and tote in the water for washing clothes. After washing, she might work in the garden, or in the field with her grand-mother. After morning chores, she would help with the main meal for the day: "Supper was a soup or stew with a piece of meat in it for taste, some meal bread, and that was about all. Every so often you'd have some fish in the dinner. Not often. Mostly just a piece of fat meat."

After helping serve supper, she would pick berries in summer or sort dry beans in the winter. All year soap was made, starch mixed, and food was processed by canning or drying. She also helped fold the clothes her mother ironed. There might be wood to be brought into the house, ashes to be sorted and saved for soap, and freshly ironed clothes to be delivered to nearby farms in Culpeper County, Virginia. Animals had to be tended. Four younger children had to be changed and fed. Floors needed sweeping. In the evening, after dinner, each of the smaller chil-dren had to be bathed before bed. More wood had to be carried in for the morning breakfast, and often garden food had to be shelled, washed, and placed in water to soak for the next day's meals.

By age nine, Marie could cook, clean, and care for the entire interior of a house and mash "wrinkles out of most pieces sent by whites to be laundered and returned." Outside, she could wash, boil, and hang clothes out to dry. In the field she could plant, weed, and harvest most crops. All of the women were fully introduced to the responsibilities of farm life before the few short years they would attend the poor, segregated schools in the rural South.

Velma Davis, who spent all of her childhood at the rear of the white landowner's house in Nelson County, Virginia, had been born prematurely and the "first child come a girl." Her father was close to her and often treated her "like a boy—with a lot of talk and play from morning on as we worked." As a small child, she remembered she woke up in the morning and walked to the main kitchen in the "big house" to eat breakfast. Her mother and two aunts would serve the children breakfast. Then she would wash, scald, dry, and put away the dishes and sweep the porch and floors with a homemade broom. Every other day was wash day, and she would fill up all the water pails, tin and wooden tubs, and, in the yard, a "big old wash pot where they heated the water."

"Mama made a fire," Velma said, "and we carried the hot water and poured that in the tubs as they washed, using soap they made with lye. The clothes had to be washed, boiled, taken out of the boiling water, put in the first rinse water, the second rinse water, and then the bluing water." On the days there was no washing to be done she had to clean up the "lock room" (pantry): "The flour was there—barrels—big barrels—wooden barrels full of flour. And one barrel full of meal. My uncles and father was farmers who worked hard, and they wanted to make sure that lock room was cleaned right." Then she made all the beds in the big house, "except the owner of the farm's bed [Mr. Mitchell]. His bed had to be just so. My mother made that one—it had to look just as smooth as this couch." The children were then sent to the field—to carry water from the spring to those who had been working there since before the children had awakened. In the late morning, the children picked vegetables or fruit from the groves on the farms. She closed her eyes as she envisioned her past:

There were two or three gardens to be worked each and every day God sent. My mother and aunt prepared the meal for everyone on the farm. It would be maybe a piece of meat with vegetables and hot bread. A little more on Sunday, a slice of sweetcake maybe. The men would break and go back to work by two o'clock. The women would do sewing on each day and ironing on the days they didn't wash.

Each day my cousin Richard and I would go out and bring the cows in. We'd get the cows in, wash our hands, and milk the cow. And some old grown person would come along and tell us to get back and strip the cow good—go back and strip her good—get all the milk out.

Then she would go to Piney River, Virginia, carrying milk, butter, eggs, and vegetables from their garden. And when she returned, she'd have money—"just about the only money my whole family'd see." And this she did every other day. What was she doing at night?

Sitting down shelling green peas or stringing green beans to take to the market. And we churned. What you talking about? Me and my cousin churned. Just soon as we finished that milk and butter, they'd put in some more. And we had to churn that too. We'd be having our fireside chat with Mr. Mitchell 'bout then, while we did our handwork—picking beans, cleaning potatoes, or whatever we was told. And, like I said—other than church, his words was the law. Now he didn't meddle with church.

CHURCH OR KITCHEN

Although economic necessities forced the employment of every able-bodied person in the rural southern household, white employers did not interfere with African Americans' regular church attendance. Aware that their bosses regarded them as social and genetic inferiors, African American employees nevertheless insisted on free time to attend church. Maybell Slaughter, born in Martin, South Carolina, recalled that her time in church alleviated the routine of work in her home community of Millheaven, Georgia: "Even working out [beyond the home], you'd go to church. Everybody did. Now most came just to hear the word.

But some came to keep from being in a kitchen somewhere. Yes, they'd hurry up and get going out of a job to be in church. They'd stay all day at Brier Creek, too. Like church or not, it was a lot better than working! Church gave you six, not seven, days of work."

The church was a pivotal part of the African American community's efforts to protect family and social life from white intervention. The church had developed its role in this regard long before Reconstruction; religious meetings had served important communal functions even during slavery. Religion imbued slaves with strength derived from direct communion with God. Slaves might hear the white preacher or the master on Sunday morning, but their real "meetin' and preachin'" came later, at their own worship services, held whenever and wherever possible. These services were grounded in a spiritual resistance to the indignities and restraints imposed by slavery. Slave religious ceremonies presented the gospel of deliverance from bondage. From Christianity, the slaves fashioned a belief system to which they could turn for strength.[29]

As Christians, African Americans could spiritually, if not physically, resist the powers that be. After emancipation African American worshipers sought to reconcile the contradictions and oppression in the social environment. They might be free to practice their faith openly now, but the sermons continued to invoke deliverance "from this world of trouble." Worship was directed to a God who had experienced suffering, just like they had. Jesus promised them rest from their labor, an end to injustice, and eternal punishment for the violent and oppressive. God not only promised to deliver all African Americans as an oppressed people but also provided a palliative philosophy to counteract the social and occupational dehumanization they experienced daily. At the same time, the worship service addressed their profound need for economic and social redemption in the present world.

Church service consisted of much more than religious ritual. Churches helped the entire community develop a sense of worth, alleviate despair, and reduce the impact of the powerful on the weak. At church, African Americans had not only a community unto themselves but also a leadership structure of their own choosing.

And just as the church was the center of the community, the women were the center of the church. Religion and the church offered women refuge and a means to express their concerns and develop their creative gifts.[30] Church identification was quasi-automatic for all segments of the African American community. In fact, the boundaries of the community usually determined the jurisdiction of the church. Bertha Jackson, born in North Carolina, expressed her understanding of the close link between church and community as follows:

I went to the old school Baptist church near Brentside, some miles from Poston [South Carolina]. Name? I never called it nothing but Brentside Baptist Church. It never had a name as I know other than that. It was the only one except the AME, and that was near First Gap, not Brentside. AME's have names cause they have bishops and districts. But a Baptist has a name where it is.

Laurlean Davis is a short, dark brown woman who was very soft spoken and hesitant as she revealed another way the local church served to define the community, even to the extent of identifying it geographically:

When I'd go anyplace and people would ask me about my people and all—not a soul had heard of my home—Lyttleton, North Carolina. Not a one ever knew that place—it's near Castalia and Spring Hope in Nash County. Truth be told, it wasn't a town or like that. But my church, First Baptist, had a preacher who traveled with a singing group and had done revivals all down there. When I said that was where I was from, then people knew my area of North Carolina. Many a day that's the only way anybody'd know where my people was living and I was born.

Further, church was synonymous with "home." Amy Kelly explained the secular significance of a "church home" or a "home church":

My church home is Antioch in Town Creek. A church home is the place you were first taught all about religion and everything else. It is the place where you really came to be in God's eyes and everybody else's. Plus, if you came from Halifax and down to Wilson [North Carolina], people can immediately know you by your church home. If people meet you and don't know you right off, your church home tells them almost as much as you name. They'll know about what area you came from, what you like and don't care for. People just know things about you that way—at home and here [in Washington, D.C.] it's that way for sure.

For the majority of the women, such as Ora Fisher, whose round face brightened at the memory of her church, the church was the only work-free haven they ever knew:

Down North Carolina you'd get there early for church meetings. For us children it was just a place to play and play. Nobody wanted you to do no chores, like at home. And I know it was the only place you could go and not feel somebody was going to make you do something other than sit down and sit still. That was a relief for sure.

But the church's significance impressed Marie Stone indelibly for another, more personally revealing, reason:

The Pine Grove Baptist Church was the only place I ever saw my mother laugh or seem happy. Even when something was funny to all us children, my aunts, grandmom, daddy—everybody—Mama would just look, say "humph" and turn her head. But down at church she'd be laughing out loud. Or smiling. Things that let you know she could be up some of the time. But it was only at church. Just there.

Maybell Slaughter sat erect in her bed at the Daley Nursing Home as she discussed her home church near Millheaven, Georgia. To Maybell Slaughter, the regular attendance of her parents, Edmond and Lulu Slaughter, was evidence of their high moral integrity:[31]

Like every person they'd be there no later than the start of every Bible study. My daddy was born near Fortsonia, so he was one of the people everybody looked for every Sunday. They'd be there all day for afternoon and late services too. Everybody, I mean the people all around there who would act good, loved my daddy and mama. If you would be just half trying to act decent, you'd be in church things, too.

As Pernella Ross succinctly concluded, "Once you saw how nice people treated Bakers' [town in North Carolina] women who were in the church, you didn't want to be no other way!" To be identified with, or to behave like, the "unchurched" or "unsaved" was to be declared a social misfit. To be considered decent was a prime motivation for attending church, as Marie Stone noted:

I can't think of anyone who wasn't trying to be half-decent. That's going to church sometime, anyway. I know many a man who'd come up from Success [Virginia] and just stand around the church—not go in once to a year—but was steady coming up to church anyhow. If you was young you had to come —because somebody wanted you to come. When you courted you came because you wanted somebody. After that, you'd just come to be a somebody to people down there in Rixeyville [Virginia]. And what you got there stayed with you, for sure, every day of your life. I know in my life it's a fact.

Church attendance therefore dispelled one of the negative conceptions of the African American female. Indeed, to this group of women, a church woman could be called a "lady."

Church attendance and activity was the basis for life's immediate and anticipatory beliefs. And it often superseded the home as a vehicle for providing guidance—defining the whys and hows of their lives. As young women, they needed to know how they could acceptably express themselves. They wanted to give their all to help the church accomplish its mission work. Experienced "old-school" missionary Mathilene Anderson, born in Virginia and ninety-nine at the time of her interview, also explained that she alone could not provide service to the sick and needy in rural Laurel Mills, Virginia: "There was too many that needed too much down there. You helped, but you'd do it with others in the church. . . . If you tried you couldn't do much of nothing because it was too much on any one body. But working as a church—might be just four or five or so—you'd get more done. And faster too."

A variety of organizations for mutual aid to the rural community grew out of the church. Pauline Crawley, born near Cross the Roads

Couple in front of a rural North Carolina Baptist church, which also served as the African American school.

[Cross Roads], Mississippi, was only four years old when her family was forced to relocate to Tennessee:

The Helping Hand gave to anybody in need. They gave to Methodist, or any of them too. In them areas of Tennessee people would sometime just be starving. Our pastor asked for food or any clothes people could give. He'd get the things in a day or so. The Helping Hand took it to the people and gave it all too. And nobody cared if you came there or not. That church helped more people.

The church also served as the community's schoolhouse, and in many cases the church ministers doubled as schoolteachers. Two of the women were educated in "one-room schools" built on land the church owned. These school buildings were adjacent to the church, and both women were taught by their ministers. Marie Stone talked at length about her father's attitude toward her education. To her, rudimentary education meant "enough that you didn't have to make a mark [an *X*]" for a signature:

If you didn't go, you couldn't read or write. Maybe a smaller sister could teach an older one, but lots didn't go to school, so they made a mark. Daddy never wanted us to make a mark, so he helped keep a teacher in homes to teach us. Our teacher was Reverend Brown, who had another church, but he'd come a few months, by the week, and teach us at our church. Our minister didn't teach, I think because he knew so little. But I know that Reverend Brown had been to high school and a trade school—so he could teach.

Velma Davis's fond memory of Mr. Mitchell, the man with a patriarchal domination over her family, changed rapidly when she explained his opposition to Nelson County's Arhenta School. With a crystalline memory, she recalled her three female teachers.[32] She also noted that forty-three years after the emancipation, the schooling of African American children continued to have sinister connotations in the minds of white southerners like Mr. Mitchell:

I loved my Arhenta School. It was one big, real large room. When you entered it had a hall where we children hung up our coats and hats. Then you go to the big room with so many benches you could not count them all! Two or four children on every one. . . . Over here were the seats for just one child. And here stood a big old wood stove in the middle of the room. And over here was a pipe going up through the ceiling. And who was furnishing the wood that was stacked away over here? The wood for the school? My father and uncle. When the wood was getting light, they would go and cut more. And they was using a ax and crosscut saw. Mr. Mitchell only got mad when my daddy and uncle went to take wood or help keep up the school. Seemed to vex him so that they did whatever they could to keep up the school.

Prudence Martin, tall and obese, is a light hazelnut brown with very broad, flat features. Her swollen arms were animated as she described her schooling in the so-called colored schools, segregated institutions notorious for their inadequate resources:

It was always in the church and for three or four months. Colored got about half the time as whites in Graveston [Tennessee]. Plus we had to help at home by seven or so. Sometimes you'd get three years—enough to read a little and write some. Colored schools was better than nothing, but not like the schools for whites. We got to go 'til I guess it'd be the fourth grade. By then you'd be sent out to work.

Forty-nine of the women had at least a third-grade education and took great pride in their ability—as Isetta Peters noted—"to read a very little and write their God-given name." Although only one woman could not sign her name, Esther Lawson seemed to speak for all thirty-one who had only limited educational opportunities:

I was in a schoolhouse twice in my life. I couldn't go because I had to work. My mother wasn't able to send us to school. And in the winter we didn't have shoes to wear. But my older sister and brother, they went to school. They had to walk five miles a day to school. School was a good ways [distance]. We were small children, we couldn't go to school.

One time I lived next to a church, and this lady lived there and taught at the school at night. So I went there. I did learn some but that wasn't much. What I learned—I learned it myself from being around peoples and you know, knowing how to read and write.

In addition to basic educational skills, the schools also taught personal hygiene, home economics, and survival strategies. Mamie Garvin Fields recalled how she had to combine elements of social work, reform activities, religion, and political savoir-faire as a teacher in South Carolina at the turn of the twentieth century. With pride and a determination as unyielding as stone, Bernice Reeder pointed to the gold-bordered cup she won in a spelling contest in about 1897: "Reverend Marshall would send you out to wash if he felt you hadn't done that good. Everybody— girl and boy—learned to cook a pot of something and how to slip a school."

Mayme Gibson, a soft brown, plump woman, was born in Mississippi in 1897. She knew that "two people went to Prentiss Institute, but not in my time. There was hardly enough money for school like that."[33] Mary Ruth Ingraham, recalling her days as an exuberant abecedarian, reiterated the common impressions of African Americans about rural educations:

They teach you to read, write, and some things about farming. Everybody had to be able to grow food to eat. They helped to see to that. Our teacher would tell us over and over that we needed to learn as much as we could to get good work. Then they'd let you know that life was hard and you had to work harder.

Even them people like Booker T. Washington and Miss Bethune, she was from right down there in Florida, worked hard. Reverend Case read books to show us, and he told us how the people with nothing worked to get up [improve] themselves. School tried to give you reading, but it was to try to make you stay in the church, be clean, and mainly get you ready for work.

TRAINING UP

Southern African Americans made great gains in literacy during Reconstruction, but economic demands inevitably took precedence over education. The need to help support the family was primary for each woman by the time she reached seven years of age. A girl's first assignment was on the family farm, caring for the children while the older females did other work.

Training is an African American cultural expression that means learning a variety of specific duties while living on a cotton, tobacco, or rice farm—duties learned early and well. When this group of women was young, it was common for female kin to assume the responsibility of training the children of the household while the mother (or mothers) worked in the homes of whites. All girls routinely helped the adult women with child care; of the group I interviewed, each recalled that she "washed, watched, and whipped" the children younger than herself.[34]

Isetta Peters's long fingers intertwined as she attempted to describe her early York County, South Carolina, training:

Lord, please give me strength. Training? It's . . . I'd say training was, down South Carolina, for sure, by six you watch somebody all the day, do some animal feeding, and a little cleaning around the house. See? By seven or so, you'd be trained to do most of the things needed. I'd say the minding children, farm field work, cooking, and you'd be expected to do some parts of the wash—by yourself.

Pernella Ross, now a prosperous woman who had recently rented her house out to a relative and moved into a new condominium, said that her life had always been hard but that her training had given her the foundation on which to build the successes in her life. During her training, her family had worked on a small tenant farm in North Carolina, about nineteen miles from the land her extended family owned in rural Union County:

They'd start you watching young ones and getting water from the spring. That's on the day you stood up! By four, you'd be doing feeding and a little field work, and you'd always be minding somebody. By six, you'd be doing small pieces in a tub every wash day and you'd bring all the clear water for the rinsing clothes. By eight, you'd be able to mind children, do cooking, and wash. If you wasn't trained full by ten—you was thought to be slow. Still, even if you was slow, you had to do!

By ten you'd be trained—our people was seeing to that. You was thought to be 'bout grown as far as your training. Especially a girl. Your training was early and hard. No girl I know wasn't training for work out by ten. From the time a girl can stand—she's being made to work. Girls are started early with work—no play ever for a girl. That's just how they [adult females] was on girls. Work, work, work. No play, 'cause they told you, "Life was to be hardest on you—always."

According to Ruth Mosley, a tall woman with flawless dark brown skin and a round face framed with short white hair, stressed that regardless of their position, all children—oldest or youngest, whether from a small or a large family—were trained. In her opinion, training benefited not her own welfare and development but the household at large:

There was no little sister or brother to care for in my house, but I had to care for the children or neighbors when I was just only five myself. Then my older sister sent her two down to North Carolina and a cousin sent her children home while she worked with a family near where my mama worked. You see, you must care for the children while somebody worked! You just did. Grown peoples had to work out as well as do the farm—so you had to care for the children 'til you worked out. They said it was training for you. No! It was just more work on top of your chores! That's all, just more work!

Because African American women in the rural South were relegated to domestic household work, both the families and the girls knew that training was intended to build the skills necessary for acquiring work in local households, that is, for "work out." Beulah Nelson described her early exposure to hard work in her training years:

When I was nine, I was doing all. I could wash, I could iron, I could cook and help Mama do all that housework around there. I'll tell you how they did it with me. They built a stool. You know, like you see these little stools here now, they built one for me. When I was nine, I had to stand on that stool, and I had to wash them dishes. I had to get up every morning and we had prayer. We had to wash up then and go in that kitchen and have our breakfast. We didn't have a cow, and do you know I had to get up and walk a mile to the neighbor's and get them two-quart buckets full of milk and bring them back home and put them down. And I was not nine years old! Now that's my life.

Often described as "near trained" by the age of seven, girls could proficiently assist the adult women in farming, cleaning, laundry, and child care. This reality applied to more than 90 percent of the African American women born during this period.[35]

Although many individuals in the community or school[36] attempted, through the classroom, to impose more liberal cultural ideas on African American people or to expose rural African American women to a broader sense of opportunities,[37] from birth on, these women faced unmitigated harsh realities by virtue of their race and gender. No matter what was held up to them, their lives severely circumscribed their opportunities. With a somber expression and tone, Bernice Reeder spoke for all the women about the unavoidable likelihood of domestic service:

Your people all trained you to do service work. It was what they all knew you had to learn—period. Now, maybe a teacher, aunt, or somebody would tell you that you could do other work, but you knew that you'd do service work. You knew, and sometimes you'd think about doing different work—but you knew it wasn't to be. 'Specially at home—service was all there was for you. They knew it. You knew it.

No matter what you'd do in life everybody knew you'd have to do some kitchen work. If you was lucky—you'd get to work in a factory. But there would still be a time that you'd do for whites. All the teachers and just everybody started work as a worker for a white. You knew you might could do better sometime . . . but you'd do cleaning or wash 'til you did!

At the core of this regimen was the parental assumption that any money earned by the children would belong, without question, to the parents. Work and its rewards were not for the individual to enjoy. All of the women remembered their brothers giving their earnings to their father or to the male head of household, except in certain circumstances, when the men's earnings went to the mother. Athelene Walker, a short, dark brown-skinned woman with cascading mixed-gray curls, lived in a very neat apartment within a dreary public-housing community. Her strong voice overpowered the constant crying of a baby in the next apartment. In talking about her earnings as a young woman, she emphatically announced that her "brothers would give Mama their money if they saw her with a special need, or if Daddy told them to give it to her for this or that. I usually remember them giving money to Daddy though."

Conversely, the women gave their earnings directly to their mothers. Ann Brown's ninety-one-year-old voice escalated from weak to forceful as she dramatically stressed:

At home your mama trained you and she took you to your first job off the farm. You knew from the first—you'd give anything you got to her. Mostly, they'd pay her your earnings when you were "in" [working in the same household] with her—you'd never see no money! If you saw it you'd not touch it— she'd give you all she had [a very long spanking] if you touched any money!

Their first jobs outside the family farm occasioned new social experiences. Each woman spoke in detail about accompanying her mother to

Amey Beasley worked with Aunt Caroline Beasley before she was placed on her first live-in servant job in the South.

her employment location and then being taught the proper behavior toward white employers. At Esther Lawson's first job in rural Alabama, she "went with Mama and walked around with this girl. She was retarded, and she'd walk around and pick up chicken feathers, and she'd walk around picking up pecans. And I'd walk around with her, keep her from falling and hurting herself. I wasn't staying at the house. I'd go home with Mama and come back during the day." Sadie Jones smiled derisively and described the cultural knowledge and behavior required of an African American "live-in servant" who was "working out for whites":[38]

At about eight, everyone [all girls] was going "in" with their mamas. You'd do pick-up[39] and watch some of the little white kids, or if she took up wash—you'd go help with the carrying and then the delivery. My mama did all them things.

Later, after every day of work, she'd tell you what not to do 'round them. When not to stare at the funny things they'd do and how to play up so as to get better pay or something. She took you with her so you'd not act out or wrong. She showed you how you was expected to be so that you'd be able to go to people [get employment] for money. You learned how you was to be from Mama. And you knew how the farm always needed everybody's money for this or that. You knew it was us they needed—so you knew you had to work. A lot of work. Early. Hard.

After two to six months of tutelage with their mothers and other adult female family members at their places of employment, seventy-two women recalled going to work for at least three months a year. And by age nine all of the women had worked in the house of a white family near their homes as servants; age nine was far too young, they reflected, for employment. Mathilene Anderson, thin and infirm after a stroke, speaks in a deliberate, slow manner. With solicitude she confided her difficult experience:

On the first job you was scared. Oh, I cried and even ran back home. But they always took you back. Most started at summer—you'd help the white missus all summer and then when school started, you'd go home. You'd get to go home on Sunday during the summer, but in fall you'd go back home. All summer you worked like a dog! They didn't care that you were a child. They saw you as a worker. And they worked you bad.

Bernice Reeder, in a disconsolate tone, echoed Mrs. Anderson's sentiments:

You hated to see summer coming. I did. In summer they'd come. Mama would call all the girls for them to see. They'd want me. I tried to hide behind the others—but they'd say "give us that one." It would be me first. My sister Julia always wanted to go, but she'd get taken last 'cause she was thin and frail. They's the type of people who wanted strong-looking girls 'cause the work was so hard. You'd work all the week . . . for just clabber and clothes!

The children all went to work early. You had to because you had nothing. I was out every summer . . . from one white person's house to another. When you was not much larger than their children! On the first farm I worked at, the overseer had children, and when I was eight I went there for a month to care for the children.

Never been away from home when they sent me and you cried all the time. But you had to wash these children's feet and mind the baby because the white mother was cooking for the owner of the place. You felt so bad, and cried. But I never went home a summer from eight years 'til I was twelve years old— and then I was sent north to work. You'd be sent every summer. They'd come to see the children to get workers—oh, in maybe late April. When they left, I'd be in the buggy with them—crying.

Live-in children cleaned, cared for children, and assisted the white wives with household work. Esther Lawson explained:

First, I worked for the peoples where our sharecropping was. Later I'd go and stay with these white people all the week. On Saturday they'd take me back to the country and spend the night with my family, and then come pick me up Sunday morning. No, I didn't like it, but I had to stay there because my mother told me to go up there to work. I didn't know what I working for. I didn't see no money. I guess they paid my mother.

Bernice Reeder described a varied, unpredictable set of duties:

You did whatever the wife was doing; sometimes you'd just stay with the wife who was pregnant. You sometimes have to do a lot; washing, cleaning, caring for any and all of the children. For the butcher I had to clean up the remains after slaughtering. That was by ten. The work was too hard, but you'd do 'cause you had to.

Family connections often enabled the girls to obtain their first jobs. Naomi Yates, a large woman, literally and figuratively, with a low voice, remembered how she reluctantly undertook her first job without her mother

with a family from down the road from where Mama worked; they were her people's kin some kind of way. They sent word that they wanted a girl, so Mama sent me. I remember they came for me in a wagon and took me so far away that I didn't know where I was.

I was so scared; and well, I cried on so that the man—I was so small—he took me in his arms and swore he'd bring me back the next day if I'd stop crying. I cried, had nose bleeds. All that just 'cause I didn't know which was home!

Did I go back? . . . Oh, you better not go back! You didn't dare go back home. I didn't dare let them take me when they said they would. They'd take you home at the weekend for Saturday night and Sunday 'til near dark. You went and you stayed. Mama trained you, and you'd go no matter what else or ever! You went!

Young servants were particularly vulnerable to abusive treatment from their employers, especially white men.[40] This threat was dramatically impressed on each young woman before she was "placed" in a home. As Odessa Minnie Barnes revealed: "Nobody was sent out before you was told to be careful of the white man or his sons. They'd tell you the stories of rape . . . hard too! No lies. You was to be told true, so you'd not get raped. Everyone warned you and told you 'be careful.'" Weida Edwards pulled her glasses down from her eyes, leaned forward and nearly whispered as she intimated her experience: "You couldn't be out working 'til you knew how people was raped. You'd know how to run, or always not be in the house with the white man or big sons. Just everyone told you something to keep you from being raped, 'cause it happened, and they told you." Ora Fisher made it clear that all her kin cautioned her about rape. She also related a protective rite of passage: "My mama told you first. Next was aunts and all. Now, then just before I was to leave with the family, my daddy just gave me a razor and he said it's for any man who tries to force himself on you. It's for the white man. He gave us *all* one. That I know!"

Early employment was an important part of African American survival in the postemancipation era. But some women, in this first generation of free people, recognized the South threatened to annihilate any hope for social or economic improvement. Their families had battled against the adverse environmental, economic and social conditions of the rural South since the end of slavery. Now, it was time, perhaps, to move on.

2
WHO'D HAVE
A DREAM?
THE MIGRATION EXPERIENCE

The "me" notion wasn't even thought about. My father's cousin came down
home and her eyes fell on me for brother. That's all I know how to tell. My
feelings . . . who'd ask? . . . You had to help, and it'll be up here instead of
down there. It wasn't for you to fall out of there like a man [could], without
somebody taking you. And I didn't follow behind no man—I was a child.
   —MARIE STONE, AGE NINETY-ONE

By the early 1900s, the South's economy—always affected by the
seasonal upswings and downturns in cotton and other staple-crop
production—had suffered a series of droughts, heavy rains, and
boll weevil attacks.[1] African Americans, like all southerners, suffered poor crop yields and an uncertain economic situation; families
were desperate in their quest to find new means of survival during this
nadir.[2] Mary Ruth Ingraham, the smallest woman interviewed, has im-
mense energy and ambition. She still drives her own car daily and recently completed a computer course. Her ninety-two-year-old voice
rings with enthusiasm when she talks about her family, her church
work, and her journey "on this highway called life." Short, hurried
conversations are important to her because she is a very active person.
Her constant activity and full voice contrasts with her physical size. Her
body is so small it seems to be absorbed in the beautiful brocade chair in
which she is seated. The chair's subdued beige, blue, and gold pattern is
exquisite and nearly matches the softly tailored beige blouse and tan
wool slacks she wears. A small gold pin accents the blouse. She revisits
every part of her life with a lighthearted, enormously cheerful style—

except those parts that compel her to talk about the oppressive poverty of African Americans in the rural South. She and sixty-four other women stressed that the lure of money greatly influenced their families' vision about migration northward. She explained her family's situation in 1902, the year of her birth:

Times was bad then, and they only got worse as time passed for my people in Virginia. Things was bad for my mama, dad, and all. They needed my mother's sisters' help and the money they sent home. It was a good thing to work and better for you to leave there to get work. Everybody was always glad for you to help.

Violence, intimidation, and suppression—all a part of everyday African American life in the South—also spurred rural families to send their young women northward.[3]

Beyond the desire for better jobs and an education, many women held personal goals of "a better life"—self improvement—up north.[4] Eula Montgomery, a woman who always smiles as she speaks, lives in a small row house with aging redwood siding. It is a two-story house with a small porch and a neatly kept yard. Her hair, parted in the middle, is curled tightly with waves down the back. Her printed dress snugly fits her very stout body. She wears thick support stockings and peach-colored, low-heeled shoes. In the view of Eula Montgomery, "People from all around Equality [Alabama] was leaving there. You saw the 'big' people going, and you wanted to go, too. You wanted to be more than you'd ever could at home, in Coosa County, and even Alabama! Just like big people." Janie Hopkins, tittering at the irony of being born near Dismal Swamp, Virginia, said, "People done better if they left. You had the chance for the first time when you left that dismal place, from down there." However, the decision and circumstances of migration were controlled by the family, not the individual.[5] Beulah Nelson sat on a wide-armed, light green sofa, a large, patchwork quilt behind her, draped over the back. She settled herself deeper into the

Photo of Sara Bassey in rural Virginia in about 1923, prior to her leaving the rural South.

cushions, mashed down from many years of use, and related her personal and parental motivations with a lively and exuberant attitude:

You couldn't really be of much help after a while. Work was there [in the rural South], but you got so little [in payment] you wasn't really helping. You got a little, but your people needed too much else. It was bad when I left in 1916. Nobody had anything. Everyone was glad when I got to come here [to Washington] 'cause I'd be able to help regular more. There was no money, and even farming was bad for my daddy. I was trained; I just had to wait my time and my turn.

JUST TRAVELIN' TALK

Marie Stone lives in a house she has converted into two apartments. The yard has a chain link fence around the back and a stone fence in the front. The house is surrounded by flowers. In the middle of the yard is a birdbath. She lives on the first floor in a one-bedroom apartment. The living room and dining room have very high ceilings, and their walls are covered with a bold floral wallpaper. The cherry and maple buffet and china cabinet in her dining room are brimming with antique silver tableware. In the living room, which is filled with her handmade dolls, a large, ornate mirror hangs behind her olive green sofa and two matching oversized chairs. Her furniture, trimmed in rosewood, is very comfortable. The beautiful hardwood floors are covered with large oriental rugs. Custom-built shelves line one wall of her kitchen, and all kinds of shiny gadgets cover the kitchen's long green counter top. Chairs surround a small white table and flowers sit in the middle of the table. In the middle of her bedroom, there is a small mahogany bed. A mahogany table with a brass lamp, a dainty chair, and a mahogany-and-brass bureau are the only other furniture in the bedroom.

A friendly woman, well known in her community and well liked by all, she is happy to receive visitors in her home. She always serves her guests food and tea or ginger ale. Whenever possible, she includes a "nip" of brandy after serving her guests. Slowly entering the living room with a brass tray, on which is a crystal decanter and two sherry glasses, she was disappointed that tea—not sherry—was requested. As she deftly refilled each tea cup, she emphasized,

The "me" notion wasn't even thought about. My father's cousin came down home and her eyes fell on me for brother. That's all I know how to tell. My feelings wasn't one way or another. Who'd ask? . . . You had to help, and it'll be up here instead of down there. It wasn't for you to fall out of there like a man [could], without somebody taking you. And I didn't follow behind no man—I was a child. My sisters all got here just like that, too!

Lizetta Prayther lives near a busy industrial strip. Although everything around her home moves fast, she moves slowly with a walker and has a calm temperament. Her brown skin is smooth, but arthritis has badly swollen her hands. There was a quiet dignity and deliberateness in her soft voice as she related, "People down Virginia wasn't never going to *do*

Kin took Marie Stone and each of her four sisters from rural Virginia to Washington, D.C. Each of the young women lived with relatives before working as live-in servants.

too much better than when I left. You're being sent, see, came out of what somebody here needed. Needs here came first—that's how we saw it for us." Velma Davis is seated next to a window with an unspectacular view of a funeral home, a chapel, a small store, and a gas station. As she sighed and turned her chair away from the window, she nonchalantly said:

You worked all week for a white family, with somebody having you in a house to do everything. When you got to the week's end and home, there was that and more still to do. No asking you about a thing. Nobody down there would. When time was to go, you'd be told what was to be what and where to go to do something more, someplace else! And bless you out if you talked too much. The thought of asking you 'bout anything never was in no mind down there. None.

Preparation for migration was both distinctive and routine. Migration was a family-regulated, family-timed process. And it was the responsibility of the rural family to reshape the young women when kin decided that migration was imminent. Lona Pitts Harris, born in Lauderdale County, Alabama, lives in a very small public-housing apartment complex. Her living room appeared to be more than half the size of the apartment, its ceiling seemingly held up by stacks of old newspapers and magazines. The room was crowded with old tapestry furniture, and dusty draperies covered the large ceiling-to-floor window. Stacks of religious books and church papers surrounded the chair in which she sat. As she ran her hands over one church bulletin, she said,

All you'd done was help somebody. At home or on a job. That wasn't different. What was different was the new ways everyone acted just when it was near time for you to leave. All over Centre Star, you got told more about things. Nobody said so much right out . . . I mean told you so much more, but they'd go over and over time and again how you was to remember to look out for this or that. Or, they'd make you stop doing things one way—something no mind was ever paid—and say "You too big to be so playful. Time now you stop and act like bigger girls. You got more to do to help us"— things like that.

"Traveling talk" started as soon as the adult kin finalized the first phase, the written negotiation. Female family members communicated constantly by mail with other family members who had moved from the rural South; they sent and received money, arranged for annual holiday "homeplace" visits, and shared kin news reports on persons who were now living in urban centers throughout the country. The women distinctly remembered that "talks and walks" with adult kin became more frequent and structured as the time neared for them to leave. Before they left, the women, now fully trained, worked on jobs outside of the family farm. And all but four of the women interviewed were at live-in jobs at the time of their migration. Cassie Hackney's stubby fingers are cracked and ashen in the joints. She has a very cordial disposition and never focuses on the infirmities caused by a stroke. She slowly explains how, just before she left Grassy Creek, "Everybody had something to say. What you was and was not to do if you ever was on the train. Or how things be at the new places. All like that."

Unlike some of the women, Cassie Hackney was aware that her mother had received letters about her leaving North Carolina. Each of the women caught up on family information during weekend "home visits" from her live-in work, but no one ever discussed when or why she would leave. Cassie Hackney, like many others, visited home from her "stay-in" job. The job was only a mile from the family farm. During her home visits, she secretly read any mail received by her family. Darethia Handy, who came north in 1916, also remembered that she was never asked for her input or opinion. Only once during a weekend visit home from her live-in job was her leaving ever discussed: "They talked about you but never to you. Money or job wasn't even talked of. I was told I'd go out with Sister and Cousin Rey. That was all said 'til past Christmas. And I was gone from Texas before that summer broke, I know."

FROM THE GARDEN AND ME

Almeda Goode of Clarendon County, South Carolina, laughed as she recounted an episode that occurred during a Saturday home visit after a week of work for Miss Coleman. She learned from a younger brother that a cousin had sent "word" from the North asking about her. Suddenly she became the center of a flurry of activity by the adults in her community, and from that point on, her weekend visits home were very different:

The talkin' wasn't bad, but then everyone wanted to give you something. And at church, my stars, how they all prayed for you. Your knees felt like they had gave out, they were just so sore. Everybody, not just the preacher now, everybody laid hands on you. You'd get a fresh [rabbit's] foot, piece of veil, a piece of money to remind me of home [a farm near Silver, South Carolina], piece of cloth for your tears—you know, that old stuff everybody had in their bags.

In the weeks leading up to the girl's departure, kin and close family members[6] also gave the young women special good-luck objects: charms and fetishes consisting of fresh animal parts or fleece, veiling, feathers, medicinal herbs, spices, and money. The family of Maybell Fannie Hunnell, after moving from Dewy Rose, Georgia, to Starr, South Carolina, maintained a long-standing migration tradition:

See, everybody got a something. Just a piece of cloth with I guess it was dirt and some flowers that smelled to know not when. It was pushed way down under your clothes right up next to your skin. I must have kept it years. First thing them women wanted to see, too, when I got back to Dewy Rose. I believe they checked me for that for years every time I came back home, too. It was nothing to tell about, really.

Only three women talked freely about the good-luck paraphernalia or charms women travelers customarily carried. Although each woman interviewed noted the taboos in her interview, such as traveling during certain phases of the moon or their menstrual cycle, only the three were willing to discuss the subject in depth. Bernice Reeder turned on the light on the table next to where she was seated, frowned as she shifted her head, and looked down into her hands. She looked up with narrowing eyes and glared over at the window sill. She held her arms tightly across her chest and was visibly annoyed by these invasive "old times, woman-talk" questions. After a long delay, this stout woman looked hesitant but whispered hoarsely:

Bernice Reeder, right, photographed just before leaving the rural South.

You'd take a good bath and wash your hair. Then Mamma took and cut a piece of hair off to keep with what I guess was dried flowers, rice and sugar. They said this'd keep you from getting hungry, sick, or having bad, you know, having female problems. Then they put all that stuff in a piece of boiled gauze or cotton. It was always white and boiled till the stiffness was out. They cooled it and then put all that in this limp piece of cloth. Tied at the top with white string—boiled just the same. You put that on right then. Under your clothes and next to your skin. Really, some things you didn't ask a whole lot about— they just did.

Virginia Lacy sat with her hands folded across her lap. She was never distracted by the slamming doors, the music in the room, or the loud arguing in the back hall. She was not disturbed by the sirens and lights from three passing fire engines. Her two grandchildren asked her questions, but she never responded to their inquiries; and, after waiting with both anxiety and curiosity, they tired of being overlooked and went away. Virginia Lacy *was* unsettled by questions that "talked up matters that only crazy people set stock in or people sporting a stink wanted to keep going." Looking across the room from her chair, she offered a strong, detailed warning against any person discussing "women's knowledge" too publicly. Then, while making no attempt to hide her exasperation, she explained:

Mamma Dey gave me a little bag to put around my neck. I asked was it to suck on because it was just like the one they used for a baby's fret medicine when they are vexed or when the mother didn't have enough milk. They laughed and laughed at me. My Mamma then said no, it was to kill germs and keep harm away. So you put it on and that's it. You wasn't allowed to ask questions. It's not like now. People didn't talk about even the women's things, you know, the period.

Everybody down there [South Carolina] had a lot of who-dos and all. All that mess. And then you didn't know. And when you're old enough to be told, you don't talk about it. That's for women to talk about, and only women, at a certain time and place. You won't do well if you talk about these things. And you should know better for your own sake!

Lottie Cooksey lives in the senior citizens' section of a dilapidated garden-apartment community. The bare tile floors of her tiny efficiency apartment are dusted and polished. In the living room are two large sofas, a high-backed chair, and an oak table. Sheer drapes and white metal venetian blinds cover large windows. A table with four chrome and leather chairs sit in the small kitchen. Mrs. Cooksey prepared tea and put two plastic cups on the oak table, setting a place for each one as carefully as she would for china. Next to each cup she placed a plastic spoon with a folded paper napkin underneath. She carefully poured the pekoe tea and then enjoyed talking about her past. Visibly startled, she rubbed her cracked hands together quickly when I wanted more detail on the things her mother, aunts, and female kin placed in her bath the night before she left and on her body just before she left the family home in Texas:

It was from the yard, the garden and me. I had not begun my woman's [menstrual cycle], so they put in this flower in the bath water and what looked like grass and seeds too. Then I was dried and Miss Veda came. She knew Louisiana stuff and all, so she put a pouch under my clothes. Just so. I didn't look in but it was soft like dirt but had a little grit. I had that thing on me when I traveled for years! Then I lost it somehow, I guess about twelve, fifteen years after I'd been here.

I can't say what was in it because I didn't make it up. And you didn't ask them then. About nothing!

THE PLEADING PROCESS

The final and most universal step in preparation for migration centered around the male head of the home. In the limited public arena open to African Americans, the husband/father/male family head represented the entire family. Most husbands were older than their wives and therefore exercised authority by virtue of both age and gender. Landowners, merchants, and government agents in the rural South also acknowledged the role of the husband as the head of his family. Landowners, under the sharecropping system, parceled out land for sharecropping to the male family head. Sharecropping contracts were based on agreements signed by the male heads of the household and the landowners. Government agency records confirm that the Freedmen's Bureau mandate that male-headed households receive more monetary compensation and larger land grants than female-headed households held true.[7] Women, who earned money as domestics and received payment for children who worked as "live-out" servants, earned more hard cash, but it was the male head of household who purchased the bulk of the family's supplies. Although men and women had a distinct set of roles and priorities, "they needed each other to form a complete economic unit."[8] And it was this complete unit that finalized the migration process of these young women.

Mayme Gibson, of Mississippi, looked over her gold-rimmed glasses as she pointed to an old picture on an old floor-model radio. Without any sarcasm in her voice or in her eyes, she leaned back in her chair and reminisced about how the "pleading and praying" foreshadowed the journey from the rural South. "Everybody left out in that way, as I know of it," she stressed. Details might differ, but the scenario surrounding the final migration decision was essentially the same. The northern family kin members, while visiting the South, conducted a somewhat contrived pleading process with the southern family to convince them that the child should go north. This pleading process usually transpired during an annual or seasonal visit by the northern kin to the southern homestead. Once in a relaxed setting, the elder northern kin (usually male) curried the attention of the head of the southern family. There were long conversations about the concerns and needs of kin in Washington, D.C. The goal was to persuade the father that one of his children was needed up north to help free other kin to perform essential duties. First, the visiting kin had to show the rural family that the travel expenses of the journey would be no burden for them. Then, the southern family had to be persuaded of the desperate need for this child up north.

It was usually argued that family members had always helped out other kin during times of trouble. This was persuasive, because the southern kin network knew that it was seen as the *only* survival support for family members living outside the rural South. And, although the entire southern family's survival and support system could not be moved north, one member—a child—could be mobile and thus an important part of the survival network. Family survival, everyone agreed, was a responsibility shared by all trained kin, including children.

As African Americans migrated north, kin obligations did not cease. Race, class, and caste prejudice impeded upward employment mobility for the recent migrants. In the pleading process, much was made of the adult kin's obligation to toil, under unfavorable circumstances, for low wages outside of their own homes. When family members moved into cities, only the extended family's cooperative spirit could further the urban family's move upward.[9] The child, nurtured to assist the family, was an important expression of the family's cooperative spirit. The overwhelming needs of the urban kin dictated that *this* particular child could satisfy that powerful demand.

During the pleading, family members raised other concerns. The parents were reassured that the child would not be a burden to kin in the urban center, the child would be safe, and she would be given education or medical attention. Most important, it was stressed that the child was not irrevocably leaving the rural homestead. A flow of letters would keep the parents abreast of the child's activities and well-being. Kin members, aware of the division of labor based on gender, insisted that they would enforce these traditions strictly. Urban kin stressed that employment would be determined and dictated by practices learned and established in the rural South. Although each head of household recognized the importance of employed children in an extended or augmented household, it was family need, not money, that figured centrally in the argument for permission to take the child to Washington, D.C.

In spite of—or perhaps to counter—these pleas, the father would recount in detail how this child needed to remain at home. He might voice the emotional burden of a "baby girl" leaving for a strange city. Despite assurances that a network of kin and neighbors would be accountable for the child, there was hesitation. In assessing the impact on the rural family, the "loss" would be great. The father's animated conversation reflected his special affection, loyalty, and concern for his child. He might express extraordinary pride in one aspect of her "chores." Finally, the father—with great and clearly perceived hesitation—reluctantly would yield and allow his daughter to depart. Despite this ritualized drama, rural southern families themselves viewed migration as a means to relieve the economic plight of their households.

Many of the woman discovered that their migration had in fact been devised and arranged by mail months before verbal consent was given. In answer to the question of whether she thought the pleading process

Southern family reading letter. Courtesy of the Library of Congress.

between her father and brother-in-law had been something of an act, Bernice Reeder skeptically answered she was sure that her father's response was fashioned for her benefit. Her voice was clipped as she described coming home for a weekend visit from the Richey family, where she was working, and seeing Brother, Ma-Sis, and, most important, a barrel. She knew the barrel was filled with things for the children, and after dinner it would be opened. Goodies to eat, fruit, shoes, and clothing were always in each barrel. She was willing to sit quiet and listen to Ma-Sis tell all about the city and her work, because she was waiting for the adults to finally open the barrel:

When Brother and Ma-Sis came home it was nice. Brother always brought us a barrelful of toys and fruit and candy, but this time there was a dress in the barrel, with lace around the front. Everybody got some candy, but Ma-Sis gave the dress to me.

The next night Mama brought me in the parlor with Daddy, Ma-Sis, and

Brother. Brother told Daddy he wanted me to go back north with him. Daddy hugged me and told Brother, "No. She can't go. You got Lillie and Mary up there. This one here's my heart. She can't go." They talked and talked. Then Ma-Sis started to cry when she was telling how she'd have to leave their two young ones alone if I didn't come. Finally Daddy broke down and said I could go.

The next day I was on the train with Brother and Ma-Sis. My mama had give me this big box of fried chicken, biscuits, and *two* sweets. And Ma Sis put a great big napkin over my new dress so the box wouldn't get grease on it. Brother was sitting next to me, and I asked him how did he know I'd like a pretty dress like this—with lace? And he said, my mama had wrote Ma-Sis long time ago to bring me a nice dress to wear back on the train.

You know, from time to time I thought on that. That thing hit me—I tell you years later. From then I knew my going with Ma-Sis and Brother was planned a long time before Daddy ever said a thing.

Such feigned activities seemed contrived to Beulah Nelson, a woman who described herself as "brazen, bold, and insolent,"[10] for another reason. She acknowledged that her migration was devised and arranged by the family through letters, but she believed she had assured her own migration before the end of the week by displaying a new-found freedom:

Before I left, a lady, who was named Miss Addie, and a member of my mother's church—my people all were sanctified—stayed home to have a baby. My mamma let me go there and I heard her say, "Just three days 'cause she going with my brother." Plus, I had done read the letters they tried to hide from us.

And I worked them three days. Why? Mama sent me, and they was paying a quarter a week! Now, you had to cook the breakfast, you wait on all of them, all the children, and get them ready for school if they had to go to school. Fix their lunch and everything. Then you wash up all the dishes. Then you had to go make up all the beds and pick up all the things behind all the children, and then after that you had to go out behind the house, honey, and pick the garden. And pick what kind of vegetables you got to have. You got to wash them and cook them. And they had three meals a day. They would eat they breakfast, and then twelve o'clock they had to have a big dinner. And then they had supper later in the evening.

But they didn't want no nigger to put they hand on their bread. Understand me good now. I set the table up and put the food on the table. But the bread be the last thing. Never bring the bread in until after they say the grace, so the bread would be seeping hot. I wait just as good until they said the grace, and I wouldn't move because I would have had to pick up the bread out of the pan, and I still would have to take knife or fork to lift it to put in the plate to take to the table, and I know she didn't want me to touch it. Right? Well, if she didn't want me to touch it, if I couldn't touch it, I wasn't going to try not to touch it to carry it to the table to give it to them. She said to me, "How long are you going to wait before you bring that bread in here?" I said, "I'm not even going to bring it in there." I said, "You put it in there. You cook it, you don't want me to touch it. If you don't want me to touch it, you don't need me to bring it in there." And I didn't bring it in there. And that's when she got mad, arguing with me so. She jumped up from table and she said to me, "Beulah, you fired." But she didn't fire me—I fired myself, 'cause I *intended* to do what I did. I said, "These two days I been in your house. You could've done—as far as you know—you could be done ate a lot of my spit [in your food]. I could have done did anything I want to do to it, and you wouldn't have never known nothing about it. But just because you could see me if I touch it." I said, "No, if that's the way it's to be—not me!" I said, "For what? Six days a week for twenty-five cents? Not me!" You see, I didn't have to do it—I was leaving.

Leave she did, and she saw many other young African American faces on the railway car headed for points north. Toting "freedom bags," heavy with their southern family's blessings and tears—not to mention neatly folded dresses, good-luck pieces, and Bibles—these young women journeyed toward maturity in the promised land of Washington, D.C.

3

NEW DAY'S DAWNING:
THE WORLD
OF WASHINGTON

Union Station . . . was so big. And when you looked up at the ceiling, you
just knew you were North! . . . The ceiling so tall and beautiful with gold all
over it. I just knew that gold was going to fall into my hands!
——PERNELLA ROSS, AGE EIGHTY-NINE

Amy Kelly, a well-respected musician in the gospel-music community of Washington, D.C., remembers the song that came to her
mind when she arrived at Union Station:

"Nobody Knows the Trouble I Seen" comes to my mind. I was so tired from
the long ride from Charlotte. Matter of fact, I thought I was up here when I
saw that big train [in the North Carolina station]. When I got here my legs
hurt, I felt so tired, and my eyes didn't see nothing special about this place.
But my brother and sister pushed me right through that big place [train sta-
tion] out to the street. I never laid eyes on so many people or heard so much
different kinds of noises. It all made me cry. Sister, now she's tired too remember, snatched me so hard and said, "Stop all that, now!" For days they seemed
mad cause this and that had went wrong when we'd been down home. When
you a child you think it's you the blame—so of course I felt worse. Seemed to
me, just one thing after another for months—I bet into the next year, before I
even liked it here. All in all, my first days was troubled!

ELDORADO OF HOPE?

By contrast, a *Washington Post* article reflected on the experiences and
anticipated rewards of white women who migrated to the nation's capi-

tal and profiled an employee of the Woman's Home Missionary Society. The article pointed out how a

sweet-faced deaconess watches as many young women leave trains alone and learns whether she has friends in town or is an entire stranger. The ignorant foreigner, women, and girls from every city and hamlet all believe that if they can get to Washington the frown that Fortune has hitherto worn for them will be changed to a smile so radiant that their eyes will be dazzled by it.[1]

According to Miss Miner, a Missionary Society employee, women faced discouragement because prospective employers were barraged by hundreds of similar applications from girls with educations from crossroads schoolhouses or young ladies' seminaries. The story detailed instances of women ending up as cases for charity; or they met "the tragedy of a gambling hall or [prostitution] parlor bedroom." Trapped in tiny Twelfth and F Street cells, women conceded their mistake of succumbing to the lure of this " 'Eldorado of Hope' buoyed with only youth and high spirits, impelled by ambition, seeking the road to prosperity guided only by ignorance which is bliss."[2] Other articles described female migrants as self-reliant, well behaved, and vitally concerned with self-improvement:

They work and like it; . . . love sports and dancing. They adore clothes—smooth, American clothes. This new army on the Potomac—bright-eyed, fresh-faced young Americans who have poured into Washington from remote farms, sleepy little towns and the confusion of other cities to work for the government.[3]

Unfortunately, these accounts did not include the early experiences of the army of African American women who also poured into Washington, D.C., from remote southern farms. Often accompanied by family members, these women contributed to the near doubling of the African American population in the District of Columbia from 1900 to 1910.[4] Once these women arrived in Washington, their expectations and hopes for a better life rarely matched what they found. For most, kin did provide help in settling into their new lives, but much of what they experienced was new and forced hard readjustments. Lost was the intimacy of the rural southern communities they had come from. Yet the women found that the old and familiar—the work—had not changed. They scrubbed floors, looked after their kin's children, and assisted the extended family as they were directed by older kin working as live-in servants.[5] In the communities where they lived, the women quickly became a part of a strong kinship network. The circle of people who looked out for them had both narrowed and widened. Although there were fewer of their own siblings living in Washington, D.C., migrants from particular southern states tended to live near one another and form their own subcommunities to provide mutual support.[6] The church also provided a constant in their lives. But it, too, was different from church down South. Like the city itself, the churches in Washington, D.C., were larger, more impersonal, and, during the women's early years in the North, less directly attuned to their own lives. Sources indicate that leaders within the African American community looked down on migrants, whom they viewed as the source of the community's problems.[7] In gentle, emotional tones, and almost as if she was talking to herself, Mary Little, like many of the women, insisted, "All I remember is that little straw bag and that big, big boat. I can't tell you how full I felt, and I won't talk about that bag." From the Potomac River at the break of dawn, Mamie Richardson's first glimpse of Washington, D.C., was a dock in the southwest covered with cargo and baggage:

Southwest was a place that many a time I wished I'd a never seen. You come up on it so slow on that old boat. You ride all night—sitting up in these big, big seats in the part for Colored. Then you got to look out and see that boat come up so slow to the land. Seemed to take forever. Some things you see far off, big buildings and the monuments. But you didn't see all that much—it was early morning. And it wasn't nice like now . . . that I can tell you! I was with an old, old woman we called Cousin Zet.

It was just smelly and people busy hollering this or that. And your eyes jumped from one sight to the next. All I had seen was a Carolina farm! But I tell you soon as you hit land things was moving. And fast too! Get this and do that, run to and fro, you up and gone.

There was no "sweet-faced deaconess" there to meet her. There were no employment agencies, no warnings of danger. Mary Little, like Mamie Richardson and Cousin Zet, was met at the dock by kinfolk, and the young women began their work life in Washington like most of the other women—by helping out in the home of their kinfolk and getting some piecework. Mamie Richardson stressed:

In what was no more than half a day I was helping do work right in the room. I remember helping light press a basket of clothes before I had time to draw a good breath. But, I got to come. In truth, I had a cousin who was older and should have been in here first. But I was here. So I learned how to make a few pieces of money walking on the muddy streets, taking clothes around in them close up places [alley areas], and on the first day, too.

Mamie Richardson, Mary Little, and two other women had their first glimpse of the District of Columbia from the vantage point of southwest because they came by boat from the tidewater areas of Virginia and North Carolina. The docks gave them a unique point of entry into the city. Between the date of the census that documented the arrival of Cousin Zet and the census that documents the appearance of Mary Little and Mamie Richardson, the percentage of Virginia, "Cacalacky" [North and South Carolina], and Deep South African Americans living in the District of Columbia increased fourfold.[8]

It was, however, by train that the vast majority of migrant women arrived. Each woman's description of the train trip culminated in what was their most memorable "new-in-the-North" experience[9]—seeing Union Station for the first time. Pernella Ross described it:

It was so big. And when you looked up at the ceiling, you knew you were North! I remember looking up, the ceiling so tall and beautiful with gold all

Union Station, with its gold-gilded ceilings, was recalled in detail by every migrant arriving by train. Courtesy of the Washingtoniana Collection, Martin Luther King Memorial Library, Washington, D.C. (hereafter noted as Washingtoniana Collection).

over it. I just knew that gold was going to fall into my hands! And so many people. I never had seen so many. Not at church or a church social. Nothing like that. We knew to wait in one spot and then the people from the street come in to help us. Plus we had stuff from home for them from they people. I didn't remember any of them, but they knew me from the time I was a baby. We went out (me still hoping that gold would fall and crying) and got a street-car. I saw the tall, tall buildings and so many more people. Streets wide, wide, wide. Then things started to not look as nice and you saw more colored people.

Mathilene Anderson arrived in Washington, D.C., on the cusp of 1910. She came with family members from Rappahannock County in Virginia and was followed by two sisters and three brothers. This family directly contributed to the doubling—in just one decade—of the percentage of African Americans in the District of Columbia. Methilene's train

Washington Channel with the Norfolk-Washington Line ship in view. Many migrants traveled by boat to Washington, D.C. Courtesy of the Washingtoniana Collection.

trip was the first of many new—and frightening—experiences in the North:

I got here with my uncle [her mother's distant cousin through marriage]. There was people waiting to meet us in this one place where you'd see the colored people stand—you didn't just go anywhere in them days. The people from her place took us to the rooming house on the streetcar. Here I just got off the first train I ever saw and was scared to death of that. Everybody made all over the new station 'cause it was so big. Now, I was scared of that and this thing, too, but they told me to get on it, and I did. But they said I looked like it was going to eat me—I was so fearful of everything up here.

They got to a place and we helped each other off the car; walked back to a street so small. I *knew* Sister, Aunt Dew, and all them never'd be in this place. Looking like they did when we saw them home for 'sociation, homecomings, or Christmastime visits? No. But in two days there she come. I didn't know what to make of a thing now. But I didn't dare ask a soul or expect any of

them to help me. I was there to do as I was told. Like a young girl would
do—and better think about a bit more.

Some, like Alfreda Baker, came to Washington, D.C., by automobile:

My brother worked as a chauffeur and two or so times a year he came home.
I heard them telling on one of his visits before I came—it was back in the fall,
before I come—all about they place. How they moved again but still down-
town; a reverend rented them his home, so on and so on.

 I came in a little car in spring. See, we didn't have anything but our clothes
to come. And I think my mother sent the baby bed up to my sister Margaret
for her babies, because she had her children here, and one or two of my sister's
children were living with us down home. So we just had our clothes to take to
Tin Cup Court. It was in a colored part, we call it across the railroad track,
but it was a nice house. Then we moved to a place at 409 P Street. I think my
older brother knew somebody who was living at that time. But I didn't want
to go to 409 P Street—that was an apartmentlike place. But 'course I went.
I had to learn to get along fast there, too.

No matter how they came, fifty-six ended up living on what Edith
Gaines, a light brown woman who migrated from Lucknow, South Carolina, called a "short street," or an alley. In a brisk, deeply accented,
heavy female voice, she explained: "We [African Americans] were living
in apartments, and in little short streets and things like that. Back in that
time you didn't have a whole lot to look forward to. People were so religious then because all their hope was in the Lord. That's how it was."
These women moved to areas already heavily populated by migrants
from the South. Sixty-eight percent of the women first lived in the
southwest, the areas adjacent to Florida Avenue in the northwest, or
near the Foggy Bottom area. By 1920 there were three migrant enclaves
in the federal city, areas that were at least three-quarters African American and close to the locations of earlier concentrations.[10]

 In one infamous area, Snow's Alley, C. A. Snow, the publisher of the
National Intelligencer, had constructed "a greenhouse and four houses in

the interior of the block just before the Civil War. Later, new homes were built to house African American families, who worked hard to develop stable family lives and employment strategies to counter adversity."[11] Alaveta Mitchell, a tall, medium brown woman with long gray hair, wore a blue sheath and a matching scarf, and her feet, resting on a low tapestry stool, were encased in expensive slippers. Behind the chair she sat in was a wall, fourteen feet high, lined with books, including many works in various languages. Her wealthy daughter and son-in-law, anxious to supervise the interview, became uncomfortable when she detailed the rough life she knew as a migrant from South Carolina. She explained how she created her own opportunity to understand life in the underbelly[12] of Foggy Bottom known as Snow's Alley:

Oh, I can tell you about a place everybody talked about and the one place I learned all about on day one. It was called Snowy [Snow's] Court, in the Bottom. A bad place, I'm here to tell. Now, I saw a dog run down there and then run out—scared by just the looks of the people who lived in there. And they told me to not even look down there 'cause them was some rough people—just too rough. And not a one from South Carolina, so I wasn't never to go in there to see for myself.

But a time or two I went in, just to see it. A small place, dirty like I can't tell you. Small houses, but people who looked out for one another. I took up with a girl who took me in there and into where she lived. So I seen the place inside to out. But I shouldn't been in there. See, if I had no people to be seeing in there I wasn't to go there or anywhere else. I did. Knowing I should stay just with or by my peoples.

Adapting to the living conditions of Washington, D.C., was a daily chore for the migrants. Alfreda C. Baker raised one crooked finger for emphasis as she recounted how she received her initial instructions on survival outside the rural South: "Indeed, what you got here first was teachings on how to make do off a farm. Every day you remember that farm—how nice it was and all—but making a way here, this wasn't nothing like farming." Another elderly woman, using a farming image to compare her experiences in Washington, D.C., to rural life, said "I've lived long enough to know that you can't grow a good potato out of bad ground. And dis [Washington, D.C.] sho is bad ground."[13] Esther Lawson's comparison of Twenty-third and L Streets to places in the South focused on feelings of social isolation:

It was lots different from down where I come from. Mostly, well, the peoples were different. Our people from home, they didn't mingle with a lot a people. You just didn't up here. Now, when we was in Alabama, we just mingle with everybody 'round 'near. Everybody knows everybody. But see here you didn't know everybody. You didn't run into a lot of people outside the building. Just like you live in a 'partment here, you might not know the people in the houses next door until you been here for a while. On Twenty-third Street you had houses with lots of rooms to rent. Yeah, it was a lot of houses, but you know a lot of people just wanna be to theyselves. And so that's the way it was, and I lived there with an undertaker shop there on the corner. But that's what it was.

Some women used biblical metaphors to describe their first experiences and adjustments. For Beulah Nelson, life in the District of Columbia "was not good like home. Crowded smelly streets, noise, and confusion was all I saw. And people talked like it was somethin' near 'bout heaven!" Queen Williams, of Gilchrist County, Florida, wholeheartedly agreed with that comparison. She said she had come "right from what's called the For Whites area of Florida to Deanwood and never saw such a place. It'd make you cry it was just bad looking. But if it'd been hell, what could a child like me do or say about it? So, you made like it was heaven—but God knows in truth it never was half what you heard or said."

Beulah Nelson lived with her sister, brother, and his family in a small apartment near Twenty-ninth and K Streets in a Northwest community called Foggy Town. She said their rooms were "on the back with nothing to see and nothing good to smell most parts of the year. I'd always think, when my sister and cousins talked about where they worked, how different a place could be so close!"

KIN AND NEARABOUTS

Kin were instrumental in the migrants' adjustment to city living. Mary Ruth Ingraham, who described herself as a "round-shouldered little woman," sat erect as she enumerated her father's network of kin living in Washington:

Daddy, he had a sister named Georgie Everts, and then Aunt Minerva Taylor was here. And then he had a brother that was living here—Uncle Isaac, who lived on W Street, not too far from Cousin Lee's brother. And when I used to come down there he'd gave me a ring. There was a ruby in it. And I let my daughter wear it and you know that was the end of that ring. He always thought a lot of me, and he gave me that ruby ring.

Now who? I'm trying to think of who else was living in Washington besides Aunt Georgie and Aunt Sam, and Ma Teag Walker.

These new communities of kin immediately became substitutes for the family members back home. Elder kin assumed many of the responsibilities of parents, as Blanche Ashby noted:

All us from around North Carolina was living nearby. Now my people from the Cumberland [County] side, just out of Roseboro and round—we all were in this area [Foggy Bottom] and most lived up from K Street—from Twenty-third to about Twenty-seventh. It was like home. You saw each other and helped each other. Now at a holiday or wedding—you did everything like down home. . . . Wasn't Miss Alice watching all girls just like my Aunt Tense did down home?

I didn't meet any people not from my home 'til I started up in Maryland. You just stayed with your people, at least for the first six to eight months when you got up here.

Alfreda Baker waved her hand above her head to stress that she would "never have made it a day if my people hadn't kept me . . . living right there was the thing that helped me from the first."

But families sometimes made the adjustment more, not less, difficult. Etherine Underwood's face is very round, brown with large eyes framed by thick glasses. Wearing a powder-blue dress with a multicolored scarf,

One of the relatives with whom Mary Ruth Ingraham
worked on her first live-in servant job.

her short hair concealed by a black-and-gray wig, she sat very straight
and recounted her first two days in Washington:

I cried a lot. I was so lonely. My brother seemed to just leave me. I knew two
or three people from home. One living down on the bottom floor. Then
some more right across the street. But he left me alone too quick. Then come
the second day so fast—too quick—my people giving me childrens to watch,
washing, and piecework to do. Then they did work by the piece and all. But

In Snow's Court, an inhabited alley, conditions rivaled the "grimmest" slums of New York City. Courtesy of the Washingtoniana Collection.

there was nobody to help me or even to talk to. Even when you worked out down home there'd be somebody with you.

But not here. You came in and they went right out. When they got days off? Out they'd go again. They carried me out sometimes, but still I cried a lot till I got to meet more people. But that, I know, was months later.

Gatha Douglass was lighthearted as she vividly recalled, in a thunderous voice, the welcome she received, which was paradoxically similar to, and yet different from, Etherine Underwood's:

My sister helped me meet everyone in the place where she roomed. I met all the people living around there from Virginia, too. She told me how to go to the market and took me on the streetcar to learn what was all around the city. I bet it was a day or more of just taking me around.

When she left me, I knew who to call for any help and everything . . . like

Beulah Nelson (and many migrants) described in detail the Foggy Bottom community, home to many migrants. This is a photo of Twenty-fifth Street, N.W. Courtesy of the Washingtoniana Collection.

home. She taught me that whole place before she left me with her and my aunt's little children for the week. Nothing to be upset about—you knew you came to do up here.

Isetta Peters is a diminutive woman with ample but dainty chestnut shoulders. In a coarse and craggy voice, she provided the best description of the new environment, especially the roles of women and men and the differences and similarities between the city and the South:

It was a small place with people living everywhere. I was just off L Street near Twenty-third. The room was crowded with so much stuff because so many people said it was home. Some came no more than twice the month, but it was a place for all us to live. Where else was they to go? So, you got here and met people. The next day you watched the childrens. That's right, the next day. Oh, they'd always be other peoples' babies with your peoples for you to mind. See they did live-in too. Now, the father of the childrens never minded nobody. No, in them days a man didn't do no mindin' for no child. Maybe a half hour or so, but somebody'd be over there quick 'cause he wasn't staying in there with childrens long. No sir. So the womens has girls come up from home. Whoever had somebody that's where all them left they babies. See, they all had to work so they all helped bring up somebody to watch the babies.

You had to pick up new things at the same time. You had a well much closer than in Hickory, yes. But, you had to carry things up steps. Nobody or place I ever lived in South Carolina had steps and things like that. So you kept a eye out and saw how everything was the same but different here. Everybody helped 'cause everybody knew you just up here. Everybody from North Bullock, Sharon, and Delsphilla lived right there together.

Newspaper articles might have associated excitement and awe with moving to the city, but Mary Sprow's diary revealed quite different feelings. In her diary she questioned the very meaning and value of work: "What is work? To clean and scrub days in and days out."[14] For African American women, migration was inextricably linked with the hard labor of domestic service.

Although many of the migrants had experienced emotional distance from their mothers while growing up, mothers sometimes wrote to express empathy with a daughter's difficult new life. The letters reveal the many ways mothers in the South provided moral support and reassured the young girls during their first phase of adjustment to the nation's capital. Bernice Reeder shared her mother's 1914 letter: "It's hard here everyday too. God's the same there and here, so he sees your problems. Everyday just remember, try as you can . . . like what you'd do here. Now's just a time to get ready for what'll be next. Don't forget that."[15]

In addition to social support, families assisted the women in obtaining their first Washington employment—home-based work. For more than half the women, their work was providing (unpaid) child-care and household maintenance. Marie Stone spoke for almost all of the women interviewed:

When you first came you worked, too. But at your people's—not out. You'd do for the children, cook, clean and all. My brother had three babies. Now

they were living-in, as most was back then. So I did all for them. And they
had two people from home rooming in, so I did for them, too. We lived just
off K Street and was doing well, too.

Esther Lawson of Alabama described her first responsibilities as a migrant to Washington in 1914:

I did linen piecework while at Brother's. His wife worked by the week, but I
helped a laundress and did for Brother's childrens. She'd send her big sons out,
and early, too! They'd bring in the work, and I'd help her. Now a good part of
the day I did Brother's house, and all day I had to mind his childrens.

GOLD FALLING IN MY HANDS

Subsequently, the women were expected to develop economically pro-
ductive lives by extending the services they were already providing for
their own kin. Their meager earnings went directly to the adult kin of
the household, a continuation of the pattern begun in the South. Pansylee Holmes declared:

When you got up here [Washington, D.C.], far as money go'd, up here was
just like home. Never did you get any in your hand. Especially when you was
first here. No, your people took that. You was helping out, but you never saw
no money that you'd earned. But you didn't know any better—it was just like
down home.

Sadie Jones came to Washington from Alabama and lived with relatives
in late 1911. She recalled living on Willow Tree Court (an alley) and
working with a neighbor prior to her employment as a live-in servant:

When you first come here you'd pull together. No money I had was mine 'til I
was working out. You raised up your peoples' babies and all. Now if you was
like us, we had people from home here, and I'd work with them to help too—
right along as I minded Sister's three—all the same.
    See, I did laundry at first. I helped Miss Lena, a lady who was living two

doors down. But my sister got that money. I don't even know how much—Sister got it. She worked by the week, and on Saturday she'd come home. She'd get that money and see 'bout us all 'til Sunday. Then she'd go back [to her live-in job].

I guess she sent it home to Alabama. But you never saw no money when your people was around, though. It was too dear for you, they'd say.

Isetta Peters recalled the many new chores that awaited the women in the District of Columbia:

You got here and you watched the childrens. My sisters and cousin did live-in—so then you'd start on to work. Right there, while you was with the children. Everybody watching babies did something: take in wash, doing ironing, doing mending . . . any piecework.

I did sewing—mostly for a woman who did dressmaking. I think she worked for stores, but colored didn't work in the store they'd have you work in home places. A big boy got the stuff by the week, and it was sent right back in a day or so. I sewed dresses, mended and fixed coats, and whatever. Real fancy work she did. Some of it was things you'd never seen. Beautiful gowns all fixed with beads, pearls, and shiny stones. I never did them—too fancy a piece of work for a child.

This is why I said you had to pick up new things all the same time. Carry things up and down steps to whoever you was helping. You didn't get the jobs . . . just helped people who did that work and knew you'd be there to help. See, people they all had something to do [in their] home or out. Down South Carolina it was like that, too. You helped as you was told to. Everybody I knew did.

Alfreda Baker compared work in Washington, D.C., to the work young women performed while in training:

Well, they had these tin tubs here like at home. You know I thought it woulda' been different—maybe white or fancy but they was tin just the same. [Laughter.] You wash and scrub with the scrub board. And they rinsed, you know. You'd rinse, but you had to go to the well and get the water. Here it was just down and outside the rooms. You'd go down there to heat your water and I mean to pick up water. [Laughter.] It would kill us today, and they lived to be old-age people.

That was the same as your grandma's, but they had to go off to a well. People home always had barrels that they filled up from rains, and they would heat water in tubs—from the barrels. That was where you keep the things cool, too—butter and milk. And that was the same way with Grandma's. They had a spring down there, too!

To Mathilene Anderson, work was a series of chores, whether she was in Laurel Mills, Virginia, or in Washington, D.C.:

You was sent to give help. That was all to it. You watched the small babies and did what was needed to keep up the place. Clean and all is what I mean. There was always somebody working round there doing what they could to get by. Laundry or mending, like that. If they worked on this or that, you did too. After all, it was work, and you came here to do work. One kind or other—wasn't no difference made. You work home or here, in or out. That's how it was for us.

Beulah Nelson, sent to live with her brother in 1922, is the mother of a very successful banker. During her interview, this very attentive son looked with amazed disbelief as his mother explained:

All my life I've been doing the object [opposite] thing. I ran away with this girl from a school [in South Carolina] my Daddy sent me to after we had a mess with that man and Grandpappy at the settle. We met these boys and I figured how we could leave that school and get us married. My oldest brother, in two days, found me and took me home. Mama got Daddy to send me here 'cause she said, "She been with that boy and soon she'll 'get big.'" She didn't know we didn't do nothing—just kissing, kid junk. But no more than that.

So after I fired myself from the Tillmans, I was sent here. My brother and his wife worked by the week and were always in a mess over money. Mama and Daddy heard all about it from people coming back home but never told them how much they knew about they mess.

So, I get here with Brother and go right to the 1900 block of K Street—in this place called Froggy Town [Foggy Bottom]. Everybody there my color except a few whites, and they was the big number writers. Nothing in that area but dwelling houses; and the Georgetown section wasn't nothing over there but colored, too. My brother took me to meet people all around there that day. The next day he took me to this lady across the street. She cleaned for the Catholics, did sewing, and was the one who would give me work and keep a eye out for me and the kids I'd watch.

The first job of most young migrants was assisting self-employed, older women working in Washington's home-based garment and millinery industries. Courtesy of the Washingtoniana Collection.

Just three days here and I'm left with his two [children] and three from other peoples. I go, with these kids now, where I was to help this lady with sewing. In this dwelling house, downstairs from where she lived, I saw a place I had to get into. I knew I had to get in there 'cause it was jumping. Next day I went right to the door of the place, told the lady my name, where I was from in South Carolina, and said I wanted to make money working. Me, bold as you please, got in there, too. She was selling liquor, cigarettes, hot clothing, had gambling games, everything. In a day she taught me everything 'cause I'm quick—remember I been to school. Now here I am, with these kids, going around for numbers or helping her in this joint place. Making money all the time!

The lady told my brother about me in this joint at week's end and he tried to stop me, but how? He had to go out working, and I'd go right back in that joint when he did. After some weeks, he messed up the money—he was always doing that! First couple times a colored man came fussing, then the white man came to put us out. My hand to God, I came cross that room and handed him [the white man] the back rent, rent due, and two months ahead. Brother ain't said a word. But then we moved down Twenty-fifth Street. And know what, I found my way right back to K Street, with them kids, making money just the same!

CITY-FIED RELIGION

If work was similar in the South and in Washington, D.C., one area of women's lives—religious activity—proved to be dramatically different. Kin prepared the migrants to expect differences in the urban church's function, beliefs, and practices. For example, most kin explained to the young women that, unlike in the rural South, in Washington, D.C., they would not have to travel far to church. Despite differences, however, just as in the South, the church was the cultural crucible and community center for all the young women. Sixty-seven were taken to church by their kin within seven days of their arrival. Marybell Slaughter, in an archetypal episode, stated,

I was here no more than a day when I went 'round to the church with them. I met people and from that day I was in church here. I wasn't out of Seven [Screven County, Georgia] no time before I was in a church. People didn't go weeks or months out of church. You got here and right 'way in church. My people home ain't having it, and my aunt knew, too.

The main difference in D.C. churches was that the religious services limited participant activity. In the rural South, religious services included prolonged periods for testifying, extemporizing songs, praying, chanting, and shouting. This new reserved worship took some getting used to, as Virginia Lacy eloquently recalled. A retiring woman, with a Boston-accented soft voice, without exception used dainty hand gestures to accentuate her spirited expressions:

Down home you got in the wagon early to go to church meeting. It started when someone sang a song. Everybody just sang, helped bring up the song and swayed with it. A lot of time they made it up as they'd go on. Feet tapping all the while. A prayer was said, and whoever could—would read from the bible. You can be sure a saint'd make a song from out the prayer or what was read in the Bible. Long and deep down slow. After a time it would get so good—somebody'd shout. Then a shoutin' chorus came up—some shouting or clapping, and stamping or crying or groaning. Church went on and on like that in South Carolina. Them people had a time!

Up here, they seem'd do everything by the board[16] or paper. Songs, they didn't get brought up by a saint. People knew what was to be singed. Church started and stopped near a time to let people get home or back to they job. Sometimes at Thursday's meetings you get service like down home. Mostly here you don't make service, you follow along. And that's 'cause people read. Most of us from down home just followed along good. And nobody made anything out of it [not reading]. Church and most people [are] nice. But it wasn't like home.

Many migrants considered these services too city-fied and dignified. As a result of such an experience with Washington churches, Eula Montgomery remains unaffiliated with a church in D.C.:

My home church is right where I lived down home—outside of Equality but on the Nixburg side—to this day because of the way people is here. Every song in a book, never an amen or shout. I'm from a church that had life. These got none and none of my money neither. If I only get to church once a year down home, so be it.

Their lack of education and poor clothing marked the migrants as different from others in the urban church, but a more significant factor in their lack of acceptance in the new churches was a bias against rural southerners. Their "shout" during the service and their theological beliefs put them at odds with urban African Americans.[17] Lovella Willoughby was uncharacteristically quiet as she explained the dilemma of worshipping amid a large number of virtual strangers:

Not too many people could read or write so good. And wasn't a soul rich enough to buy more than two dresses new, and couldn't go in but so many stores, anyway! So what was education or clothing? The real problem? If you do a too wild shout or anything with people you don't know, who knows what could happen? People can do things to you and church ain't no different.

Spirits, good and bad right there, waiting to possess you. I know people went to a South Carolina church, went to doing a "one-legged" shout, fell out, and ain't right yet! What was done? I don't know, but people back then knew to be careful in a church filled with people [who] didn't come from no place near you.

The women attended a variety of churches in their communities. Thirty-nine of the young migrants attended churches they identified as "large." Alfreda Baker's face brightened as she recalled the awe of first attending a large Washington church service:

Want me to tell you something? To be honest the real first thing I remember? Nothing about the service. I remember first that at that church they had a place where they could feed people, instead of going home. Home? Mama always had a big dinner that we fixed and we had dinner at home. But places here had you eat, I mean sit right there and eat, before evening services and all. For a long time I thought it was free, too. It was nice for us to get out when we could go on Sunday afternoons after Brother and them came back from work living in.

Only eight of the thirty-nine women who began attending "large" churches continued their affiliation with congregations established before 1865.[18] Most of the women eventually joined smaller, newly organized churches, located within walking distance of the members. Those who stayed in large congregations felt relegated to the periphery of activity, but at least they had a close relative who was already a member of the church when they joined. Five of the eight women also had at least

three years of school in the rural South and were therefore considered
"educated," as compared to the other migrants. None of these eight
women felt ostracized by other church members because of her employment[19] as a domestic worker; as Marie Stone observed, few women
had the luxury of escaping domestic service:

Who didn't do domestic work? Even the teachers did it for one while in their
lives. Many people couldn't get teaching jobs here cause they went to schools
in the South, so they had to do domestic work, too! I know ladies with college but got good pay and did domestic work to make that money. Everybody
in Fourth Street had mothers, aunts, and cousins working right with you at
one time or another. People didn't look at that so much as how you presented
yourself. Good home training and people being ladylike, nice. That's what
people down there look at. People who say this or that about my church never
been there once.

Alaveta Mitchell shared important observations about the workings of a
small, community-based church:

It was a small place on the street. Started by a man from home, his name I
can't recall. He preached in his house. People from all around, even from
Snowy Alley, came to hear him. He had a painting trade, but he'd preach. And
have Bible lessons on Thursday and Sunday. Right on the first floor in the
front room with a piano. A small church you'd say, but its where we go'd. On
other days people in Bible units, clubs, and prayer bands—some together today
started right there. He helped start kids out in teams that people still have. It
was just nice, I do remember that.

Reformers of this epoch authored works that explored African American religious activity with the expectation that religious worship created
"either white Christians or no Christians at all."[20] These demographic-
and social-reform works chronicled the migrants' religious activities in a
negative manner.[21] During this period the studies found that small congregations in dilapidated buildings, improvised pulpits, itinerant preach-
ers, primitive wails, frenzied rituals, and other chaos created a saddening
travesty of Christ's religion.[22]

Marie Jefferies lived with her brother Charles Jefferies and his wife Lilly Diggs Jefferies, pictured here, and cared for their three children soon after she came to Washington, D.C.

Esther Lawson also believed that her small church strengthened her community's social life:

The best church in Washington, D.C., was on Twenty-third Street. It was in the back, you had to go through the hall to get to it. Church was like home for me. Good singing and people there most nights in prayer meeting or missionary meetings and so on. They always working to help this one out of a problem or to give that one a hand. The name I cannot remember but it was like New Baptist Spirit something.

Church life augmented women's perceptions of themselves in both their sacred and secular worlds. Blanch Ashby gave vivid details of the church she attended in the Deanwood section of Washington, D.C.:

Bible-reading classes were on Wednesday and Tuesday. Thursday is prayer-meeting night. And I saved them. I *saved* the Thursday night services—went house to house to get peoples every week for this. Sunday we have services sometimes all day. We had a choir, a piano player, then we got a piano an' a drum [laugh]. It was Reverend Phillips. I worked with him, from my first day in that church. Anybody 'round there today or 'round church will tell you about me working with Reverend Perry and Deacon Hall. Deacon Hall had cooking, sewing, nice sing-a-longs—just always something to do every night. It was fun to go. He's dead now, but he was the one who was there every night with us. He was *the* deacon. We got three young deacons after about ten years. Yeah, some still there and they'll tell you about me—now.

Through church and kin connections, migrant women were involved in a myriad of community-based activities. Their kin and geographic nexuses instantly connected the new migrants to beneficial organizations located in their immediate residential areas. Mary Ruth Ingraham found these community-based organizations an important part of her urban experience:

People from home had the best horse shows. There was a group of people who formed a club—I guess it was better than thirty years before I came in 1917—and they used to have shows. There was colored "Fourth of July" show all colored people had. And we still would go to the horse shows, picnics, and what like that. And then there were ball games, and the circus and things. Oh my, and the parades.

Our people, just was neighborly. And had a little club called Citizen's Club. And those people would go there and sew, knit, and crochet. They sent stuff home and made patchwork blankets. I mean, quilts and things. People used to do that years ago. And in the same way visit around. Well, when I first came to Washington and we used to love to go to the home things they'd do here. And I used to feel I'd gone back home—it was just like I was at home. Food, games, singing groups, just some of everything. Oh, people liked a big meeting on a Sunday and outside all day. Oh, they could run the picnic here!

And, oh yeah, in winter and cold we visited after church quite often. Sit and talk and eat. Then on New Year's Day, like I said, people used to go 'round and give everybody something for luck. I'd be just there waiting. They'd have a piece of money to hand out. We were in home clubs—Sunday or holiday clubs, it was nice us just here then.

Female migrants participated proudly in Washington's African American street parades and celebrations, events the newspapers saw in a hostile light. The *Washington Bee,* reporting on a celebration about the time Mary Ruth Ingraham's club began, described it as massive display of the "class of colored people who live in poverty and spend all their money for one day's festivity."[23] Even the city's African American leaders questioned

the tinsel show, gaudy display and straggling processions; thrusting upon public view a vastly undue proportion of the most unfortunate, unimproved and un-progressive class of colored people, and thereby inviting public disgust and contempt, and repelling the more thrifty and self respecting among us, is a positive hurt to the whole colored population of this city.[24]

Many young girls, however, were too insulated for the community's disdain to register with them. Athelene Walker of Tennessee commented, "I didn't know people. I knew my people, and the church people, or those who lived right around us. That's all."

But the nation's capital was quick to express its limited acceptance of young female migrants. In some cases, they were blatantly accused of being the "real cause" of the myriad of problems confronting the African American community. The education of migrant workers, for example, was a major concern to civic leaders. With education, it was hoped, these women would no longer "appear at work in soiled clothing, run-over heels, tattered stocking and hair uncombed—to arouse sympathy they insist."[25] Many citizens expressed concern about the influx of migrant children into the already overcrowded and segregated school system. A 1900 government report raised concern about the intrusion of the new arrivals. The report noted that the migrants were "a detriment to the District of Columbia colored schools. Uneducated they come . . . and they are hastening the demise of our schools."[26]

Migrant workers themselves saw a need for change, but local reform crusades generally emphasized changing the workers, not the work. This particularly racist concept of reform was called *servant education.* One early reformer advised African American women to learn their

Sign listing the weekly schedule of a community-based church in Washington, D.C. Courtesy of the Washingtoniana Collection.

work well because women "in the humblest employment must fulfill their employers' needs and regard their service mission as serious." Another reformer recommended that servant education begin in the employment agencies, which, she claimed, exploited household employees because they were uneducated migrants from the rural South. However, because the vast majority of African American women had obtained their positions through the community-based network, such reform would have been meaningless to them. Migrant women had to look to their own people for educational and occupational reform.[27]

The migrants' arrival was considered the reason for exploitative housing costs and deterioration of property values in Washington, D.C.'s segregated communities. They were considered educationally inferior, and urban African Americans thought them crude and "country" in their social graces. Even African American businesses would not initially employ college-educated migrants because they were "poorly educated by northern urban Washington, D.C. Negro standards."[28]

Beulah Nelson was one of only six women who straightforwardly divulged how the established African American community of Washington, D.C., viewed migrants. Her loud voice became quiet and filled with contrition as she recounted how her carefree attitude could change in the presence of those who were not migrants. She demonstrated how she carefully emulated their pronunciation of phrases she had never heard and expressed her embarrassment about her limited formal education. Occasionally, she encountered situations in which her inability to converse in polished English made her genuinely self-conscious of her rural southern origins:

I wasn't scared to be alone with small childrens. I did that [at] home, and then was with the Craigs for a year. They took me to meet the people around, too. So I knew people and had no fear of them from home. But them from up here [Washington, D.C.] was different. My talking was so bad. Everything was different, and my brother didn't try to help me with one thing. Them kids helped me find the store, or go here and there. No, I wanted to get back to the room quick 'cause I heard them talking. Oh, they sounded so different and nice to me. It was clear and sweet to hear, like music. And hold their head to a side and all. And then I heard me just talking so bad. I didn't like to talk to them, never. And what could I have to wear? Old things stuff from down home. Around my people from home, yes. Not other people, not them from up here.

Mary Sprow's diary referred to such people as the "good boys and girls that can find something else." They were the lucky children whose kin had given them an education early in life and prepared them for other opportunities. Within fourteen months of her arrival, Mary Sprow noticed that her relatives were preparing her for "new" work. In her diary, she stated that she was being prepared to work as a live-in servant in the home in which her older kin were employed. She recalled each stage of her education on the rules of "the senator's" home, where her relatives would place her as a live-in servant. They drilled her on the innermost details of the senator's household during the month before her duties were to begin: "You knew every crack and cranny, about work long before you got there. Why? 'Cause you was to be ready when your place opened." Reminiscent of the way these free-born descendants of slaves listened to the stories of their former-slave grandparents while in the rural South, these women listened to *and gauged* the advice of their older kin in Washington, D.C.:

They talked about that place whenever they came home. Who did this, what and how to not do that, but mostly laughing about the others. I listened to how they got by on they job, but let me get by on my work? No, no, no. So you listen at how they got 'round them people but you'd not try to get 'round the work they had you doing while they away.

Born in freedom and having tasted the fruits of one aspiration—migration—migrant women could not obligingly accept the despised calling of live-in domestic work with the same passivity and resignation as their older kin.[29] They might have appeared to have learned and accepted the subordinate servant's role, but they remained more independent, less focused on winning "they good jobs," than the older migrants, as Beulah Nelson remarked:

I listened many a day to everything they said. But in my mind I was going to do different. More than them. I didn't know when and sure enough how . . . but I knew I would not work over thirty years and end up like them. That's the truth as I live. Imagine me with such a mind. I had it all my life, too.

No aspect of this period of transition was by chance. Even the arrangement of their tote bags, which they carried to the job, resembled the manner they were taken from the South by older siblings. Just as each girl had carried a freedom bag when she was taken on the train, she was now given another freedom bag to carry to her first live-in job. Somehow, her new identity was folded inside that bag. And because there was as yet no fit place for her in society, she carried her own identity with her from place to place.

Each woman knew when and how her period of working "at home," in the confines of her small community, was to end. She was now expected "to clean and scrub days in and days out," living, as Mary Sprow described, "little different than a slave."[30]

4
A' ENDLESS MIRATION: LIVE-IN SERVICE

The things you made to do, how they'd act, how you had to act with them all . . . And you learned that the first day [on a job] . . . no peace, quiet, or semblance of order. Just a endless miration to be there.
    —MARIE STONE, AGE NINETY

In many ways, live-in service work in Washington, D.C., replayed an anachronistic master-servant relationship. In a diary written in 1916, domestic Mary Sprow wrote despairingly, "To clean and scrub, days in and days out. . . . Work is all for a poor girl like me."[1] A local D.C. poet described these domestics' work as "entering backdoors, scrubbing them floors, changing them sheets, taking all the lickings and turning other cheeks."[2]

ENTERING BACK DOORS

Like seventy-four other women migrants, Velma Davis was turned over to her first employers by her kinfolk. She maintained a practiced nonchalance throughout the interview, but all the time we talked about "that" job, she solemnly stared at the floor:

I'd been in Washington near a year. By then I helped a lady do wash and minded my people's childrens. Then my aunt Rose's people needed a helper for the nurse at number three Bradley Boulevard. Now my brother and two sisters, they worked at number one Bradley for the doctor, and my aunt came and took me for that doctor's son. She came to get me in the morning and by noon I was put on that job. I helped in the children's nursery for nearly three years there.

Kin placed migrants in domestic jobs and taught the girls the conventions of service, but no amount of preparation matched the realities of live-in work itself. Eighty-seven-year-old Annie Brown of Mississippi, a woman who worked more than twenty years for a family related to the DuPonts, had heard about her future employer long in advance of her arrival:

Oh, you'd be gotten ready for your work. And my brother talked about that house near a year before I was there. But it's not 'til you're there you really know what and how to do for her. It's something you can hear and think about how it is, but it's not real—for real to ya'—'til you there working.

For a moment, Lovella Willoughby's calm, doelike eyes almost betrayed her emotions, and her powerful voice hardened as she discussed "her":

It wasn't my people I lived with but my Aunt Dell, who took me to work first. See, my dad was raised by her mom when his grandmom died. They were really cousins, but they were raised like sister and brother . . . when I came they took me to meet her where she lived . . . because she hadn't been home for three years. I'd been here for seven months when her people needed a nurse's helper. Aunt Dell sent word for me. Brother's people hadn't needed me—so he let me go. She came in on a Sunday, and I started that very next day with her.

Six women had their first employment experience with persons from the neighborhood, as was true for Esther Lawson:

The lady lived just off Twenty-seventh Street, so she was a neighbor of ours. They needed somebody next to where she worked, and she took me. Didn't know what I was to do. Nothing. Mr. Levi [her husband] knew my brother from home and all. He asked my brother for me, and I was just sent off with his wife. I worked right by her over three years way up Wisconsin Avenue.

Invariably, the new employer immediately made clear two indelible facets of live-in service in Washington, D.C., namely, the stigma placed

Marie Jefferies, far left, pictured with kin while working in Massachusetts at
the summer home of her employer.

on African American live-in servants and the master-servant nexus the
employer required. These elements of employment stemmed from a
widely held belief that class distinctions must be sustained in every
home.[3] Employers believed in the inferiority of the servant and demanded subservience from their "retinue of vassals."[4] Esther Lawson, an
immaculate woman, is an impeccable housekeeper. Her small home in
northern Virginia was meticulously clean. With great lament in her
voice, she recalled her first live-in accommodations:

When I got there, the first thing they done was take me to "my place." This
woman had me a room fixed up in the basement. Well, it was more like a
garage. No door on it, or nothing. They pulled the car right in—just like you
have your room, put all your tools and things in, a little room. I guess that's
what that was. When I'd go down at night from the kitchen I'd go right in this
little room. Car sitting up there. That's where I slept.

Then my sister came where I was. And she stayed there with me, [while working at] a job with a lady right back of me. Anybody could just walk in off the street and come on back there to that little room, but nobody never bothered.

From the moment of their arrival, the young women understood that the typical house was divided in order to minimize contact between employers and servants.[5] The migrant women believed that this distance was important to "big" or "good" employers. "Good" was determined by the employer's social status as well as by the quality of the work. Rather than working for *any* person who could afford to feed and compensate help, as these women had done in the South, migrants to Washington were taught that high-status or prestigious employers were better employers. Interestingly, however, the servant's own social status did not increase by virtue of their employer's social standing.

The employer's social position was important for several reasons. First, the women believed that through their association with people of wealth and power, they could ensure future employment for their southern relatives. Second, high-status employers were able to pay salaries promptly and provide fringe benefits, such as paid vacation or holiday bonuses.[6] Finally, household workers believed that a family of high status would have had prior experience managing household help and would therefore be both fair and generous. Experienced, self-confident employers were not usually inclined to browbeat and belittle servants, whereas lower-status employers sometimes resorted to bolstering their egos or reassuring their social positions by mistreating their servants.[7]

As Annie Brown put away the sample of her Lenox china service that she had received from her "good" employer, she explained:

When you was just new here and still working only for your kin and near-abouts [extended kin family], you'd hear everybody telling stories of how and why you had to work for a big family.

No, not size—but big. They know all the big names, likes people in Congress or the president. See, you'd get with them and you'll not get worked to death and then handed a pile of old clothes or half your week's pay. And when they has to travel they pay you something, too. They got the real money and power, and that's who you'd be put with. People who was big in this town. I was.

Mary Little described what a good employer was as she sat her cup of tea on a small antique table with stiff, lacy doilies. Her face, dark and filled with deep wrinkles, contained striking deep-set eyes and a very full mouth. As she talked about her many employers, the employer's amenities always figured prominently:

You'd be to know that good people was all your people had been with. They was the tops of this town. They go and stay in to help get they money and to help bring people up [facilitate migration]. For years and years they stay on a job to get the good pay and the time-off pay, too. They get a lot. Good families had the money. Those big houses and just everything in them to keep them up. You'd get with them 'cause they had. Some had ten and fifteen people living in. See, these people had real money and treated us like they was used to help. They was who you'd get with—people with real money. You was right there working with your sister and all. You'd be all working together on the staff.

Each woman remembered being taken to the employer, who then lectured her on the definition of a "good servant." Good servants were to be efficient and meet all of the rigid standards of the household. The introduction unfailingly emphasized the employer's lofty status, unparalleled standards, grand moral obligations, and unbounded benevolence. The main message, of course, was that a good servant must assume the role of humble subordinate at all times, as Faustina Zellers of South Carolina recalled in her low-pitched voice:

My sister-in-law used to like to go to dances with people from down home. She met this young man who told her about this job. She told him I needed a job, so they took me there. I was hired immediately. From the minute I got there I was so scared, because the missus stressed *she* was the wife of a senator. (As if to say, what did that make me?) She told me he was from Arkansas (meaning he didn't like coloreds), and all about the house, and her rules. See,

that was the first job I had. This job with the senator. And after that, I'm taken
to my place. One side of a room in what was a basement type of a place—
with just bed cots and a small place for your things. A small bath we [the ser-
vants] all used, and that was it. From day one you knew what you was to try
and be when you working there. I worked for him and, I must say, that wasn't
a pleasant job.

These women were accurate in assessing their employers as powerful
members of the Washington white community. In fact, two were members of the Supreme Court, four were United States senators, and three
were members of the House of Representatives. The others included a
State Department official and former diplomat, a high official at the
War Department, four lawyers, three doctors, and five businessmen of
some prominence. Even those men not officially part of the federal government had close ties, both professional and social, to those who were.
For example, one woman remembered her employer, a doctor, being
called away from the dinner table when President Woodrow Wilson was
taken ill. The wives of these men played golf together, served on committees that oversaw various charities, and met for lunch. Through
money or political power, or a combination of the two, these people ex-
erted considerable influence in the federal city.

As she thoughtfully spoke about her life, Eula Montgomery was
clearly a woman you earnestly listened to but never felt intimidated by:

He was the baby doctor for all of them congressmen and senators. He'd know
them because of they childrens. I guess that's how he got to go around to so
many of they parties and stuff at night. She [the wife] golfed with the wives of
two people in Congress nearly every day in summer. All during cold weather
they went to teas and luncheons all day—they claimed they was to help this or
that home for childrens [charity]. She was a great helper because *we* cooked,
cleaned, and cared for all them!

I'm here to tell you that they both ran around with them Congress people .
. . out and about in the days and the night times, too!

Darethia Handy's first employer was the president of one of Washington's largest banks. In Texas and Arkansas her mother had also worked

Mrs. Spooner, wife of Senator John C. Spooner of
Wisconsin, an employer of Bernice Reeder, and a member
of her family.

for a banker. She was sure this was why her employer was comfortable
with having nine of her kin working there: "Every night him and his
friends only talked about all that the government was doing. I guess it
was because his office took up so many cases with the government. He
didn't have no elected place [position] or nothing . . . but he knew
everything they [government officials] did."

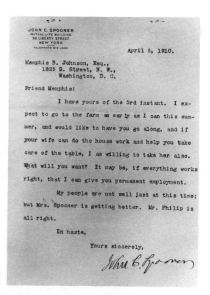

Senator Spooner and a letter he wrote allowing the wife of his yard man to accompany his family to his summer home with the understanding that she would work as a servant.

GOOD HELP IS HARD TO FIND

Many families, especially after 1870, employed servants because family tradition and social status required it. Until World War I, to the employer, the word *servant* meant a live-in servant. This group of women worked on staffs consisting of both men and women. Men were employed as butlers, outside caretakers, chauffeurs, footmen (or chauffeur's helpers), furnace men, coal men, handymen, and housemen. Women were hired to be personal maids, chambermaids (upstairs maids), nurses, nurse's helpers, cooks, parlor maids (downstairs maids), waitresses, and pantry girls (cook's helpers). There were also non-live-in, full-staff workers, such as the laundress, tutor, and social secretary. According to the women, the latter two categories were always filled by white women. To live-in African American servants, those positions did not constitute "work." Essie Octavia Crockett enjoyed telling about her days as a live-in servant. She is medium brown, of medium height, with medium brown hair cut to a medium length. Yet everything average about her quickly disappears as she firmly describes, with no hint of servility, the lives of live-in servants:

In that house only colored people worked; did everything. Now she sometimes had a white lady to make up her menu for her fancy parties. Or she'd [the white employee] come there to do her [the employer's] invitations. Some came to do fancy writing for Christmas cards—like that. These is things they'd never want us to do because we might have to sit down or get talked to like a human person.

But they didn't work. No serving, running for this or that, in uniform. No, whites didn't do that then. I heard that before colored people came out of slavery times they used white girls as maids. But I started work in 1918, and I never worked with none here nor saw any serving for a family. No, they don't do no work.

The bright yellow sunflowers on Nettie Bass's dress fit her self-portrait as "a worker: somebody who has spent my life working in someone else's garden." She had spent long days and nights as a live-in after her migration from North Carolina in 1909. Afterward, she had lived a year and a half with a brother, his wife, and their three children on Westminster Street in northwest Washington. We discussed the differences between the employment opportunities for African American and white females prior to World War I:

They [white workers] got better jobs than servant work by the time I got here. My brother's first wife worked with whites—people'd said near Thomas Circle area. I helped a lady do piecework, and no whites were over there that I knew or saw. Ever. Where Brother and his second wife took me there was nothing but colored people. Some people had whites in other places, but they'd be too old to do better. Young ones? They'd only stay 'til a better job would come along—a store, factory, or office—somewhere would take them. Plus, them people had to pay whites more. A butler made the best money. And a white maid—my God they made ten times or more what we did. But we [African

Americans] knew we'd always do housework, and had to take any little bit we got. If not, what? They [employers] know'd you was never getting store, factory, or government work. You was there for life. I know that's how they look at it.

No job description came with a live-in servant's work, although some tasks were universal and consistent. But many additional duties were assigned to servants simply because of the capricious demands of the "mister" or "mistress."[8] Bernice Reeder's eyes narrowed as she announced that it was a "wearisome task" to catalogue the sundry duties of the twenty persons who served with her during her seven-year tenure as a live-in for three families in the DuPont Circle-Massachusetts Avenue area: "When you live-in, you must do everything but chew they food. Do this, do that, run here, run there, and when you get through —do this!" Weida Edwards, in her soft voice, affirmed the unending demands of live-in service work:

You had to do everything, twenty-four hours to the day. You was up with the mister—if you was upstairs you got all the fresh linen for him. Everyone downstairs prepared the food, waited his table, or got his car ready. 'Cause the outside had to be just so when he came out.

Then the children had to be cared for and, of course, she'd finally start calling for this and that by about ten or eleven. The whole place is cleaned daily and all meals are from scratch. They'd have had lunch served and dinner readied. Everybody put on dark uniforms, and us upstairs served the childrens in they room and they parents ate downstairs. After nine or so—after dinner they'd go to the parlor with they friends in or go out. You get them kids to bed, and by ten help get all the dishes done. Now she'd be up to all hours worrying everybody to do this or that. Why not? She'd sleep 'til noon if she wanted to—it was you that had to be up, dressed in your gray by six-thirty.

THE MISTRESS

The American white mistress and her African American servant formed a complex partnership that both resulted from and contributed to the worker's social stigma. In this sense, relations between female servants and employers functioned much as they had in slavery; as in slavery, those relations were strengthened and stimulated by racial prejudice.[9] Mistresses held stereotypical, prejudicial views about African Americans; white employers, men and women alike, viewed them as dirty, slack looking, corrupt people with clear limits beyond which they could not be educated or trained.[10]

Live-in domestics, for their part, saw the white household as a weapon in the hands of the white woman. Many of the tyrannical indignities imposed on domestics by their mistresses came about because employers were cautioned against creating a kinder, more humane environment. For example, magazines and newspapers of the day encouraged women to use the management principles of commerce, industry, and shops in the home.[11] The mistress took seriously her responsibility to manage money wisely; stories abounded of women who triumphantly explained how they fired a fifteen-dollars-a-week maid and got another "who gave prefect service for $6.25 a week."[12] The mistress maximized profits for the household by minimizing labor costs and exploiting their household servants.[13] She made all the decisions regarding a servant's duties, hours, and rewards and directed all facets of the live-in worker's life. Frances Pollard used a spurious tone and feigned gestures as she described the mistress' multiple demands:

I was a chambermaid and was to keep sleeping areas clean. Expected, now! However, my mistress would expect me to re-dress and to serve dinner. Now, my younger sister worked across the street, and she was a chambermaid, too. But she was to change and cover the door [serve at the door] so the butler could serve the meals. And we made so little money.[14]

In the South, white men directly supervised the servants' work and personal space, but in the District of Columbia, the male head of household was an "absentee manager." Overwhelmingly this was noted as the major difference between live-in service work back home and in Washington, D.C. Velma Davis recalls that her mistress' husband was "never home. He'd leave everything to her [the mistress] mainly. He'd be served and not say much. Down home they order you *and* her around. Mr. Mitchell was in charge of everybody 'round there. That's the way he made it for all my life and my daddy's too. But not up here."

Unlike her southern counterpart, the Washington mistress' personality and temperament dominated the households in which these women worked. Live-ins were required to learn and respond to all of the mistress' idiosyncracies and demands, as this 1901 pronouncement of a Washington mistress made clear: "My servant is hired to do whatever she is told to do and to be at any time subject to my command."[15] Domestic workers often came to the job already versed on their employer's character. Virginia Lacy groaned and slapped her cheek lightly as we talked about "that woman," Mrs. Green:

My sister always talked about Mrs. Green this and Mrs. Green that. But its not 'til you're in her house that you really learn how she is and what it's like to work for her 'round the clock. You hear about them, but it's not 'til you start work you learn what you have to do—day and night—for that woman!

A good household worker, according to these women, was not necessarily one who completed all assigned tasks well, rather, she was one who knew how to please the mistress. Employers might rattle off a list of tasks, but the women knew that it was the worker, not the work itself, that was really under constant scrutiny. Odessa Minnie Barnes's soft voice became unnaturally stilted as she remembered the message she received from the footman, a migrant from South Carolina like herself: "Forget what you are to do and just keep *her* happy. The work and such, that'll kill you never. But she and them kids is your worry all the time. This ain't like home." Such advice was commonplace—and useful. Shaped by their experience in the South, the migrants had come to Washington, D.C., expecting to show more deference to the husband than to the wife. They clearly had to relearn the household order.

Slowly, through trial, error, and the advice of other migrants, the new household workers learned to respond to the desires of the wife instead of to those of the husband.[16]

Servants maintained that mistresses maximized their control by never adhering to a given schedule or routine. And it was usually the caprice and whimsy of the mistress that determined how soon and how success-fully a worker could complete her tasks. In an emotional Texas drawl, Darethia Handy recounted:

She'd ask for her beds to be done one way on Monday and another on Tues-day. She'd just keep you doin' this or that to have something to say or do. She really didn't care about the house—she just wanted you running and doin' for her. Like my people talked about when they was in slaves times in Cookson. That's just what that woman wanted—a slave. I know that to be true, too.

By employing domestic servants, middle-class white women gained a sense of superiority and lost the feeling of being a drudge.[17] With a tinge of pathos, Beulah Nelson intimated that she knew her psycholog-ical value to her employer: "You was there to do for her and make her to have somebody. They man and kids pay them no mind. But you had to listen . . . or they'd really act up with you." In effect, the staff often saw themselves as an frenetic audience forced to attend the mistress's performance. The home was the wife's stage; it was the only setting in which she could feel legitimate. Domestics saw the white woman's domination of household workers as a transparent exercise of the only kind of power she had.

All of the migrant women felt that female employers took advantage of them because of their financial obligations to their families, which limited their mobility and opportunities. Velma Davis had worked for a woman whose conduct toward migrants was especially harsh:

She knew you was from down home, working to help them [your family] to survive. So she'd feel free to work you harder and longer 'cause you wouldn't never quit. So you and your people worked in one house years longer than people from up here [northern-born workers]. We had to. This being so, that woman worked us and just plain ran us to death near about. And only with us did she really act up.

Never did she talk up to her husband, or to them kids when they got size on them. Or them people, like the laundress, who came by the day. Not them, 'cause they'd quit on her. So she'd give us [the live-in servants] the devil—especially if you was from down home. She knew you'd take it and be glad, too.

If you ever did get sick and say something—now your people working right there, they'd get you straight quick! They'd dare you to speak up and make them look bad. No, they'd keep you quiet. We didn't want to get nobody else in the family in no trouble—so you took all her stuff. That's how it was your first years here. For everybody.

Faustina Zellers described a senator's wife's trickery with a male servant:

She was after him. Just always trying to get him into something. And he was telling her no, no. And she walked around behind him and once dropped a key. And I saw her, so she said, "Well, you go on and do your work"—talking to me then, you know. 'Cause she didn't want me to say, "Now you dropped that key for him there." See. And I said, "Now they're going to accuse him . . ." And I think this was probably why she had him there. Then they'd accuse him and work him for nothing. If he didn't do it they'll put you in jail. See. Now maybe he's [the senator] going to do this to me. See? And I'm always thinking, "I'm going to find out how to get away from here."

Ellamay Carter of Georgia had not changed much from the thirty-year-old photograph on the wall above the chair I sat on. She was still stylish, with dark red lipstick. She sat almost as still as a picture during most of the interview. But she suddenly came to life when asked to describe her tasks in the home on Connecticut Avenue where she worked as a live-in from 1919 to 1921. Mrs. Carter rose from her high-backed, brocade chair and graciously demonstrated her ability to closely dust the perfectly "dust-free" mahogany end table and its many contents for more than fifteen minutes. She would stop and lean in, slowly exaggerating an inspection of her handiwork, then she would move an inch or two around the table and begin dusting again. She explained each detail of this elaborate subterfuge through unsuppressed giggles. By the time she had finished, we were both laughing uncontrollably. She sat back down and said:

You learn quick how to be busy at nothing. At first when you asked, you only say what really needs to be done. And then get a lot more added to your work 'cause you from down South, and they expect you to always do more! So you learns quickly how to always be real busy all the time. You don't wait to have work 'signed [assigned]. No, not if you from the South—'cause they'll work you the most, to death 'cause you just suppose to do more, longer, harder. That's so.

The women all expressed mastery of the skill of always being "real busy." They knew how it annoyed employers to see any household worker idle.

Employers were demanding and insensitive to worker's needs partly because they did not know the amount of work involved in the tasks they assigned. More to the point, however, white women demanded more from poor, southern-born servants because they knew these young women were accustomed to intense, exhausting work. Only the "good" servant avoided the mistress' unpredictable wrath. The women I interviewed articulated their ideas of what a "good servant" was—a label they all had diligently aspired to attain. Good servants, Bernice Reeder brusquely explained, were "always busy. They had plenty to do in they gray or black uniforms. They was always busy." Mathilene Anderson's feeble voice painstakingly defined a good servant as

always moving. They never are sitting when anybody white is around. I mean the mistress or anybody. They'd keep moving, dusting, doing her errands . . . but talking and laughing with them all the same. They'd just be doing nothing, but they made it seem so much to the whites.

Now we knew it was nothing and when we were around just us [the staff] we'd laugh. Those of us from down Virginia would get them with better stories of how we'd get them down home. We'd fool that woman from dawn to dusk. The very *best* came from down South. Seems you was the goodest of the good! You'd be busy longest doing nothing! But talking and laughing all the

Mathilene Anderson recalled how Grace Batson (pictured) taught her the idiosyncracies of the Thomas Clark family before she was employed there.

time. A good servant living in does nothing more than anybody else but they knew how to *look* busier. It's funny!

The good servant was rewarded in various ways. She received extra money in tips, earned paid holidays, and was usually assigned the less-difficult household tasks. And she had more time to acquire vital information about the mistress.

To be successful, servants discovered, meant satisfying far more than the labor requirements of the job. Employers seemed to need a self-enhancing relationship that came from having an inferior at their disposal around the clock.[18] To their surprise, the women who came north were expected to appear more subservient than in the rural South.[19] Velma Davis stated that "at home they was white and they knew it. Wasn't no need to be on you to make them feel more white. Up here they knew they was white too, but they seemed to need you to make-up to them to keep reminding them how white they are."

Mary Ruth Ingraham, at age ninety-two, remarked that even in the racist South, African American privacy was respected:

Down home you worked and very hard too. But you was to do your job and mainly that's all. You were a worker. After that you was free. Even when you live-in. You'd work and they let you be mostly. See they saw you as no better than they animals. So after you'd worked you be let to rest—like they cow or horse.

That's so, but up here you got no peace living-in. Day or night no peace from them people. They have you running for no reasons. Just don't sit or stop, never.

Perhaps nothing symbolized this new role of servant more than one essential prop—the uniform.

THE UNIFORM

After 1900, the uniformed servant became one of the most visible and valued signs of a white person's social arrival. Washington's nouveau riche demanded liveried servants, prominent symbols of the aristocratic decadence and foppery important to them in the "City of Magnificent Intentions," as Charles Dickens dubbed the capital.[20] The demand for livery marked the major difference between servant work in the South and their role in Washington. Unavoidably, the uniform contributed to a total identification of the individual with a symbol. Velma Davis's eyes were steadfastly fixed as she said:

You just do they work down home when you was sent out. Up here it wasn't the work—though it was a lot, at times. Up here you served. It wasn't like your job only. You'd have to do more just plain makin' them happy. Now at number one Bradley Boulevard it was that way. You'd just be there to make them look good. Tell her how she looked so nice, the kids being so this or that. Dear God.

A live-in did more play than work. Your uniform seem to make them expect you to do all that. When they saw them clothes they knew how you'd be acting. And you had to act they way playing up to them. You must—always do it.

Live-ins felt the stigma of the livery.[21] Uniforms announced their low status[22] in the workplace, and uniforms meant waiting at a white person's "beck and call," in the words of Ophilia Simpson:

You learn first gray for day and black for night. White cuffs and collars was always used in good homes, too. Now during gray times, as we'd call it, you did your heavy work for the house. When you in your black you'd do mostly serving or waiting. You know, fill they plates, passing they refills . . . all that table-side work.

The uniforms, it made you at they beck and call. Down home, that white man he'd make you work, work, work. But like any animal you get your rest-up time. Up here it wasn't so much work, but it was more running to suit the wife. It was all hard, but the uniform made it different up here. Still, the work was better up here, but living in made life not be better, too.

Josephine Moss explained how employers used uniforms to distinguish their "retainers" from those of other employers[23] and to lay claim to servants as their property:

Uniforms catch the dirt. You'll prowl through the house to clean the house up and the uniform catches the dirt. And everybody tried to have they servants different from the next one—to make you look like their's. A bow here or a frill on the apron there. Like I said, to make you look their's.

As long as you got that uniform on like she wants it—when somebody comes to the house—they looking for Miss So-and-So-and-So—but she not here. But her slaves are here. That's the only thing they had it for. That's the only thing they can keep because they can't keep nothing else. Blue with white collar, black and white hat—a bonnet like a nurse cap. That's the slave look on you.

Alaveta Mitchell never took a breath as she told the functional aspects of the uniform:

Most of the time [when] they cooked, or stayed in—they had 'em. I stayed in and I wore uniforms then, but she furnished the uniform. I stayed in a live-in job right off Connecticut Avenue, jus' the man and his wife. I lived in and I wore uniform. They had a striped one to work in, they liked me to do the laundry and the cleaning and the scrubbin' in that. It was gray and white stripes that what she had, but you know lot of 'em had different colors.

You had to change that uniform when time for you to serve their food. Years ago for some you had to have a black uniform and a white apron and a white bag [rag] round your head. On Connecticut Avenue, her uniform was dark gray [with] a white apron and the bib and the tie back in the back. Well, that's what I had then.

Vada Lancaster's voice was full of energy as she proudly maligned people who felt that the uniform was the established way to present oneself, no matter what the time or place. Although embittered about her treatment while working as a live-in servant, she generally concealed her rage in witty stories.[24] Her thoughtful and revealing account goes to the heart of servants' repugnance for this attire:

I have had to get up in the middle of the night to get something. She'd sent him to the top of the basement steps to call you and say, "Mrs. Sommers wants you." You had to get up, put that uniform on, and go upstairs get what ever they wanted right then. You couldn't go up stairs in your duster or a robe. No! They wanted you in that uniform at all times. You were working so you had it on. Never did you get any rest with that thing on. I meant work, work, and more work. As long as you had that on you couldn't sit down or take a rest.

Rowena Morgan is a tall, solidly built woman with a large face and oblong, light brown eyes. At eighty-one her voice, strong and resolute, left

Amy Bundy in formal servant uniform.

no doubt about why servants rebelled against this attire. She said it served to remind the migrants that they always had to obey and to remain subservient to the will of another:

In front of people, she'd do a little better. But you'd have to always be running here and there for them. I guess it [the uniform] made them seem big or they thought we was just they toys.

People like to feel they over somebody else. Lots are like that; and if you work living-in, you really have something on you all the time. I tell you, I don't know why they needed people to order around so much. But they did, and you had no choice but to do for them. They way. All day and night. Not work, but just here and there and that. Just running.

Marie Stone shook her head and slowly said:

From the start—it's a miration[25] whenever you put that thing on. And, it had to be that way. In that uniform—the things you made to do, how they'd act, how you had to act with them all—it's just that everything was going to be a mess. And you learned that the first day but what could you do? This was how it was living on a job—no peace, quiet, or semblance of order. Just a endless miration to be there.

SETTING THE NET

The on-the-job educational process had yet another dimension—learning how to work with other staff members. A multitude of rules governed staff relations, such as: never question the authority of the butler, but follow his directions quickly; cheerfully run errands for the personal maids; do not talk when the personal maid is explaining the schedule of the mistress for the day; and do not show impatience with the laundress—ever. But all of the migrant workers observed one cardinal rule: never antagonize persons who transmit news about the mood of the family or those who have news of the outside world. These persons carried the information the staff needed to gauge the mood and movements of the family, and of the mistress in particular. Always defer to these workers, because they can facilitate your adjustment to the working environment.

Power over and respect from the staff were based on the ability of a staff member to transmit two types of information: the mood or the movements of the wife. The more access a staff member had to this information, the higher he or she was in the hierarchy. Workers with this type of employer intimacy forewarned other staff members of an impending "very bad mood," or of the periods when the family would be outside the house. In this way, they allowed the workers advance preparation for a stormy work day or the opportunity to plan activities for the "free" periods, including accomplishing tasks that were easy or stress-free.

In 1909, Mary Ruth Ingraham came to Washington from Virginia and lived in a room with her mother's aunt on Westminster Street. She assisted a neighbor who did laundry and child care for the neighbors. Later, as a live-in with a very wealthy family, she learned quickly how to define the two basic groups of staff workers in the large home located close to the White House: "You had two kinds of people in a house, just two. There was them giving orders and them taking orders. That was all when you lived in."

Mayme Gibson attached great significance to these two groups in the household[26] where she worked as a live-in in southwest Washington, D.C. The Mississippi native was self-possessed as she explained, "I know this is true as of today like before—it was just them and us workers. That's the live-in jobs' way. It'll be like that forever, too."

Essie Crockett was a self-confident worker with no hint of obsequiousness in her mannerisms. As a servant she felt,

You was asked to do more a lotta time when you was from down South. And when you was new, you don't know the two main rules. You don't know why nobody talks 'til after dinner (you want to always appear busy until the male head of household arrives to divert the mistress' attention). Or why you have to get to know the cook or pantry girl (they can get the worker extra food or desserts). Once you worked as a live-in you learn this stuff and you can change about. But you got to do the work to know!

A second social network was formed by the staff's relationships or connections with persons outside the work place, particularly family relations. Most "full-staff" persons had other family members employed on the same household staff, often performing specific limited duties. These specialized workers held positions of respect within the staffing network. Annie Pansylee Holmes was the daughter of Freeman and Martha Collins Holmes. Her mother's family were very well respected in the Alabama community of the nation's capital. She described her work within the migrant community: "I wasn't never a cook, live-in or not. No never. But even in my first job, when I worked off Thomas Circle, nobody ate a cake I didn't make! See Collins, they's bakers and they knew me to be one. So I baked—but mostly for us." Velma Davis recalled how staff members communicated nonverbally to other workers:[27] "Now, a laundress came once or twice to the week. But she'd know Mrs. Cameron's ways. She'd know good when that woman had a nasty spell on. Couldn't help but learn; you'd come and see how we's acting—you'd know what that woman's mood was."

A third social network was formed by "staff insiders," an inner circle who congregated in the kitchen and pantry areas or in the "staff quarters." The insiders were "the group from down South," the migrants, as opposed to those born in the North. As servants discussed "down home," they shared the experiences and responsibilities of this special network within the household. Everyone in the household was either "born up here in these ways or outside of them," as Queen Williams remarked.

Most migrant women perceived the household workers born in the District of Columbia as having advantages that they lacked. For one thing, the northern-born women had their entire families nearby, which meant better access to resources and assistance networks. Amy Kelly had nearly forty kin members living in Washington, D.C., but it was not the same as having one's immediate family to turn to:

Up here you had some people, but they had *all* their people. They'd be able to help each other better. If I could a had my mama, daddy, and my aunts and stuff up here like them—I'd been better off, too. We'd pull together as best we could but that's not like having your family up here.

Eighty-nine-year-old Beulah Nelson, who began live-in work in 1905, said, "They [people born in Washington, D.C.] had everybody right here so they had help. I just had a little part [of her family], so I got such small help. You're better off if all your people are here."

Native Washingtonians could, and often would, leave unsuitable employment without wreaking economic havoc within their families. Dolethia Otis at eighty-four is proud of her home and its manicured lawn. Her freckled face flushed as she conceded that her husband's pension gave her a "good" life. She acknowledged her long employment as a live-in servant but admired the independence of her husband's family:

They'd get so they wouldn't take what she [the employer] dished out. They'd leave. They had people who'd let them come on home and take a week or two to get new work. We couldn't. Once you started work you knew people was dependin' on those few pennies you earned. You dare not quit for no reason. That's why I loved them people so!

Odella Scott of Georgia expressed her regret about working all of her young life as a live-in servant. She felt the limited education available in Mitchell County forced her into "nothing" work. After the first few minutes of conversation, her apprehensions eased and she commented:

Girls from here didn't care about no job for too long. They could go home. How am I going back to Hopeful [Georgia]? Just made it up here, in truth. But for them home, it was just a streetcar away. Like they got one job, they'd get a new one. That's how they'd act and tell Mrs. B. too. They were lucky to be working home.

On the other hand, many of the migrants felt that prospective employers disliked the independent, "uppity" attitude of native Washingtonians. Naomi Yates was convinced that employers preferred young women from the South:

A girl from North Carolina could get a job in Chevy Chase quicker than they [women born in Washington] ever could. All them people knew we'd stay on the job and were trained better too. We was the ones who never had to look long—they did. And that was because everybody [employers] knew how

Staff of persons, including relatives of Mary Ruth Ingraham, in a large
Washington household.

they'd walk off a job over something we'd never! I guess in that one way we
had it better.

Nevertheless, the migrants were unequivocal in their agreement that
women born in Washington, D.C., attained superior education, which
provided them greater opportunity to acquire employment as cleaning
persons in government agencies or businesses. Ora Fisher's experience
corroborated this feeling:

I remember when they first started taking colored at the laundries or to work
cleaning government buildings. Every one of them that got on came from
here. They had been to school more, that was the reason. They sure couldn't
work no better than us the world knows. But who from down North Carolina
got a chance? None, and I know it was because they had more grades in they
school up here. Most went up to six. At home they couldn't get three most of
the time!

Mathilene Anderson, at nearly one hundred years old, remarked:

By the war [World War I] nobody in Georgetown hired a girl unless she came from down South. They [employers] knew that as these jobs got open up them girls from here was going to be gone. They had better training, and when they could do cleaning at the army hospital or anyplace they'd leave a family and never look back. Pretty soon people'd only hire someone born and trained-up in the South. Them people knew you'd be there for good right along with all your people.

Mayme Gibson remembers that the only differences were cultural:

We'd get together and talk about growing up on a farm and life down here. They people born up here couldn't say a thing. They didn't know about that. So they'd listen. That was the only thing I remember "different" about them. They didn't know about down-home food too much either. But how could they? They didn't grow up down there like the rest of us [staff members] just talking late at night in the kitchen.

Knowledge of the rural life distinguished southern servants from the "citified" Washingtonians, but the migrant women did not harbor any personal antagonism toward their urban counterparts. "Everybody got along because we was working," replied Mary Little as she checked the silver wave clips in her hair.

When the migrant women took live-in positions in white homes in Washington, they were following the path trod by their kin (or extended kin)—the people with whom they worked on their first jobs. As live-ins they found the perpetuation of many elements of the master-slave relationship, yet in some ways their role in these Washington households was more degrading than what they had encountered in the South. At all turns, efforts were made to impress on the live-ins their subservient status, most graphically represented by the uniform they were required to wear. On call twenty-four hours a day, with little opportunity for privacy, live-in workers turned to positions that offered a chance of greater autonomy and personal freedom.

5
THE TRANSITION
PERIOD

I thought to myself time and time again I wasn't going to take this place. I wanted to do better. I knew I just could. I seen my way out long before I left her. But my time had to come. I waited too. My mind knew to wait 'til I had new work and all. But I was leaving them houses, and I made up my mind to do it even if my brother was mad. But I did wait 'til I was set.

    —ODESSA MINNIE BARNES, AGE NINETY-FIVE

Wearied of the soul-destroying hollowness of live-in domestic work, African American migrants yearned for change. For Beulah Nelson, religious conviction underscored her resolve:

Here's is my hand to God, I knew living on that job wasn't for me no more than two months after I got here. God revealed it to me time and time again. And I knew no matter what, it was a some way to make my work better—change it. And do better than all them. I knew God would deliver me. Just like he got me 'way from home, he'd bring me through here. Didn't know how—but he would.

TO BE AS BETTER AS I COULD

The sadness I had first sensed behind Velma Davis's dark eyes rose to the surface as she explained her sentiments about perhaps the most difficult, degrading aspect of live-in service—the utter lack of privacy. She captured the women's universal sense of the work as something not their own; it was they—the employer's—job:

Living in you had nothing. They job was for them, not your life. [From the] time I could, I started to try to get something that let me have some rest. A rest at the end of the day. That's why you try to live out. You'd be willing to take any chance to live out to just have some time that was yours.

Even fictional accounts of domestic service repeated the infringement on African American servants' personal space, as one of the protagonists in the novel *Like One of the Family: Conversations from a Domestic's Life* asserted:

She [the employer's daughter] got to be 'bout grown now and just like her mom and grandmom she's just tryin' to nose in my business . . . or to poke fun at me on the sly. They ask you, "How's your boyfriend?" Like it's funny as all get out that you should have a boyfriend! Or save money? "Do you people like this? . . . do you read?" "Do you do this or that? Now, by "you people" she means colored people, and I tell you she can wear my nerves pretty near the breaking![1]

This heedless disregard for the servant's human dignity and right to privacy further alienated the African American migrant from her employer.

After an average of seven years, all of the migrant women grew to dread their live-in situations. They saw their occupation as harming all aspects of their lives. They dreaded wearing the uniforms that formalized their subservient status. They detested living in an environment in which the representative authority, the mistress, lacked respect for their needs. Virginia Lacy puckered and scowled as she summarized her disenchantment with live-in work. More than once her fist banged the arm of her chair for emphasis:

Look, I got tired. Just running here and there with no rest. I could stay down home for that. No, I wanted to go 'round and do. Well, be able to go to church on Sunday, like that. I got tired of one woman trying to make me near 'bout a dog. You got no rest from them. So time you got set—you'd leave. You came 'way from all that. It was the North, and you'd just want to be able to do better and more.

Many women voiced their repugnance for their live-in situation with the much-used phrase "they job." They described their time as live-in workers as being "on they job," or referred to a particular household by saying, "when I worked at they job." In these phrases the women refused to "own" those jobs, to consider them extensions of themselves. Their outrage at the indignities of wearing uniforms further underscored a refusal to identify with the servant role, even while on the job.

Among the many pressures causing job dissatisfaction, constraints on church participation figured strongly. Live-in domestics were rarely given Sunday off. Live-in servants could hardly maintain an active church involvement. As Amy Kelly exclaimed, they "never knew what it was to have all day Sunday off. Not living in!" Amy also remembered live-in servitude as limiting one's social interactions with other church members:

You lived in a room in the attic. How could you be in any of them clubs? You couldn't bring nobody over there. No you never got to be in a fellowship. That was for people who had a good job—where they got off on Saturday and Sunday. They had a nice place to stay; and to have people over to—not no kitchen. A kitchen was all I had living in for a parlor or anything else!

Live-in servants did not get Sundays off, but not necessarily because employers were opposed to church attendance. According to the women, unlike in the rural South, northern employers simply had no respect for the religious and personal needs of their live-in servants. Bernice Reeder observed the hypocritical contrast between her live-in employers' devout Christian activities and their blithe disregard for their servants:

Now they'd get up and go out to Sunday morning church as sure as I sit here. He'd (the husband) act like Sunday was such a holy day around there. No loud talk, no laughing or nothing—he'd say was foolishness. He made it clear Sundays was a day of rest. But us? We'd work like dogs just the same. We didn't get no rest on that day.

Virginia Lacy, who worked for an Orthodox Jewish family, confirmed that even in homes in which strict adherence to religious practices was a

Young woman working in the home of a Washington, D.C., government worker. Courtesy of the Library of Congress.

way of life, such behavior applied only to the employer, never to the servants:

Now Jews would have them big dinners and tell they childrens all about getting saved from slavery and death. That's they passover and such. But they'd not a bit more care that you was working day and night—for nothing. They never cared, none of them, if you got to see the inside of any church. They holiday or not, you worked.

This federal government charwoman is pictured at her "big job." Women employed in any area of government or industry had greater prominence in church or community service work. Courtesy of the Library of Congress.

Like an apparition, Virginia's former longing for participation in religious services overshadowed her comments. "Every Sunday you'd hope to get to an evening service," she said. "You never dreamed of going to day service. You'd be out of there if you was done by four or five."

Not surprisingly, church attendance sometimes revealed who did or did not have a "big job"—a realization that sometimes caused envy and further dissatisfaction among migrant workers, as Beulah Nelson observed:

Anybody who went to church every Sunday had a good job. They worked maybe as a messenger or cleaning in the government or something. People who went to church every Sunday was doing good.

A live-in got off when they could, so they went to church when they could. Anybody who got to church on Sunday was doing good. Even if they worked for a family they must have been really liked—if them people let them off every Sunday! You was a big shot if you could say you was in church every Sunday.

Mary Person, who was very religious, believed that

big people, like government messengers or people working in a colored business office, that's who'd be regular at Sunday day services. They didn't work but a half day on Saturday and none on Sunday.

They could be on the church's special committees, too. And how they'd speak up at any of them meetings. They could 'cause they be real active in First Baptist; they couldn't help but have a say. Us? We'd do good to be at one service—on Thursday. You couldn't really be doing much else.

If you got every Sunday off? It showed you had work that you didn't live at. To any live-in, you'd be somebody most times for that right there!

Regular attendance at "day church" also symbolized having work that was less restrictive, thereby affording a person more leisure time. And for a married couple to attend church together on Sunday, this signified their status as nonservice providers for their children. Madree Hershaw deeply sighed as she said:

People with good jobs got to have time with they people. Now if they had kids they could all go to day church services. And in summer out for picnics. Nice things. People who had good jobs was living high. Nobody working them to death day and night, six days a week. Never'd you have every Sunday off or holidays as a servant, living in.

Sadie Jones's voice went flat as she explained that "you couldn't be active in church work. Your days off were different from week to week."

Velma Davis clarified the effect this work condition had on the local church:

You'd have every church packed on any weeknight. See, the women usually got a weeknight off, so they could go to church that night. Big churches and small, all had weeknight services. Now, most churches had two services on Sunday—to let people who got off late or worked parties get to church. It wasn't like now. Churches was always open through the week. Had to be, 'cause we only got the weeknights off.

BREAKING THE NEWS

Their families certainly depended on and respected the benefits of live-in employment, but these women were fed up with subordinating their personal needs to those of their employers. They were tired of serving people who they saw as encroaching on their rights and as taking advantage of them. Unlike the earlier generation, this group seized the opportunity to gain more control and dignity in their work and to establish a clear boundary between their public and private lives.

But in seeking admittedly more difficult, though more satisfying employment, the migrants ran afoul of their families' expectations and instructions. Most women had received clear messages about staying put once they found live-in work; in effect, what they heard was "get work as a live-in with a well-paying white family and remain there, even after marriage." The women believed that their kin wanted them to allow the employer to become the domestic's own family, and she was expected to stay with them. Beulah Nelson exclaimed incredulously, "I was to stay with them forever, they [her kin] musta' thought—like *they* did."

Any alternative employment plans were considered either unnecessary or impossible to achieve. Velma Davis's family's consternation was typical:

My sister kept telling me to stop saying I was really lookin' to do better than number one Bradley Boulevard. The others there too tried to make me see this was how it was for colored girls. I didn't care what they thought, I knew I'd leave that woman. I figured my way out long before they knew too!

Exposed to a diverse community, the women began to realize that not everyone had to stay with one family forever, and that not everyone had to be directed by the will of their kin. If others could choose from a broader palette of occupational options, why shouldn't they?[2] As they explored other opportunities, however, they found that few people shared their vision. Kin and friends rejected outright self-directed missions for improvement; other live-in servants also spurned them, content to remain[3] the stereotypical "faithful servant girls." Thrust outside the social and cultural mainstream, these pioneers of African American labor created a unique subculture that actively redefined and reshaped their futures.

This new awareness of options alarmed their employers and their families. On the employers' front, in 1924 the president of the Domestic Efficiency Association of Baltimore denounced African American women's desire to live in their own homes in paternalistic language all too familiar to African Americans by the early twentieth century:

The desire to live out so prevalent today among the Negro workers should be discouraged for many reasons principally on the serious question of health.

Negroes are notoriously easy prey to disease, particularly to tuberculosis, a veritable scourge among them. Most Negro women who demand to go home at night do so for two reasons. Either they really do go to their homes to do the work they must neglect during the day, or particularly the younger ones, want to amuse themselves and spend much too large a portion of the nights at dances, movies, festivals, etc. In either case, they are trying to burn their candles at both ends, and their health suffers, while the employer suffers from a tired servant utterly unequal to the requirements of her day's work.[4]

Family members proved hardly more sympathetic. Thedella Crockett reported her kin's response to her own efforts:

Mary Sprow in maid's uniform serving the Naubuck family.

You'd try to talk to your family or them people working in—to say you wanted better up here. They'd laugh and just make you up to be nothing. They would. You'd feel like they was mocking you and how you'd feel about getting out to do more in your life. You'd be made to feel like it was too much to want. They didn't see it, so they made fun of it.

From 1900 to 1920, servant employment shifted dramatically from live-in to live-out work. African Americans largely occasioned this change, as historian Katzman notes: "As blacks became the dominant group in service in the urban North after 1900, they played an essential role in

Castleview, Thedella Crockett's place of employment for
five years.

shifting service to live-out and daywork there."[5] Slowly and deliberately,
migrant women reoriented their thinking toward more personal aims.[6]
Virginia Lacy made the hand-on-hip declaration: "Look at my family—
how they stayed in [performed live-in domestic work] all they work
days. But for me, I thought about it and knew when I got any chance,
I'd go—like a lotta girls was doing up here." Odessa Minnie Barnes had
also acted with patience and deliberation:

I thought to myself time and time again I wasn't going to take this place. I
wanted to do better. I knew I just could. I seen my way out long before I left
her. But my time had to come. I waited too. My mind knew to wait 'til I had

new work and all. But I was leaving them houses and I made up my mind to do it even if my brother was mad. But I did wait 'til I was set.

The idea of working on a job that allowed you to leave at the end of the day was both liberating and terrifying to Naomi Yates:

When you thought about living out, you know'd maybe you'd not get people, or not get paid or just not make out. It wasn't so sure like being with a good family. My brother said that over and over. But me, I had to try. He loved them people and they work. Truly, he'd be there now if he'd lived. Not me. They made me so tired and sick I just was going to try. Like I said I got set and in near a year I left and started on my own. You know it's not easy but you decide to just try, I guess.

Not knowing where a decision might lead characterized urban experience in the first decades of this century. In modernizing America, at a peak period of migration and immigration, a vast number of people had left their home places—places of emotional, if not economic, security—for better opportunities. African American domestics, like others, encountered a world in which the unknown loomed large. As Peter Berger notes in his volume *The Homeless Mind,* individuals in modern society not only feel uprooted but also run the risk of never regaining the sense of "home."[7]

The tremor in Weida Edward's high-pitched voice revealed that, for her, to undertake such a transition had been an act of valor. She struggled with security in the form of guaranteed wages and the presence of kin, versus freedom—and the fear of not finding work:

You'd be scared of two things. One, you had to be able to get work to keep yourself and help Mama down home. Now if you wasn't set and all, you'd be doing harm to more than just you. You had to get your job lined up good—to not be loafing or have to go home for a handout. Not getting work scared you bad. You was most scared of not being around your people. Now, you'd work living in away from each other's sight but you was all in the same house or the same family. You'd have them right from my part of Florida too. So you was with *all* your people—kin or no. It was good, and they'd help you and just make sure you was OK. Now by yourself, you didn't know who could get you or do harm to you! People told of girls going out and finding trouble, but you hoped it didn't find you. That's what you was scared by.[8]

For Athelene Walker, looking for daywork was a hallmark of personal triumph:

Oh, you'd be scared at first. Now your people here didn't help—they wanted you to stay with they people and never leave. Not me. No, I was there only about two years when I started to ask people I worked with—and even them who just came to that house—for days work, about making money day to day! I'd come from home and made it. I was going to try here, too. I guess you are young and don't really know any better. All I had was me anyway, so why not? I didn't care but I knew I had to try to get out of that place. And I did, too; just like I said to them, too.

Getting set is the expression[9] the women used to describe a transitional process toward day work. Velma Davis defined it as

the ways you get yourself ready to get your day work. You'd first try to set more money aside for yourself. Now, I didn't spend no money on me for near a year. None. I sent four dollars down home and saved up all the rest. No buying nothing, 'cause you was scared when you left your live-in place you'd not get all your days for work right away. Then you learn how to ride streetcars. You'd go 'round and 'round just learning how to go places. Now that was on your off days, of course. Soon when you heard the staff talking about this or that street, you'd know exactly where it was. When Ora [the laundress] helped me get set she'd asked me how to get to so and so—just to see if I knew. First, I didn't, but after a while I knew this town! And I learned myself, just going around on one day of the week, too!

Next, you'd go on your day off and try to see people who needed a day worker. See, I'd get they names from Ora, who knew when people all around this town needed help. So you'd go. But it'd take a while for [before] anybody'd hire you, mainly 'cause by my day off—Thursdays—they'd have gotten somebody else!

Others described this process in similar terms. According to Annie Brown:

I started to saving more and more. One day, when I had carried sister over there, too, the lady said to me: "You really been saving up since the summer. You getting yourself set for daywork soon?" Sister didn't say anything then but later she said I was going to be sorry for leaving Mrs. Kelly. I told her I was leaving, but it wasn't 'til she knew I was getting set that she tried to scare me—telling me I'd do bad and be wrong to leave Mrs. Kelly. But I never let her stop me. And I was gone from that place by the next summer, too.

Beulah Nelson defined it this way:

Getting set? Oh, well it's really just learning to put money aside. Now, I know that's when I started saving in a penny savings club. When you had enough to keep yourself for nearly a month or so, you'd start going 'round the city and learn the streets. I'd been here over seven years, and it wasn't 'til then I started to ride the streetcars to see the town. Now I knew how to go to work or to Sister's from work, but that was all. My people didn't want me to do anymore neither! But after all them years, I started just going on the streetcar—just for me to learn to go here or there. For me. Well, then you'd get with somebody who'd help you find people needed cleaning by the day. It'd mostly be laundresses or other people who'd do work by the day—pick-up work. A lot was in my penny club, and they was the ones to help me get my first work, way up on Sherman Avenue. You got yourself set, to be truthful. You had to do for yourself and all.

Two institutions that assisted the women in getting set were the church and the penny savers clubs. The church, of course, had been central to their lives since childhood. As in the South, church life in Washington provided, beyond spiritual benefit, opportunities to establish social relationships; church connections also oriented many migrants to African American urban culture. To some extent, the church perpetuated the communal intimacy of the rural South, despite the obvious differences between the churches back home and in Washington. Ellamay Carter, a prim and somber woman, lived in a house that was always too dark. Her recollections of entering the urban church were clear:

Dad and Mama took us to church down home in Georgia. When I lived with my sister, Miss Carroll [a neighbor] took all of my sister's kids and me to

Mount Saint Paul every Sunday. I got to make my first Washington friends up there. Through the year they'd raise money to help people out. At Christmas they gave almost everybody the food we'd eat. Some got clothes. The little ones got a toy, too. I liked it like a home.

In addition to church involvement, which necessarily suffered from their obligations as live-in servants, the migrant women developed a second support network beyond the family—the penny savers clubs. In large part, migrant women still supported rural family members, but they also invested small portions of their earnings in these clubs. Based on financial need and modeled after the extended family's cooperatives, these penny savers clubs were African American mutual-benefit associations that provided social activities and sickness and death benefits to members. As savings organizations, they served an important function for the migrants, whose small deposits were not acceptable at local banking establishments. When migrants from specific regions of the South settled together in areas of the city, they formed these citywide mutual-benefit associations along state lines. Active membership in the clubs usually was limited to persons from the specific southern states. Eula Montgomery, for example, had helped organize a club from Alabama:

I helped get my group really started. I did it because I knew people from other areas had penny savings clubs for death or accidents. The colored girls didn't trust no insurance, and they couldn't go to no bank with them few pennies. So we started collecting, mainly us working in Georgetown. Every maybe Thursday and Saturday you could meet the girl collecting and she'd check the book "paid." We pulled together like that in them days.

The Mite Savers Club had several branches in Washington. An Alabamian, Mary Person, quietly declared that the

Mites was just people from Alabama putting their pennies together to help each other. It wasn't important like the Tuskegee Club,[10] or like that. Just people who worked in homes up here putting money up to save.
    I'd save at where I lived—at my sister's rooming house. The lady there

checked ours in. But it was just pennies, no real money like now. You couldn't bank that little bit, so you'd save it by the week.

Mathilene Anderson, aged ninety-nine and listless from a stroke, gleefully recalled her Virginia club's activities. After two months of looking, she had found a picture of the women with whom she saved. Her eyes danced as she recalled, "She was at the streetcar stop. No matter how little, you'd save some with her. She was nice and had the news from home or just talked about this or that. Eva, no I can't recall her name but I can't tell you all the ways that club helped me." Savers clubs, like the Mites, also sponsored benefit social gatherings, which helped foster and preserve regional loyalties. Mary Person, a thin woman with soft brown, finely wrinkled skin, continued:

You'd hear the Mites were giving a party at somebody's house or in summer a picnic near the river. You'd go—if you was off that day or evening—and see all your people and [a] lot more all just from down home. The food tasted just like it was from home. You'd pay a little to get in and for food. Now, we never had drinks, like some.

But it was to help, you know, people from down home who were up here, and it raised up money for the sick fund, funeral expenses, and burial plots, too.

The penny savers clubs drew friends and kin into a circle of mutual assistance and reciprocal obligation. Some of the migrants even admitted that club members often substituted for their absent family members. Through the clubs, they renewed childhood friendships and found persons who had been close friends of their parents in the rural South. Bernice Reeder described her visit to a club-sponsored picnic as a "family gathering," and to Bernice, club-sponsored fund-raising events "seemed like socials, or more like my kin's reunion." Ora Fisher laughed as she described her club as

just a group of live-ins from North Carolina. It was just sick and death insurance—but not with a big company. You was almost just with family or really the family of family and all. You was just up here and trying to put a few cents

Penny savers "social" with four live-in servants, including
Mathilene Anderson.

aside, or help with funeral expenses or help people from home. That's all—it
was just something we all did. We wasn't from here so we had to pull together.

Velma Davis, who eventually pursued an active social life in her club,
initially joined it because of her friends' persuasion:

The only way I got in was a lot of us were working in Chevy Chase. These
girls was all from Virginia, and two worked in number three Bradley Boule-

Photograph of Virginia penny savers club account clerk.

vard. They kept talking to me and telling me to join in . . . so finally I did. Now they all knew each other from home. I knew just one from home when I started. But they wanted to keep up the friendliness and all that from home—so they put in with all the people from our towns and around.

Because of their large membership, penny savers clubs were often so-licited to assist the philanthropic organizations in African American communities. For instance, state clubs would relieve the plight of new migrants from a particular region. The clubs helped migrants find friends or relatives in the city, in effect relieving some of the loneliness of living in a large metropolis.

Penny savers clubs also engaged in philanthropic activities, such as lending support to needy persons who came from rural areas. "We had to help out," Amy Kelly said, because "we would be turning our backs on our family if we didn't." In 1927, for example, a terrible disaster hit Mississippi. The *Minutes* of the Blue Plains Industrial Home School recorded the proposal to involve "the many former Mississippi residents in the District of Columbia. Miss Ware notes many servants of this city will spare nickels for relief to aid their home state. A special note is to be directed to Mrs. Drake who can reach their savings club for an appeal."[11] The July 1927 *Minutes* noted that $29.39 came from colored women, collected by Mrs. Lester and Mrs. Drakes.[12]

Unable to attend regular church services on Sundays and facing exclusion from the social life of their churches, migrant women felt sharply the intolerable restrictions of the live-in life. As painful as these restrictions were, however, they alone might not have compelled the women to leave. But spurred on by some economic leverage by way of the penny savers clubs, many women indeed had "gotten set" to escape the deprivations, humiliations, and oppressions of live-in work.

ASK MAY ONE DAY

Only one staff member consistently encouraged and supported the young migrant women's endeavors to obtain daywork: the laundress. Providing both a role model and a support network,[13] the laundress never (unlike the other full staff members) ridiculed them in their sometimes-awkward struggle for economic improvement and self-betterment. Mayme Gibson has fond memories of Miss Dee, the laundress who served her Georgetown employer:

After a while I could talk to the laundress. See, they worked house-to-house, always, and they didn't care. They'd do it and didn't feel like it was just pick-up work neither. They really made good and didn't have that woman on they backs day *and* night. Now they'd know where jobs was. Not doing piecework, too. This one called Dee helped me find my very first work out. She was nice, but it was over a year before she helped me and another girl get set and in some day work. The others didn't do nothing but make fun. But me and my friend left and never went back to that house. Never.

Weida Edwards nodded and smiled softly as she remembered:

A lady that was just coming to they house to do laundry really helped me. Well, this lady, I can't remember her name, just told me to keep trying, but to be quiet and she'd help. It took nearly a year and a half for her to help me get out, but she did. She even helped me find a room by the week at first. She was so nice.

They wasn't like laborers or that. They had steady people, but they just didn't live-in. My people saw it like not having a family and all that. That's wrong. You had work, but not like they jobs where you was always there. But doing day work was not here-and-there work like people try to make it all the time. It's not.

Annie Pansylee Holmes confided her hopes to the laundress May:

After I'd been there, oh, maybe a year or so, I started to think about leaving. But not to go home but to make it up here. So, I just decided to ask May one day. She did all the laundry and did they parties at times, too. She said she was glad not to stay in and told me how she set herself out to do for more than Mrs. I'd do just that, too. So when I was set she helped me to get two days with a lady and her daughter way up Georgia Avenue. That was how I left down Thomas Circle.

All but two of the women used their relationship with the laundress to make the transition to household worker. (One received help from a distant cousin who belonged to the same penny savings club; the other, from a fellow church member.) The laundress held a position and status very different from those of a "washerwoman." A washerwoman commonly was a married woman who did wash in her home to supplement

the family income while carrying our her responsibilities for her husband and children.[14] A laundress, on the other hand, went from house
to house on a regular basis. Dolethia Otis was filled with a rosiness and
her many freckles appeared darker as she offered this explanation:

Washerwomens was in the South! They did wash at home. And it was most
old women who didn't live-out. They'd mind grandchildrens and take in
washes. Up here some did it too. But they washed for anybody and got them
pieces back in a day or so. For them it was all [done] from their rooms or
apartments.

Now "good" families like the Kent's never sent they piecework out. They
had a laundress who came and did just that. A full staff always had a laundress.
Now laundresses never live-in, and I know they was on the staffs of more than
four or five families. But these good families wouldn't no more have they
piecework sent out than die. No, they had all they jobs done in they homes.
They had money and the staff was full. No cutting corners—for what? They
had it and didn't want no sending out for they stuff. No, not a good family.
Them people had money to keep they jobs done—right at home too.

Laurlean Davis was emphatic about the distinctions between the two
professions:

Ora was a laundress, not a washwoman. You see, first a laundress wasn't no old
woman. She'd be up here with small kids, like that. They live-out, always, and,
often they'd be able to serve in the houses of five or six families. With a schedule she'd work; and, by nightfall go back to her own childrens. They'd be
young and able to get around to they works.

A washwoman would be down home. Just washing for money with no set
people. They did for most anybody. A laundress had just her set people. A
washwoman might have some few set people, but all the same she's more than
real glad for anybody else's wash she could get to do in her own place.

As a stable, regularly employed woman, so different from a person who
performed "pick-up work," the laundress ranked high in the staff hierarchy. Bernice Reeder noted that the live-in staff felt that "pick-up
work [was] just work people'd get. You don't know from day-to-day if
you'd get work. It was just lazy people who'd go house-to-house and

Mrs. Fannie Dodson, respected Georgetown laundress, pictured in her son's (Dr. Joseph Dodson) yard. Courtesy of Barbara Dodson Walker.

get anything. They could be colored or white trash too down to get a job." To the migrant women, the laundress was like a private contractor with regular clients—someone to respect and emulate.

Except for the laundress position, house-to-house work carried a stigma of being precarious work performed by persons of dubious character who were not otherwise acceptable to employers on a long-term basis. Marie Stone pinpointed why pick-up workers were held in such low esteem:

Look, they'd be just around. Not good enough to get work by theyself, or they had no people to help them get good live-in work, so they just go door to door like a beggar. They do any job for a few cents and be sent away. They went place to place 'cause no good family'd have 'um. I guess.

Such workers were generally considered uncommitted to the prospect of long-term employment. They were believed to be less skilled and less tractable than live-ins, or simply unable to submit to a routine. In other words, free-lancers (as they might be called) presented few of the attributes an employer sought in live-in domestics.

The conflicting factors of day work weighed heavily on the women's minds. On the one hand, they had learned from birth that predictable employment made a person complete or "full." On the other hand, they perceived the position of laundress as highly desirable, for several reasons. First, although she was not a live-in, she commanded the respect of a full staff member. She was accepted as an intimate and learned all the problems confronting workers, including their private feelings about their employers. Second, she served on the staffs of more than one household. Like other staff members, she had a specific role and tasks, but she served a variety of families on a weekly basis. Third, her work allowed her to leave at the end of each day. And, of utmost importance, she had clearly defined work hours and duties. She arrived, completed all the laundry, and promptly left after her tasks were completed, escaping the innumerable duties expected of the live-in staff. Velma Davis wistfully recalled:

You'd never be done, not like them leaving. You rip-and-run from morn to late night. They had you there in they jobs. They wanted you to never have any peace. Up and down, here and there for this and that. And mostly just a lot of nothing. But a laundress never had that bother at all.

Employers likewise valued the laundress for her unique access to the social and occupational life of various households. Her independence assured a measure of fair treatment by employers. Beulah Nelson tartly recalled, "I tell you she didn't act up on the laundress and people who came by the day. They'd quit on her."

Despite the staff's high esteem for her and her profession, winning the laundress's respect and confidence was no easy feat. Laundresses often tested the live-in servant's commitment to pursue day work. Initially, the women listened as the laundress brought news to the live-in staff about the most recent church changes or scandals. They then learned to pay particular attention as she discussed activities in the other household staffs she served. It was important, each woman recognized, to listen to the laudress's opinions before divulging their own desires to obtain live-out work.

At first the laundress ignored the endless questions about the availability of live-out work. She would admonish the women privately and often publicly display her annoyance with their questions. But determination and persistence would eventually sway the laundress's confidence. And after she had observed and questioned these persistent women for at least a year, she would finally offer to assist those who had gained her approval. A laundress explained her role in helping live-in servants attain independence:

I never tried to get them girls away from a live-in job. I'd make them almost beg me for months before I'd listen to them. Then I'd watch the way each one worked on a staff. She'd have to really be able to do a good job and show she could work on her own, not act slow-witted or seem too big acting—them things. After a year or so, then you'd help them get set, and then they'd go away from working for just one family and start with three or four people to clean for the week.

Household workers were neither prisoners of the past nor masters of their new environment. Rather, they sought to resolve the sharp disjuncture between the commandments of their culture and their own urban experience. The past—the South—had shaped their first responses to Washington, but experience had taught them lessons their families had not foreseen.[15] No longer immobilized by poverty or familial obligation, these African American women claimed full responsibility for their own destiny.

6
THIS WORK HAD
A' END

The living-in jobs just kept you running; never stopped. Day or night . . .
never a minute's peace. But when I went out days on my jobs, I'd get my
work done and be gone . . . that's it. This work had a' end.
—DOLETHIA OTIS, AGE EIGHTY-SIX

By the early 1920s, two major shifts in domestic work had taken hold
nationwide. Few native-born and foreign-born whites peopled servant staffs; African Americans served in most households. And
due largely to the rise of apartment living and of new technology
for maintaining the home (spurred by the domestic use of electricity),
employers no longer required the continuous service of live-in staff.[1]

JUST DIFFERENT WORK

African American women experienced transition from live-in service to
daywork as something far more significant than a mere minor change of
tasks or hours.[2] Daywork radically altered their self-esteem, relationships
with other employees, assessment of employee-employer relations, and
ideas about what constituted satisfactory completion of tasks. They consistently heralded the pronounced differences between live-in service
and daywork. One was the daily ritual of traveling to and from work, an
experience most Americans took for granted but one new to domestics.
The other was the ability to wear personal clothing in the work place,
likewise making domestic work relatively equal in status to the work
done by other Washington residents.

The transition from live-in servant to household worker was not a panacea for African American women. To curtail any predisposed, rampant optimism I might have about daywork, the otherwise timid, quiet Nettie Bass set the record straight concerning the place where the rubber of daywork met the occupational road of these migrant women. When I asked her how daywork made her life better, she became quite animated: "Life for a colored woman didn't never get 'better.' The most it got was 'different.' Daywork was just different work. Period. More time just meant more jobs at more places. One in the day. Party work at night. And sewing on weekends for extra money."

But the new path of their work did raise their collective consciousness about personal and social change and about their right to effect such change. This new awareness would eventually stimulate women to build a movement for collective action to change domestics' working conditions.[3] Buxom and dark brown, Thedella Crockett spoke to the important issue of choice in the two sorts of employment situations: "Living-in, you had no choices about nothing. You was told what to do, and you had to do it. Period. But working out, you'd be able to pick homes, days, and kinds of work you didn't do. You always work. But you'd have some say in it. That's better." Daywork enabled the women to use their personal freedom for advancement. They perceived their new life-style as an opportunity to fulfill personal choices and responsibilities. No longer was identity ascribed to them at birth; instead, they might achieve by their own efforts.[4] Velma Davis clarified the progressive aspects of becoming a dayworker:

Once you got some work by the day and got around people who only did it, you'd see how you could get ahead. Get better things, doing the same work. Living-in was going to get you only so much. Don't matter how you try to or nothing. A servant on they job will do only what's been done before on Bradley [Boulevard]. Period. Working out, you'd see how to get more and more days, some party work, extra sewing, stuff like that. Huh, not in that house could you get to do more for yourself. Never.

Mathilene Anderson also sought to get ahead—an impossibility as a live-in:

Living in you'd do cleaning and serving 'til you'd drop. They was never going to give you an hour extra off or any more chances to get ahead. And they good and well knew you was trying to help your people at home, too.

When I started working days, other people'd [household workers] show you how to get a few extra dollars. In this town you could make more money and they'd sure show you. But living in you'd only clean and fetch for whoever you worked for. Ain't no way for extra to be made.

Being a dayworker meant the difference between doing a "job," or "work," and "serving." As she contemplated her experiences, Odessa Minnie Barnes tightly pressed her dark fingers between her knees and rocked forward slightly. What mattered most to her was the chance to be treated as an individual with assigned *limited* tasks, no running to and from "doing a lot of nothing":

You'd be by yourself, working for the day and a day of pay. That's not serving—no running for this or that. You was doing a job, work. No serving—running back and forth to hand them this and that. In daywork you got a job to do; you do it, and that's it. No running around doing a lot of nothing.

When you was living in they'd never let you forget you was just one part of they staff. You'd do this one day and some of that and this the next. You never felt like you had one job for just you. Then they'd got so they gave my little bit of money right to Brother every month. Brother's was no better. Always you was just one of everybody in his house. I mean that, too.

Now time I got my first days of work, it was different. I did the whole place myself. They told me what to do to my face, and I'd get to talk right back to her. Plus I got my money every time it was to be paid out. Right to me. That's what more to yourself means.

Eighty-four-year-old Weida Edwards described her first taste of independence after leaving live-in work:

I was on my own for the first time. Down home Mama put you on them jobs. Up here your people took you to work with them, when they was ready for

Many women were proud to wear clothing they felt chal-
lenged the negative images people had of service workers.

you. But doing daywork you got to do for yourself on a job. . . . I been working over seventy-five years, and after I left live-in I never went back. You
wasn't working in a good way. I know that. It was you and too many other
people doing a lot of nothing, making no money, having no say to nobody!

All the migrant women reported a striking difference in the process of
obtaining a daywork position: each was hired without an acquaintance

"Better things" often translated into clothing for young
women. Bernice Reeder is pictured in her first "new" outfit
she purchased after leaving live-in servant employment.

or relative present to introduce her to the prospective employer, in stark
contrast to having kin take a girl to the mistress for the first live-in job.
Ora Fisher viewed this as an early indicator of her newly acquired freedom and responsibility as a worker:

When you go to do live-in work, at first, they'd look at you as So-and-So's
sister. It's like they really wanted to be hiring them again, but in your skin.
You were to be like So-and-So. They hired you because of So-and-So. So

now if you were a problem, So-and-So'd be told first, then you. Now, when you got daywork, they'd hear of you. *You* was who they hired; you'd be told direct if they didn't like anything. It was your job; you got it, and you'd have to keep it. Wouldn't be nobody else to speak up for you.

For most of the women, an acquaintance had referred them to their prospective employers prior to their applying for the job. Contrary to the informal process by which they started their first live-in jobs, the women were subjected to extensive personal interviews for daywork. Annie Brown stretched her round eyes and bristled as she recalled how surprised she was that her first daywork employer "wasn't like Miss Kelly. That woman [the daywork employer] questioned a body to death from the first." This first interview for daywork was a landmark for all the women, because it was for a job that required them to perform specific tasks and assignments, rather than for work as a staff member who was on call around the clock to "step and fetch." Velma Davis described the particulars of her first interview in these words:

Ora's [the laundress's] cousin knew of this woman who really needed a person by the day. This lady had a place up Georgia Avenue. When I first started daywork, she'd been told about me and just told me how she wanted this and that done.

Reference? Nobody checked that if you'd been sent by somebody they knew. That's how I always got jobs, through people. I guess if you got work in the papers they'd check, but never if you was sent. Let me say I, and nobody I know of, was [never] checked up on if they was sent to the people by somebody.

Amy Kelly thoughtfully stroked the freckles on her plump cheeks as she discussed her daywork interviews:

They'd talk to you and make sure you could work like the person who sent you there said you could. Then, on my first job, they told me when they could start me and gave me time to leave my live-in lady. That was all.

It wasn't no government work, so it wasn't no great big interview or something. They talked to you to make sure you'd be able to do. Now they knew you'd been sent to them by somebody they knew—it was no problem. Now they'd watch the first month to be sure you was honest. After then it was no nothing.

Another benefit of the new employment was that on-the-job performance could not reflect on one's kin. If a situation did not work out, or a dayworker had some conflict with her employer, no one else stood to be hurt. This was a great relief to Marie Stone: "Daywork was your job. Not because anybody 'got' you the work, so if you wanted to speak back, or leave, you wasn't hurting nobody. The family wouldn't be shamed about how you acted. Plus you didn't 'owe' anybody anything with days [daywork]." Then she added happily, in her husky voice: "It was finally me, doing my job—not just a lot of playing up foolishness."

Most had *no* idea what they earned as a live-in, because kin received their monthly pay. In fact, no live-in worker was ever paid directly for her service. Not surprisingly, then, each woman described a happy adjustment to receiving wages, and seventy-nine of the eighty-one women interviewed recalled *exactly* her first wage.[5] Marie Stone said, "I worked all day and nearly fainted when that woman put the money in my hand. Fifty cents and I near died." Wages varied, depending on the demand for workers, the housewife's budget, and the desperation of women glad to take the job at any price. Nevertheless, receiving wages at the end of each day helped make the hard work and long hours bearable.[6] Marie Stone insisted, "I could never go back to working and somebody else getting my monies. Them few coins, when she put them in your pure hand—well you'd near died of joy."

Whatever else daywork might bring, one commitment never faltered: the women continued to send their monthly income allotments home to the South. Throughout the first quarter of the century, despite the vast changes in migrant work experiences, their family survival strategies remained stable. This strong umbilical cord between migrant women and their southern kin sustained them through the many personal and professional crises they faced after the change to daywork.

Daily work eventually realigned the women's most significant personal relationships. For a while, most of the dayworking women continued to live with their families, but inevitably their feelings about both their kin and their restrictive living arrangements began to change. Their new work schedules afforded them far less personal contact with their relatives during the week and little, if any, social time with them. For example, Velma Davis's "brother and his wife came (home) only on their day off. I'd see them then at night, but we didn't talk." Furthermore, as their social horizons broadened, the women soon grew bored with the tedious, employer-centered conversation of live-in servants. Annie Brown detailed her experience of a growing gap between herself and her family members:

I still lived in my aunt's apartment till the next May. And I kept right on working days, too. I'd see them once a week but that'd be late. Plus, I didn't care about what went on at the Kellys no more! So we didn't have much to say. I guess for all that time I mostly just slept there. If one of the kids was sick at night, I'd help. Other than that, we had no need for a lot of talk. Our work was different, so we was, too—I guess.

Once you got to leave live-in work you'd still have to help out your people. Since you'd be home every night you'd feel like they even wanted you to do more for them [more household related duties] than you'd do that one day you got off as a live-in. But I didn't care. I was probably doing more work, but I wasn't having to be a live-in.

It was not long before these women felt some pressure, whether internal or external, to move out of their first Washington homes. Within a year or two of getting daywork, most of the women moved away from their kin and into boardinghouses or the homes of friends from their rural birthplaces. Ellamay Carter recounted her own decision to move:

I was working for myself and really wanted to move. I just did. Things got to be too different. It's hard to make you know, but moving was best. Everyone did the same work but me. It was good when I was working with all of them. But when I got my own work and all, I wanted to move.

Many women, before they moved away from kin, faced
added family and child-care responsibilities. Pictured are
Hester and Wilma Bundy, nieces cared for by Bernice
Reeder after live-in service employment.

Another reason for moving was to permit kin still in the rural South to "move up here, get trained, and then get put on a live-in job," as Zelma Powell explained. Annie Brown believed that her move served both her own and her family's interests:

I knew when I got daywork I'd want to do more. So I asked a girl who'd stopped doing live-in, and she told me firm to get me a room. I listened, too, because when I left the Kellys' house I got me a room with Miss Williams from down home on the next May! Sister didn't care neither. I think she was a little mad, but only about me leaving them Kellys. But mostly I think she didn't mind because my cousin wanted to come up. My half-sister was trained and got my job when I left. So they'd need my cousin to help with the kids and all. From Miss Williams I worked every day, six days a week. I went to three people, twice to the week. I worked hard too. But they was my jobs and my jobs was better.

Similarly, Velma Davis remembered:

Nobody'd be mad that you got daywork. But I planned my money so that when I left Bradley Boulevard, I'd leave from Brother's house too! I moved off Pennsylvania Avenue, them places are long gone now! I moved with the cousin of my pastor from home. She had rooms for girls up here. I was glad to do daywork but I missed the people out Bradley Boulevard. But I wasn't going back. Not there, to do live-in? No! I just made it. I got steady work, five days too. And I didn't do pick-up work. I worked day-to-day, but it was steady and for good people. As long as you was working steady and not doing pick-up jobs nobody'd be mad you'd do daywork and get a room. They'd fill that space with somebody from down home too quick to be mad long!

Of course, because "getting set" had included preparations for finding new places of residence, the women were somewhat prepared for these moves. But their real frontier challenges lay in adapting to life away from home.

For the first time in their careers, household workers could dictate their own pace, set their own priorities for tasks, and complete assigned chores as they saw fit. Autonomy and job control were very important to Mayme Gibson:

When I got work by the days I'd work in jobs where I'd be doing all the cleaning, my way. Nobody'd be looking over your shoulder, saying what you was to do. I didn't want that no more, not after I left out from living in down southwest. What was the need leaving sister and everybody if I was only going to work back with somebody else watching me? People took daywork to finally get to work by theyself; to get away from people telling you how to do every little thing.

Virginia Lacy relished being left alone to do her work efficiently:

She'd [the white employer] meet you at the door most times. She'd tell you what and how she wanted her house done—and she'd be gone. You did the work without her. When she was there she'd be in the way slowing you up. Slowing you up? In daywork that's when somebody is asking you to do this, and don't forget that, and asking why didn't you do the other. On a day job we knew how to get everything done—but in your own way. Having anybody around will make you work slower.

One hazard of daywork, however, was the possibility of not being paid after a hard day's work. Lottie Cooksey's small, rough hands clenched together as she recounted a particularly unpleasant incident: she worked three full days assisting a family in preparation for their religious holidays, only to have the woman (whose husband had given his wife the money to pay the maid in full for her services) give Lottie Cooksey some of her old clothing in lieu of money. Mrs. Cooksey was enraged and returned to the house later that evening when the husband was home. However, the man would not make his wife pay her the money. "From then on," she proclaimed, "I always insisted on being paid at the start of the job, not when I finished."

Employers usually hired someone other than their own former live-in servants to do the daily paid household work. Domestics understood this arrangement and, on resigning, both they and their employers tacitly agreed that no future offers of employment would be forthcoming. According to Darethia Handy, "People who had a full staff only wanted full-time live-in workers. When you said you wanted to work days—

you left there. She told you you'd not be able to come back. It was OK, cause you'd got all set and could go on where you'd be working next."

Still, three women did return to service work in homes where they had previously worked as live-in servants. But the relationship with the employer was different: a woman worked for wages and no longer accepted the belittling live-in servants faced. Nettie Bass's recollections demonstrate how profoundly daywork changed many women's perspectives[7] on the old household routine:

They called me to work days after her children got in school for all day. I saw Aunt L. Still there with them as a live-in! She used to seem so busy and so nice. But after I went back she just seemed silly. Just running for her [the mistress] and not really doing a thing. When we was all working in, it seemed like she was doing something. But after I went back it just seemed like kids' junk she was doing. Just back and forth to look at her new dress; or to check on her this, or her that. Not me. I did my work and just didn't want no kid junk. No more. They needed me by the day only. To work. They had all the others to run back and forth, night and day.

Women who returned to their former jobs also found that their interactions with other staff members had changed drastically. For one thing, dayworkers had no time to "waste" on tasks not assigned by the employer. They were, therefore, not comfortable sharing tasks with persons who were not concerned about completing their work. In fact, some domestics criticized live-in servants over their unspecified assignments and postponed completion of tasks. Anxious to finish their work so that they could go home, daily workers felt a disdainful superiority because live-ins were not given well-defined, specific assignments. When Nettie Bass returned, her Aunt Letha appeared to be more of a "go-fer" than a worker: "They tell'd her to do anything—go-fer this, go-fer that! She wasn't doing a job, she'd just be serving, lapping up to they 'you-know-what.' I didn't like that no more neither. I was doing better than that!" For the first time in her forty-seven-minute interview, Costella Harris abandoned her indifferent tone and attitude as she avidly noted how different her former live-in household seemed:

If they got a smaller or a lot bigger place, and if you did good, they'd call you back—even if you doing only days. Funny, they kids and all was not so cute and all. They seemed to get in the way so much more! It's a funny thing to tell to you. I guess you just was meaning business and work—not there to play with them or to fill up the day with them like you do when living in. The family seemed in the way more to me when I went back there. I guess I just saw them kind of different.

THE GOOD PLACES HAD STRONG BAGS

As the new dayworkers emerged from their live-in cocoons, they simultaneously shed their uniforms like old skins. Carrying their own work clothes to the work place became for them a symbol of advancement. Pernella Ross, a tall woman with tiny hands and feet, explained the close link between wearing a uniform and losing ground in the path toward improvement:

At home you better not try to do no better. It wasn't for colored people to be much of nothing. But up here, I knew different. You had chances to do so much more. Every time I put on uniforms I knew in myself it wouldn't be for always. And it wasn't just me. All us came here to do better. Living-in wasn't better—you saw that every time you put that uniform on.

To them the uniform was fiendish. In the uniform the women felt trapped in a constricting role, and they expressed their discomfort about wearing one many ways: "You'd put you in a black uniform for this" or, "In the gray uniform you couldn't even do that." By shedding the dreaded uniform, the women disassociated themselves from the major stigma they associated with live-in work. The right to choose what they would wear while working symbolized their freedom to direct their own lives.[8] Darethia Handy spoke with passion on this issue:

When I got my first day job, I told them right off that I wasn't wearing a uniform. Them things are what really makes you a live-in and a part of a staff. I had my own work dresses and all. They just as nice. And don't you just know, the lady said she didn't care what I wear—just so as I cleaned like she said!

Bertha Jackson's neatly styled hair was "messed up" because she moved her head back and forth quickly when she talked about the uniform. While her head moved, she tapped her cane on her oriental rug for emphasis and reiterated others' sentiments about the uniform:

I'd go to whatever house I'd have to be to work at. I'd change to my work clothes and then clean the house. I'd not use no uniforms when I'd do work by the day. See, when you got your own work, you'd not be using uniforms and such. That was better. At least for me because I never liked to be in the uniform. Well, once I got my own work, no more uniforms. I guess serving in a uniform made you be back on the staff. And you wasn't, so you'd just not want to wear that uniform. The uniform made you staff, like a live-in. Wearing your own clothes—that's like you being your own boss. Or, well, you wasn't staff. You was on your own job for a day and pay. Then—go on home.

To these women, their shopping bags full of work clothes meant no less than their hard-won personal freedom. In fact, Sadie Jones reported that women often referred to their clothing bags as "freedom bags":

When I got to carry clothes I was finally working in what I wanted to. Not no black or gray uniform. Not in no castoffs, that's what you'd have to wear down South. Down there they swore you had some bugs or something, so soon as they took you to they farms they put some old rags on you. Sometimes badder than your stuff. Now when I got to work in what I wanted, I knew I wasn't just to serve or belonging to anybody.

It's a funny thing to tell. . . . Well, I put my stuff in a bag at home. My freedom bag was always from a good store—'cause that's where it [the clothing] come from. Even if it was second hand. Who knows? You might have got it there [laughter]. Plus, good places had the strong bags. They wouldn't tear on a street car. Mostly I guess I wanted to show I didn't wear a uniform. I wasn't a servant.

Even their modes of speech registered the psychological and cultural changes resulting from the transition to daywork. In recounting their earlier history, from their lives in the rural South to their first years in Washington, they used the pronoun *you* a great deal. In effect, *you* implied that the speaker was not a particular, real person, but someone, anyone, in general—any young migrant from the South who migrated North to be a live-in household servant. For example, when asked to describe her first work as a migrant, Darethia Handy replied, "You was brought up here, and you'd soon be worked near to death." And Nettie Bass said: "You was put down on that floor quick, too. They didn't ever offer you no mop. Why? You wasn't like a person, to get respect or nothing. On they jobs? I couldn't start to tell you what was done to you. And you better never even blink—let alone talk up." Whether describing migration or live-in servitude, these women always portrayed themselves as being moved around like cargo or, at best, like nonpersons.[9] They made statements such as "you was put on the train" or "you wasn't in that house one hour before you was put right down to scrub," which reflected feelings of passivity and subordination, the sense that they could do little to offset the power of kin, or employers, or of the migration experience itself.

Similarly, household workers reported that they had staunchly stated to employers, "*Your* job is over too late" or "I can't do *your* job Saturdays." The *your* denoted a derisive refusal to assert ownership of the job, or to permit any one household to become the woman's soul, or to fully identify oneself with the work. By erecting this verbal barrier, African American women sought psychological sanctuary from their employers' continual insensitivity.

Daywork brought more personal power, and this sense of power permeated the women's words about work. No longer was it "they job," as Isetta Peters explained in defining her experience:

When I say "my job" I mean a job I got and I'd keep if they acted decent. Now that is always by the day. Nobody trying to work me to death. "They job" is for them. A job that you did and did, more and more and more. From most one thing to another, from early to late, and just being worked to death. It's hard to let you know what I mean.

Dolethia Otis, sitting rigidly and speaking very slowly, was forthright and firm as she distinguished clearly between "they" and "my" job:

The living-in jobs just kept you running; never stopped. Day or night you'd be getting something for somebody. It was never a minute's peace. But when I went out days on my jobs, I'd get my work done and be gone. I guess that's it. This work had a' end.

In their house you was always working. You come here and they'd work you like a dog. The houses was big, not like now, so they'd have a full staff—to serve day and night. Big people with big money, and they have everybody working from dawn to way after ten. Back then dinner wasn't 'til eight! They jobs was just too much. And for only five dollars a month!

Now on my last job I got fifteen dollars a day. I hear now they pay up to thirty-five! Even with my party work I never made that kind of money in one day. It's better now—really it is.

New housing, new kinds of mobility, new relationships, even new ways of expression—so much had changed from the live-in social world. A cadre of young dayworkers with a distinctive set of life experiences found one another—at boardinghouses, on the job—and created a new network of support.[10] Annie Brown, recalled that

people in Miss West's house helped me out a lot, from the very first. Stuff I thought I had to do, like sweeping outdoors, they was the ones that told me don't do it. And if I ever got done wrong or anything—they'd tell me what to say to the woman the next time she'd try anything.

Them girls was good to me. They really helped me if I needed help. . . . And it was only after being around other girls with days that I knew my live-in days was gone. That's when I learned to get my work, my way. Right in

Miss West's is when I learned to make my own way working out. And I was still just a girl. They really helped me.

Bernice Reeder learned much from her companions:

When I moved in, the girls at the boardinghouse was all doing daywork too. They took right to me from the first day. Soon I was doing just about everything with them! I didn't see Sister much because really I was with them. We'd ride together in the evening, and on weekends they'd go all around to the saints [Christian friends].

I know I didn't see Sister till near Christmas! I just liked being with these girls who was single, nice—not wild or drinking—and doing things. I guess that's when I started to feel I'd finally left home.

And the not-as-demure Beulah Nelson further admitted:

I moved from my brother's in late 1923 and got in with Miss Williams. She knew everybody 'cause she wrote numbers [ran a betting establishment]. She had girls living with her and just one man in the basement. Now she'd let us have parties and she'd sell liquor, but it wasn't no fighting or bad.

See, they was Catholic, so drinking was not sinning. I lived there for over three years, and I didn't see my brother much at all. I liked the girls, and we was all from different places too. And nobody was bad. We had fun and the best old parties; full of people. At first I didn't know them but, baby, soon everybody knew me. Them was my best days, and that's how I met my husband!

Though the majority of the women fared rather well, some of them confessed that many of the fears and remonstrations of their families had been well founded. For instance, Virginia Lacy had "up and left" live-in service to marry "a perfect man," against her family's hostile admonitions. Sadly, she recounted the outcome of her heedlessness:

My husband beat me the day we got married. I left that place in Georgetown and went right down to hell. I never knew what a minute of peace was like. I went to work everyday for some peace of mind. My brother and all warned me, but I was not to be told a thing. I got better work, but that was all, honey. My life was not worth nothing 'til he [her husband] died.

Ruth Mosley originally left her live-in position to marry a man she subsequently lived out of wedlock with for two years. Her conduct brought

Room-for-rent sign in a dwelling or rooming house in Washington, D.C. Courtesy of the Library of Congress.

despair and disgrace to her family, who painfully reminded her that moving out from the live-in household had been her downfall. But Ruth Mosley just flashed her beautiful, doe-brown eyes and declared that she was "still better off having the freedom to be hurt!" After her "downfall," she eventually got married, but it was not to the man she had lived with.

An unwelcome surprise was the high cost of the new life-style. Worked started between 5:15 and 8:00 A.M., and the women cleaned, cooked, and cared for all of the children until after the dinner was served. The women then cleaned the kitchen, capping off a twelve-hour day.[11] Most had to take in laundry or sewing or serve evening parties to earn enough money for clothing, streetcar fare, and liberated recreation. Dolethia Otis, who had one son to support when she left live-in work, twisted her red hair into a bun as she recalled working at night to augment her income:

I left there and never looked back. I'd hoped to one day have more children, but that house and that work took all my babies from me, I know. I worked days and baked and cooked for people nights, but I'd sleep in my own bed every night—and that made it worth it. If it was only for two hours, I was still in my own bed.

Sadie Jones depicted evening work in a less-romantic light:

After I left the Bailey's home, I never figured to have to work day and night again. But I did. I took in wash and everything. The work never ended in service or when I took just days. It was good that I worked my night at home I guess. All in all, work day and night is work day and night.

Blanche Ashby arched one bushy, silver eyebrow as she described the high price of her freedom:

I'd hoped to do a lot more when I left living in. But I didn't do half as much as I hoped. I knew I'd have more time and money. The streetcar took up most of the time I got. People gave more, but I spent so much more when I had to get a place for the kids, James [her spouse], and me once and for all. Before that they lived with my cousin, and we lived on the job. I didn't do that much better, but it was something more for us. Not a lot. Just something.

But Blanche Ashby was relieved to remove her child from an abusive situation in the home of a cousin who watched the son while she worked as a lived-in servant:

I didn't see at first how bad my boy was being treated by the cousin he was left with. He was dark, and they made a bad difference between him and my girls, who was light skinned. . . . I hated that I'd left him at all. . . . he'd been done so bad. I guess that's the difference—you'd see more of the ugly of everybody and everything when you worked out.

Yet freedom tasted sweet, for the most part. Eula Montgomery's pecan cheeks rounded into a smile as she shared her first moments of social freedom: "On my first day off, I walked in the zoo and then went to church. I had never known what it was to get up and not have Mama, Brother, or Miss Lawson telling me what to do." Eula Montgomery became the very close friend of another dayworker, Pearl Evans, who introduced her to Washington's nightlife. Fortunately, Eula Montgomery confided, she "quickly learned how it was better to go back and forth to church and not in and out of 'juice joints.' Pearl went on to have three children and never marry anyone. I had too much of her ways quick—I began to see the good and bad of people in a way I never did before."

Pernella Ross is a celebrated entertainer who laughed as she explained: "My friend and I got a room and did we enjoy it! We could play cards, dance and, well, we felt free to do anything there!" And as she tilted her head to the right and pointed to an antique upright piano in her neat parlor, she stressed, "We got a piano and I still got it and my old radio— right there to remind me of my freedom living in that room! Oh, the good times I had there." Urbanization brought commercial entertainment into contact with southern African American culture; and the radio and recording industries that bloomed during the 1920s were fundamentally influenced by "the black southern music . . . of the migration."[12]

One casualty of the transition to daywork was the migrants' relation to the penny savers clubs. These mutual-benefit associations had done much for the migrants, but they figured much less prominently in African American community life after the early 1920s. During the Depression, African American savings associations suffered from a greater demand for benefits at a time when members found it hardest to keep up with their dues.[13] More significant to the women, however, was the attraction to conventional banking and insurance organizations. The women wanted to conduct their business like other salaried workers, and the symbolism surrounding penny savers clubs bothered many: dayworking women associated the clubs with their old and undesirable role as live-in servants. In contrast, having a bank account was a public acknowledgment of their new status as independent workers. As Ellamay

Pernella Ross enjoyed "freedom and real good times" as a young woman not employed as a live-in servant.

Carter said, "Those clubs wasn't for workers; it was not for us—people getting their pay day or every week." Many women would have used conventional banks if they had had the chance earlier; now they might have that chance. Helen Venable of Virginia said, "I'd have used them [banks] earlier, but with that woman [her live-in employer] you never got no time to go to a place like that. I know I didn't." And Matilene Anderson gave this explanation: "I used a bank [as a dayworker] because it was on my streetcar line home. I couldn't go in there before, because Brother got all the money when I lived in. You didn't see no money in your hands ever." Annie Brown also stressed the importance of this move to banks. "I started to save my money with a bank," she stated in her soft voice, "because it was better than them clubs. They was for servants. Banks was for people with jobs. That's what people's said, and it was true."

Yet their movement away from regionally based, mutual-benefit associations did not mean a decline in support for rural kin. The women generally increased their economic assistance after they left live-in servant work. Velma Davis, for example, said, "I sent more money home after I left Bradley Boulevard. Every month I sent nearly ten dollars, didn't miss a month even when I started working days. That's why I got myself set before I left live-in; never missed sending my share home." With stamina, persistence, and perseverance these women workers were able to "hold back the ocean with a broom."[14] Dayworkers learned to provide for themselves, their families, and their communities. The newly independent African American woman made it, as Toni Morrison said, with "nothing to fall back on: not maleness, not whiteness, not ladyhood, not anything. And out of the profound desolation of her reality she may very well have invented herself."[15]

For the women of this book, family was a universal index of success. The true rewards of freedom, as Zelma Powell said, centered on her family life as the mother of four sons:

My boys are my life. I started living when I could raise them myself. I could go around to all they things at church and take time to go to school things, too.

I loved it the first day I worked daywork. I can't tell you how it felt to just walk out of any house and the sun'd still be up. I will remember that feeling as long as I live. To see that sun hitting me as I left to be with my boys.

The women all became mothers by adopting or actively aiding in the rearing of at least one child. Seventy-four became natural mothers. Seventy-one married at least once; of the ten who never married, two lived in long-term, common-law marriages. For all, families became important emotional anchors. Many women minded the caution, expressed by Mary Little, of becoming "too close to the [white] family . . . and get too used up by them."[16] By moving into daywork, they distanced themselves emotionally and practically from their employers and resisted the limitations the employers wanted to impose on their lives.

SUNDAYS—FREE AT LAST

On the historical scale, the transition to self-employment marked only a ripple of advancement from the lowest and most exploited work in this country. But in the women's own lives their courageous movement re-warded them with the dignity and personal power they deserved and enabled them to contribute more visibly within the larger African American community.[17] Dayworkers grasped at the opportunity to in-crease their attendance at and participation in the African American churches of Washington; in turn, their church activities directly shaped the community through social programs and other benevolent work.

Prior to their emancipation from live-in work, the more educated or affluent African American women had dominated the church leader-ship. With the influx of new dayworkers into the local churches, how-ever, both the number and size of Washington church organizations grew rapidly. After stripping off the stigma of the uniform, the migrant women triumphantly donned hats and dresses and presented themselves at Sunday day church to celebrate their arrival in the promised land of free society. This jubilant clamor of the dayworkers at the doors of the local churches may have been muffled by conflicts within the African American community, but as they worshipped together on Sundays,[18] urban African Americans from all walks of life birthed a vibrant kinship. Pansylee Holmes's deep-set stare went to the floor as she detailed the significant mix of class backgrounds at her church:

Most women down at Mason Street Baptist who were real active were edu-cated good and had jobs like teaching. A few working people might be doing a lot, but it was mainly people who did laundress work, and it was only a few of them. Almost all the other women worked live-in and could not do much there.

As people got more away from live-in now, you saw a lotta different people in all the things that church has. I know for me I didn't do down there till I got daywork. Then more and more people got in the church's clubs or work.

Odessa Minnie Barnes, as she proudly handed me a copy of the 1924 *Shiloh Baptist Church Bulletin,* will always remember how gratified she felt when she saw her name listed as a participant in the Sunday school program honoring the Northern Virginia Baptist Sunday School

Union. "This was just my second month after leaving live-in work," she proudly declared.

Church participation did not necessarily mean that the women had easier or lighter workloads. Rather, it meant that they chose to exercise a variety of options in their new-found leisure time, however modest it was. Odessa Minnie Barnes shared with me the 1926 letter she wrote to officially resign from many of her church activities because she needed to work evening "party-work" as well as daywork to support herself. As Velma Davis pointed out, many workers had to accommodate a full-time and part-time working schedule, even if they were active at church:

Ora [a laundress], who was very active in her church, worked hard. She'd have four washes to do: white, coarse white, flannels, and the colored ones. She'd have her tubs of hot rinse water, too. Then she'd have them heavy irons for ironing them. She worked. But she'd still be able to get to church. When I joined Correy Way, the laundress out of number one Bradley [Boulevard] was in almost everything in that church. She was on so many boards—and she'd speak up in a minute at any of them meetings, too. She got to do that 'cause she was off every Sunday. She worked real hard for six days, but every Sunday she was off. Then too, she had some evenings to herself. That's how she got to be so much down there. And she was somebody big in that church for years and years.

Perhaps predictably, the dayworkers' encroachment on established turf stirred some resistance. Beulah Nelson shared some of the problems she faced at the first church meeting she attended:

I had been working days for about two months. I'd promised I was going to join the B Club all during the time [two years] I went to Third Avenue's Thursday night services, but I couldn't because I was living in. Well, Pastor said the meeting was to be on Thursday night. So I went. I got to the door and had to drag myself in—but [I] didn't let a one of them see it, now. I was just scared of them. I was never in nothing with people who was teachers or clerks or in other jobs; all I knew was people living in, mostly.

But, baby—you know how bold I always been—I got in and just acted like them. Soon other people [dayworkers] got in, and then we really working, too. The people that used to run everything acted funny and all, but they

This church bulletin, cherished for sixty-seven years by
Odessa Barnes, lists the first time she participated in a
Sunday meeting and afternoon fellowship activity.

didn't complain. Nobody new was impudent; we just was there at first. But
we slowly got moving in that church.

Now Third Street got all kinda people in everything. But it wasn't like that
always. No, it wasn't 'til girls got time by working days, that you'd see anybody
but real educated people in different [church] organizations.

Beulah Nelson graciously employed a euphemism—that migrant
women "slowly got moving" in churches—but Mayme Gibson (who in
her eighties had sworn off shyness "because God convicted me, so I

must speak") frankly declared that "even to this very day" social elitism remains an obstacle to domestic workers in some local churches:

I was nearly seventy before I could speak up. They'd all but laugh at you if you wasn't a teacher or a laundress or had a government job. We [dayworkers] couldn't hope to be seen as much of nothing—none of us. Everybody hopes to be able to do better. But you can do better and people might still treat you like nothing. In some churches I know it's true because that's what happened to me.

Isetta Peters, however, contradicted Mayme's testimony with her description of the sweeping changes wrought by the migrant women's participation in her local church:

When people got daywork, that's when my church started having clubs. Before then, most people didn't have no time. That church was closed up except on Thursday night. After people got more day-only work—that's when all these clubs, circles, and aid groups got going. Now church is open every night for them meetings!

Alfreda Baker rubbed her small, veined hands against her apron and talked about her success as a human being. She, like the other women, took great pride in the fact that none of her children (even those currently unemployed) was forced to accept live-in service work. As she spoke, Mrs. Baker picked up a large-print Bible from a nearby table. With the free time she gained by becoming a dayworker, she said, in addition to attending day church on Sunday, she had spent Tuesday and Thursday evenings at Bible class. For her, church attendance meant the glorious opportunity to develop her abilities:

My niece would help me get to the passage, and I'd listen as people read the Scriptures. Then I'd memorize the words as they read. In fact, the reason I joined the church I did was because they read long sections of the Bible on Sunday and in Bible classes. That's how I learned to read this well.

Then she read aloud from the Book of Saint Matthew. "And everyday God sends," she said, proudly closing the book, "I learn more and more."

7
KNOWIN' WHAT
I KNOW TODAY

I n the summer of 1983, Virginia Lacy's plump face shone above the prison of her daughter's cluttered, unkempt living room. Her three great-grandchildren scampered noisily back and forth through the broken screen door as boldly as did the flies that buzzed around the head of her eldest grandson lying in a stupor on the sofa. This was the second time I had attempted to interview her. The first had been at her own home while her disapproving husband was still alive.

THE CASTLE

The Black woman had nothing to fall back on: not maleness, not whiteness, not ladyhood, not anything. And out of the profound desolation of her reality she may very well have invented herself.
—TONI MORRISON, "WHAT THE BLACK WOMAN THINKS ABOUT WOMEN'S LIB," *New York Times Magazine* (1971)

Watching Mrs. Lacy darting around trying to clear a space for us to sit, I wondered what an elegant, princesslike woman like her was doing in a place like this. Her rich silver hair was rolled into a waved pump atop her head. Although she spoke broken English, she maintained her refined dignity by speaking distinctly. As a lady, Mrs. Lacy was aptly concerned about appearances amidst this squalor of confusion.

She wore a conservative navy blue dress with a ritzy Peter Max-type scarf and a rhinestone brooch and earrings. Her tiny feet were in navy blue flats with clear "red fox" stockings, and her nails were well manicured and polished red. She had obviously dressed up for this occasion and was disturbed that her granddaughter had not come to pick up her children on time, as she had instructed her to do.

As we finally settled in a corner on two well-worn and soiled easy chairs, she explained that her daughter, Patricia (who owned the house), worked three jobs, one of which was at the State Department. This Patricia (whose "shiftless" husband had left her three years ago) had never done daywork, and Mrs. Lacy was proud of that.

One of Virginia Lacy's sons had been a drug addict, like the grandson: she nodded wearily in the direction of the young man asleep on the sofa. Her other son was in jail. And her granddaughter, age eighteen, was the mother of the three wayward youngsters she was presently sitting for. All in all, with her three other nieces and two nephews, I silently counted twelve people who lived in that broken-down, four-bedroom, two-story, frame house in southeast Washington.

The granddaughter finally arrived, giving me a long, curious once-over as Mrs. Lacy hustled me out of the living room, through the clothes-strewn dining room, into a dish-infested kitchen, and up a dark, narrow stairwell to a dimly lit hallway. There she pulled a set of keys out of her bosom and unlocked a door on the left side of the hallway. When the light came on inside the room, I was utterly amazed.

There in front of me was a massive mahogany poster bed overlaid with a luxurious, eggshell white, ruffled bedspread and matching pillow shams. The two windows facing the door were hung with lovely ivory eyelet priscilla curtains and sheers. All of the mahogany furniture was highly polished, and a magnificent circular mirror adorned the 1940s double dresser. To my left stood an elaborately wrought brass-and-marble vanity table and an ornate brass stool with a white velveteen cushion. Diagonally facing the bed was a white satin chaise lounge, and beside the bed was a marble-topped night table with curved French legs, a lacy doily, and a crystal lamp. The floor was covered with plush ivory carpet. It was breathtaking. Mrs. Lacy smiled triumphantly as she beckoned me to a seat on the chaise lounge. She pulled up the vanity stool.

An area where Virginia Lacy and her family lived early in her marriage.
Courtesy of the Washingtoniana Collection.

Here was the princess I had always suspected her to be. And this was her
castle.

Virginia Lacy had known much pain and tragedy. At sixteen she had
eloped with the dapper, soft-spoken gentleman who had come often to
visit her at her live-in job, only to have him beat her on her wedding
night and every day thereafter, until he died in 1982. Although she bore
no physical scars from this prolonged battery and abuse, she confessed
that during his convalescence, she was silently grateful that he could no
longer get up to lay his hands on her. She was not glad that he was dead,
she explained sheepishly, but she did feel relieved and much freer with
him gone. (He was dead. Good! I thought.) She was very sad that one
of her sons had recently died a violent death, and that her youngest
daughter had died in "questionable" circumstances in 1975.

Virginia Lacy did daywork every day of her married life. En route
home she was forced to stop at the corner store, where her husband and

his drinking buddies hung out, so that he could check the time she arrived. If she was five minutes late, he promised to beat her when he got home. She would then go straight home to fix his dinner, and she would not come out again until she left for work the next morning. That had been her life until he died. I had met her husband, Charles, when they were living in their own house. He was a silent, light-skinned, heavyset man with cold gray eyes. She was in the kitchen frying fish when I arrived, but she was extremely guarded and only spoke about three words to me in his presence. Now that he was dead, she would have the interview.

Her father had also abused her. As a child she had worked in the fields for him. He beat her, and no matter how much she begged and cried, he never let her go to school. Handsome Charles, with his shy smile and good looks, had been her first ray of hope. And his telling her he loved her had simply swept her off her feet. She was sixteen at the time, and he was thirty-four. Then she "up and married" this dream man despite the heated objections of her family. Consequently, her family's attitude toward her marital woes had always been: You made your own bed, so lie in it.

She believed their kids became delinquent because Charles would never let them move away from the crime-ridden, drug-infested neighborhood where he and his cronies drank and caroused. In his view, if that neighborhood was good enough for him, it was good enough for his kids, and certainly good enough for an uppity, hypocritical woman like her. In fact, according to Charles, she was "damned lucky" to even be there.

She left Charles once. Walked out one morning just like she was going to work. Only instead, she moved to Florida with a family. But after about three months, he tracked her down like a bloodhound and dragged her back home. After that she resigned herself to a hard life of beatings, wayward kids, casual religion, and an occasional treat of cheese and matzo crackers. Though it would mean a certain beating, after work she sometimes stopped at a Jewish delicatessen to buy Kosher snacks and crackers, on which she would nibble delicately during the streetcar ride home. The money she spent for this treat was a sacrifice, because she paid the bills and bought clothing for her kids with her daily wages. What was left from her husband's drinking and carousing with other women barely covered the rent. So the major household expenses fell to her.

At the time of this interview, Mrs. Lacy was still doing daywork three days a week. She had helped raise her daughter's four kids and was now babysitting for her great-grandchildren. She paid no rent at her daughter's house and was saving part of her husband's retirement so that one day she would have a place of her own.

Three years later, in 1986, she telephoned me to say she had finally gotten her apartment and wanted me to come by. It was on a perfect Sunday afternoon in May that I went to visit her. The address was in a clean, tree-lined, working-class neighborhood in southeast D.C. Her spartan, one-bedroom apartment was immaculate. In the living room was a nondescript chair, a turquoise sleeper-sofa, and a coffee table on a fringed throw rug. A Last Supper tapestry hung on the dining-room wall above a small walnut dinette set. Everything was new. But I grinned openly when she showed me that her ivory castle—the ruffled mahogany bedroom—was in place exactly as it had been in her daughter's house. Only now, she did not have to lock her door.

"This is the first time in my whole life I've ever lived alone," she confided. "I was scared and had a real hard time getting to sleep my first night here. But, Honey, when I woke up that next morning and found out I was still alive, I said, 'Ginny, you can do this!'" We laughed like schoolgirls over iced tea, cheese, and matzo crackers.

She remarked that she felt household service work had exposed her to the etiquette and life-styles of "better families." And the money she earned had enabled her to finance her children's education, although they had not availed themselves of the opportunities Washington, D.C., afforded them. She said she had no regrets. She sincerely believed that her childhood training and service had prepared her to live happily ever after. Then she laughed infectiously, "After all of that, I can sure appreciate happiness!"

Then she walked me to her bedroom window to see a very special "new" item. On the parking lot below was a 1978 Dodge Dart, dark green with green vinyl seats. To me it looked like an old, used car, but to her it was "new," and she kept it waxed and spotlessly clean. She said her daughter and grandchildren had accused her of using her husband's insurance money to buy the car, but she swore she had saved the money during the months she stayed with them.

As we said our good-byes, I could still see the scars the hardest years had left in her face, but my last triumphant moments with her had struck a satisfying peal of joy in a symphony of pain.

THE PONDEROSA

I have great respect for that unsung army of black men and women who trudged down lanes and entered back doors, saying "Yes, Sir" and "No, Ma'am." . . . [T]hese Black men and women knew that the job had to be done, and they put their pride in their pockets in order to do it. It is hard to believe they were in any way inferior to the white men and women who opened those back doors.

—JAMES BALDWIN, *The Fire Next Time* (1963)

Journal entry.

6 October 1986. Mary Ruth Ingraham is always busy when I come to interview her. Today she is wearing a beige satin blouse and tan wool slacks. It is quite sunny outside, but she says her day is short. Her secretary is waiting for her to relieve her at the office. Mrs. Ingraham's late husband left her a thriving contracting business, which she manages along with her brother-in-law and nephew. Therefore all our interviews have been short.

Her lushly landscaped property is called "the Ponderosa" by family members. Her brick rambler is situated on nine rolling acres in Rockville, Maryland. She says her husband Jim bought the lot when it was still farmland. Behind the house is a large redwood deck and a built-in swimming pool. Jim and his brother built the house themselves, and now that Rockville has become a popular suburban community, her acreage is worth a fortune.

Mrs. Ingraham is very well traveled and has just returned from another trip to Europe. Previously, she has shown me picture albums full from trips to Hawaii, Kenya, Ghana, Germany, France, London, Mexico, and many of the Caribbean islands. Her favorite place is Japan. She said, "The Japanese people are always busy doing something. My husband and I knew they would take over the world when we first went there in 1963." (She has belonged to the same travel club since the 1960s and takes at least one trip a year.)

She showed me through her twelve-room, custom-built home, proudly pointing out special carpentry work that her husband had done—the recessed wall in the dining room and the special closet in her bedroom just for shoes and handbags. Her living-room suite was imported from England. Large oriental rugs and runners cover hardwood floors in every room and hallway, and the china and crystal stemware in her lighted Belgian breakfront (the reason for the recessed wall) are valuable antiques. They were priceless to her for other reasons.

The most conspicuously displayed item in her Belgian breakfront was a carving set with floridly embellished, mother-of-pearl handles. This carving set (and many other items on display) was owned by a former employer who went bankrupt during the Depression. Mrs. Ingraham bought the carving set, and several pieces of her former employer's furniture, at an estate sale in 1968. She also has a choice collection of hand-blown crystal figurines that she bought at various estate sales and auctions.

At age ninety-two, Mary Ruth Ingraham drives to town once a day

In its early years, James and Mary Ruth Ingraham's business was located in the basement of a building that also housed a church and rooms for rent. Courtesy of the Washingtoniana Collection.

to check the bookkeeping work at her business. Except for occasional overnight visits from her thirty-six-year-old grandson, she lives alone. She has a woman who comes in once a week to "help straighten up" her immaculate house, but she still does her own cooking and laundry.

In 1916 she met her husband on a live-in job. He was a gardener/chauffeur/handyman, and she was a maid and, later, a cook. After they married, they continued living in as a couple, but when Jim decided to launch out into home-improvement contracting, she started doing day-work so that they could bring their two young daughters up from her home in Florida. Her younger daughter died in a car accident in 1960; her older daughter is married to a successful CPA and lives in Potomac, Maryland.

At the close of our interview, Mrs. Ingraham unceremoniously grabbed her briefcase and dashed to her Lincoln Continental, which was parked in the circular driveway of her estate. "Sorry to rush," she apologized as she started the engine, "but my secretary is waiting."

THE HAPPY BELIEVER

She gave me everything: clothes, furniture. She was genuinely in love with me because I made life easier for her. . . . She was giving so much both because she wanted to keep me as a housekeeper, but they did love me too. A combination of both. And she needed a friend. . . . She wanted me to be her housekeeper forever. She said after the boys left and got married she hoped I would give them each a day.
—JUDITH ROLLINS, *Between Women* (1985)

Eula Montgomery loves white people. She especially loves the way white men worship their women. "Like goddesses," she said. During the interview she repeatedly sighed, "I'm always happy. No matter what. I'm just happy." She was happy when she worked for the mean white lady on Wisconsin Avenue who never let her take any time off.

She was happy when that caused her only boyfriend to leave her. She was happy that she never married, never had children, and never had a personal life. She was happy when the family she had worked for nearly thirty-one years simply let her go one fine day—without notice, severance pay, or pension. She is "just always happy."

Now she lives alone in a tiny row house on East Capitol Street. She wears a peach print dress, with no jewelry, and, white sandals. She is short, light-skinned, and quite stout. Her short hair is blonde, curled, and well oiled. Although she is "happy," the telltale wrinkles around her mouth are not from laughter. And the constant twitch in the lower corner of her right eye is suspect. She frequently pauses in midsentence to stare vacantly out the window, especially while describing "her people" (the family she worked thirty years for). She loves to tell how she cared for their nine children, who are all grown now with children of their own. She is happy that "her people" still send her a dollar in a card every Christmas and continue "to this day" to bring their old clothes to her nephew's children.

She discussed in great detail the inevitability of hard work for African American women and compared the work of a live-in to that of a day-worker. Her voice was high-pitched, and she spoke with ingratiatingly sweet affectation. The result was an unnervingly shrill, Butterfly McQueen-type whine.

At eighty years old, she still does daywork. But her two sisters and other family members accuse her of letting white folks and everybody else walk all over her. Eula Montgomery said she disagrees. Then her fingers started making busy movements in her lap again. She pursed her small, dry mouth, and her shiny eyes glowered as she insisted that she could not remember one time in her life that she had been mistreated or abused by anybody. Not even the time she had missed her sister's wedding because "her people" would not give her the day off, even though she had given them four months' notice of her intention to take that day off. But to make up for her having to miss the wedding, hadn't they

Eula Montgomery, like many household employees, recalled reporting for work on many holidays. Courtesy of the Washingtoniana Collection.

taken her on a trip with them (and let her babysit) the very next summer?

She had never liked how her sisters talked back to white folks. It was not right to treat white people that way. After all, there was good in everybody. It wasn't that she practiced "turn the other cheek," she just "liked to be happy and not make anybody upset."

Eula Montgomery never spoke up. She never fought back. "Her people" took whatever they wanted from her. She did whatever "her people" wanted, whenever they wanted. As long as they left her "happy," she did not mind. When I left her she was still staring blankly through the window. Her right eye was still twitching, and her empty fingers had begun to busy themselves in her lap again. From all appearances, I left her as happy as I found her.

LIKE A MEMBER OF THE FAMILY

Afro-American women . . . have continued to be portrayed from outside . . . . The shaping of black women's story has revealed much more about the pictures in the minds of its shapers than about the diversity and complexity of her realities.
—PATRICIA MORTON, *Disfigured Images* (1991)

A young white woman who shared a desk with me at the Library of Congress told me about Nellie Willoughby. When she learned that I was researching black domestic workers, she insisted that I meet the woman who had served her family for more than fifty years. "Nellie," she said, "is just like a member of our family." Nellie had been included in everything her family ever did, and they just "loved her so."

I accepted the telephone number the young white woman offered me, but instead of using her introduction, when I called Miss Willoughby I said that I had been referred to her by my great-aunt, Mrs.

Robinson, who had also worked for a family on Connecticut Avenue. (Miss Willoughby did, in fact, attend the same church as my aunt, so the name Mrs. Robinson was vaguely familiar to her.) I told her about my project researching working women, but she replied gruffly that she had never done anything but daywork and could not possibly tell me anything of importance. Then I mentioned that I knew she went to John Wesley Church with my aunt, and she consented to have me come by. (I never mentioned the white woman who gave me her number.)

We had scheduled the interview for ten o'clock on a Tuesday morning. And as was my custom, for obscurity's sake, I dressed in plain slacks and a sweater with no jewelry except my wedding band. As it turned out, however, the woman at the Library of Congress had given me a wrong address. So I telephoned Miss Willoughby and told her where I was. "Miss Robinson thought I still lived on Tennessee Avenue?" she asked. I had to fudge and mumble some feigned response. "I haven't lived there in fifteen years," she laughed hoarsely, giving me her correct address. "I guess Miss Robinson is like me—getting old," she mumbled, hanging up the phone.

Miss Willoughby had moved to a high-rise, senior citizens' building in northeast D.C. Her efficiencylike apartment was a living room that served as a kitchen on one end, with two doors that led to a bedroom and a bathroom on the other. She lived alone and yelled for me to "come on in!" because she could not come to the door. Inside I found this enormous, dark-skinned woman in a brightly flowered, snap-up house dress, her thinning gray hair tightly pulled back into a braided bun. She was perched like a great bird atop an overstuffed chair, with her dangerously swollen feet propped high on an ottoman and two pillows. (The circulation in her legs was so bad from chronic diabetes that she kept them elevated during the entire interview.) Her living room seemed overcrowded by two heavy, high-backed chairs, like those found on a church pulpit, and a winged sofa fit for a giant. She occupied one of the chairs, and I sat across from her in the other. Several framed pho-

One section of the Willoughby home, located on Eighth Street, N.W. and purchased in 1916 while the family was still "in service."

tographs of white people were strategically placed around the room.

She is not a fat woman, but she is big-boned and powerfully built, with absolutely mammoth hands and feet. She has a loud, boisterous laugh and very thick lips. And her small, wide-set eyes are so severely crossed as to be almost comical. Her speech is peculiarly slurred, and her voice, which begins in a soft tone, graduates steadily, until at the end of her statements she is nearly shouting.

Miss Willoughby was very generous with details about her former life down South and what she had done in her eighty years. Memories of her trip to Washington were particularly vivid and lively. Then she began to show me pictures, including those of the white people. She told me they were her employers. Then she described each person to me. She said that she kept their pictures around "like people go to scary movies, to remind me of them people I hate." When she saw my shocked expression, she laughed, "That's the truth, honey!"

She also brought out her old uniform, which she still kept in her closet, though she had not worn it in forty years. To her the pictures and the uniform are like war relics or scars from a painful surgery. They are macabre mementos of the things that pained her most. She said that her hatred for her employers helped her keep her life in perspective.

Needless to say, in light of the description I had received from her employers' daughter, of "good ole Nellie" being "just like a member of the family," hearing her pronounce her hatred for them was a real jolt. She went on to reveal that the father of the household in which she worked was an important Cabinet member. He was not just a mean, racist man, but she insisted that she suspected him also of sexually abusing his daughters. "He never bothered me because I'm so big," she said, "but I sure felt sorry for them little girls."

She still worked for the mother but was glad to be away from her on the days she was off. The only reason she went in at all, she said, was to keep the woman from calling her on the phone to talk all the time. She said she would go over there and prop her legs up "just like this" and listen to her poor, lonely employer talk on and on and on until it was time for her to go home. She did "nothing but waste time and pick up money."

She had started out with the family when their four kids were very young. They were still in a big house back then. But once the kids were grown, they moved into a condominium. They loved her so much, after more than twenty-five years of service, that on discovering the condo had only one door, the father had declared that he "wouldn't have no nigger coming in his front door." He paid a contractor to have the plumbing rerouted so they could cut a back door in the hallway for Miss Willoughby. "And from that day to this, I have never used nothing but that back door," she said bitterly. "Don't tell me about them people."

As far as traveling with them, she said she hated it. She had once gone with them to the daughter's graduation—presumably to lay out the clothes and prepare. But in reality it was just to "show people that they had enough money to bring a black person with them." Later she went with them to a son's wedding, this time to show the in-laws that they were bringing not only Miss Willoughby but also a black man—their driver. "They were putting on the dog," she mimicked with a raised pinky finger, "by bringing their niggers with them." The last time she traveled with them was to Florida on vacation. They had asked her to accompany them on every vacation since, but she said she did not want a vacation well enough to play "their nigger" in an atmosphere that was supposed to be relaxed and restful. "I'll sit right here in my own place with my own friends and my own everything before I'll ever go another place with them." She enjoyed knowing that she had this big façade. She was proud that they "didn't even know where I lived." She did not consider them nice people, friends, family, or even good employers. She worked for them strictly for the money. Period! Yet they insisted that she was "just like family."

She said she really felt sorry for the wife. As I listened, I supposed that her employer probably felt sorry for "good ole Nellie" when she came hobbling in on ailing feet three days a week. But Miss Willoughby felt even sorrier for her because "her husband and kids all hate her. I know what he did to them girls, and I hate to think of what might be the real reason them boys so troubled. And that's why them kids hate her; and she's mean so she don't have a friend in the world, 'cept me."

She told me how the family used to give their servants the ends of the roast beef to eat. "One day I guess they felt guilty," she snickered, "so they gave me a piece of the middle part of the beef, which was red and cooked the way they liked it. Then they got mad because I didn't eat it. . . . All this time they didn't know that black folks don't like that raw meat. They been thinking they hurting us by giving us the ends of the roast 'cause they well done, when that's the part we likes anyway!"

Nellie Willoughby is very active with the senior citizens in her community and in her church. She said she believes in "fighting for her rights." She actively participated in civil rights marches during the

1940-70 period. She is most proud of pictures showing her protesting in the 1968 Poor People's Campaign.

As I left her apartment, it occurred to me that had I told her that I had been referred to her by her employer's daughter, I might have encountered an entirely different side of Nellie Willoughby. I laughed out loud in the elevator down to the lobby when I imagined the "good ole Nellie" who might have greeted me had I said I had been sent by the white folks.

MAKING A HARD WAY FUN

[A] person is more than what he or she does; a person is not merely the sum of his or her work or achievement or talents. . . . No, the people who are sources of nourishment and clear vision in this world measure a person in a different way.

A woman is a good woman, over all she says or does, if she knows . . . her *woman-ness*. Knowing that she moves or does not move; if perplexed, she can instantly be reminded of the inscape of her *is-ness*. Knowing makes her easy, still, resilient.

—ELEANOR W. TRAYLOR, *The Fabulous World of Toni Morrison* (1983)

In 1915 my great-aunt Mary Sprow kept a diary in which she described "a summer of blues" and herself as "a poor maid that has toiled many years for a living and has really become tired of it, but still see no way out of it but to give up my life, to give up life." She believed her "life [was] not in many ways as good as a slave." "If you give us our daily bread," she asked God in a prayer, "Who made work? to clean and scrub days in and days out. Above all who made the people that we toil for that never knows what it is to want and yet is never thankful for nothing that we do. No matter how hard. No matter how we try to please." She concluded by stating, "But I go where, when to who. Every place has no better news for me."

When photographed in 1910, Mary Johnson Sprow,
like nearly 90 percent of Washington's gainfully
employed African American women, worked in
domestic service.

For our videotaped interview in 1980 my aunt adorned her full, four-
foot seven-inch figure in a fancy red dress with matching lipstick, a long
strand of cultured pearls, and rhinestone-and-pearl earrings. Her short,
mixed-gray hair framed her face with delicate curls. She patted her soft,
fragile fingers on the arms of the Victorian chair, displaying painted
nails and a beautiful diamond wedding ring. She resisted moving from
the chair, however, because her steps are slow and awkward now. And

Mary Johnson Sprow at age ninety-three. She was a
domestic worker in Washington for nearly eighty
years.

because we promised not to put the camera below the waist, she wore
her comfortable black lace-up shoes.

My great-aunt owns a semidetached, corner brownstone in the
northeast, near Catholic University. The second floor of her house has
been converted into an apartment, which she rents out to college cou-
ples (preferably with children). You enter through a narrow hall. There
is a marble-topped oak table on the far wall and an oak-framed oval
mirror over the table. The living room is filled with antique furnishings.
The wood of the coffee table is so similar to the wood on all the other
furniture that it is clear that she took great care selecting each item in
the room. Heavy floral drapes are drawn back from sheer panels on the
large window, letting in plenty of sunlight. The room is close but comfortable.

A large, oblong mirror with ornate gold trim embellishes the wall
above the sofa, and all over the sofa are small stuffed animals she made
herself. As she sits amid them, it is clear that these stuffed animals give
her joy. She introduced each of these jewels to me by name. She consid-

ers them her "children." There are, in addition, at least seven ceramic figurines on every table, and each of these knick-knacks has a history she is glad to tell.

The dining room hosts a large cherry/maple table with six chairs and an antique china cabinet filled with beautiful tableware and crystal. Silver candlesticks and a silver tea service rest atop the buffet. To the left of the buffet is a cherry/maple secretary covered with letters, family pictures, pens, stationery, and yesterday's junk mail. Right beside the secretary is an early sixties color television set. Large Persian rugs cover the beautifully stained hardwood floors. An enclosed porch has been converted into a small burgundy-and-pink floral bedroom with a single bed and a bureau. A small table with a lamp and cut flowers is tucked in the far left corner. A large window, which takes up the whole right side of the tiny bedroom and overlooks a tiny, neatly trimmed yard budding with seasonal flowers, is hung with ornate burgundy draperies and pink sheers. The entrance to the bathroom is at the foot of the bed. Over the bed hang pictures of her parents, Jesus Christ, a French pastoral scene, and her late husband, Luray Sprow.

The 1950s kitchen has all-white cabinets and appliances. On the red-and-white formica table are animal salt and pepper shakers and a "white cat" napkin holder. The four chairs are chrome and diner-red vinyl. At the rear right is the door to the back yard. Knick-knacks are all over the wall leading to the back door. Animals are everywhere in this accumulation of "small things forgotten."

Unlike the young woman in her diary, at eighty-eight Aunt Mary professes undying love for candy, brandy, and laughter. In that order. And she never lets a day pass without at least a little nip of each. "No one should go a whole day without some candy," she whispers seductively to my two-year-old daughter, pressing a piece of hard candy into her palm, despite my protests about too much sugar. She cautions me about needing to laugh more with my daughter and at life.

Aunt Mary is sorry her mother never laughed or seemed to enjoy her

Ladies club members.

life. As a child she was often chastised for her light-hearted nature. Her mother fretted about her "being the first girl [after five boys] and still not taking life serious." Just before she migrated, she remembers her mother nearly beating her for being too "childlike and playful." But now she is glad she retained her sense of humor. She says it is probably the main reason she has so few ailments today, and why "so many sweet children come visit."

She married Luray Sprow in 1918 and was widowed in 1934. She purchased one house with her husband in 1932 and bought the one she lives in now in 1950. She never had children, which explains her attachment to her stuffed animals and figurines. But she has a genuine love for children of all ages and is truly entertaining in her playful antics. Aunt Mary could make a mummy laugh.

During my visits she has shown me at least three boxes of keepsakes from her church, Asbury Methodist. (She was a member of several church and civic clubs, in addition to the renowned Twelfth Street Bible Club.) She has at least ten boxes of pictures of family members, which she also takes great pleasure in showing visitors. A "good life" to her is one of love, honest work, manners, and support from her parents, husband, and sixteen brothers and sisters. She now passes this legacy of love on to everybody she meets, hoping to make them feel better about their life and their world.

When Aunt Mary talks about her life and work she punctuates her conversation with smiles and reassuring gestures. Unlike the girl in her diary of 1915, she is convinced that her life has been a good one, well lived. And she has a priceless philosophy about employers and domestic work: you do the best you can, but it is a job that is never done—you leave it, and then enjoy life. She also talks with great pleasure and exhilaration about her life-long love—her ladies' group. Before we ended our interview, we confirmed our plans for me to attend the next meeting of that ladies' group, the Twelfth Street Bible Club.

8
THE SOUND STAYS
IN MY EARS

What does it take to survive? What does it take not only to survive but to triumph? . . . We must see where we've been to know where we are—so we cannot be lied to. At the same time . . . a need arises to celebrate historical figures—not just famous persons, but people in our own families, [who] we have seen survive with strength and dignity.
> —AMIRI BARAKA, "INTRODUCTION," IN *Confirmation: An Anthology of African American Women* (1983)

As the daughter of a woman who spent five of her forty-five years of employment as a dayworker, the granddaughter of a woman who worked many years as a live-in servant, and the great-grand-daughter and great-great-granddaughter of slaves, I have traveled back to my own foundations, to the very woof of my African American heritage. Looking back at the wonderful, giving women who contributed their precious time and experience for the sake of this book, the sound of their voices stays in my ears as I recall my own journey toward an understanding of my family's struggles and successes. I recall clearly the day sixteen years ago when I, in the company of my great-aunts and great-uncles, stepped across the fallen fence and with my adult eyes saw the time-battered but beautiful three-winged house. It loomed in the distant clearing amidst grass high and yellowed from neglect and the July sun. Aunt Marian said that passing through that fence (it had been strong and white back then) was the last thing the children remembered leaving behind the day they rode the train north to Washington, D.C. These children of two former slaves left this rural home many years apart: the first to leave was Memphis, who left in 1897; then Mary, who left in about 1900; Marian, who left in about 1913; and finally Lewis, the seventy-eight-year-old "baby" of the family, who left home last, in 1918. Each sentimentally recalled that passing beyond that fence marked the egress from the homestead into the new world called "North."

But my attention remained fixed on the abandoned, once white, then red, and now aged, brown-frame house that was home for my grandmother and her thirty-two siblings. It seemed so frail in its dilapidated abandonment. It was small by city standards, but the L-shaped frame was still sturdy, and all three wings were intact. There was a wing for each of my Great-Grandfather Peyton Johnson's three successive wives and a small place added on for his mother, Winnie, my great-great-grandmother. Peyton Johnson's third wife was Eliza Stewart, the mother of the great-aunts and great-uncles I was accompanying on this family visit to the old homestead.

My great-aunts and great-uncles explained that all of the thirty-three children of Peyton Johnson mailed money home each month to help the family survive and build these three wings. Their mother's wing was built last, and it was the tallest. With pleasure they related that it was built by the seventeen surviving children of Eliza Stewart Johnson. Her children looked proudly at their wing, with its parlor on the first floor and bedroom on the second. All this had been built by the sweat of the brows now scowling in the sun.

As they surveyed every inch of the house and grounds, Aunt Marian gently pulled me under the massive oak tree in front of the house. "It was right there," she whispered, pointing to the shaded, overgrown grass under the tree. That spot was right where she was sitting the day her childhood ended. There had been no third wing on the house back then, she explained. She was only three years old and was fiddling with the dirt, pretending to help big sister find chips for the fire. Then sud-

The last members of the Twelfth Street Bible Club at an annual social they
have organized, or jointly sponsored, since 1913.

denly her grandmother Winnie and her mother emerged from the front
door of the second wing. This eighty-eight-year-old woman showed
me exactly how her mother had held the new baby, Jeff, and how her
grandmother Winnie's hand had motioned to her. "Come on quick,
girl," she was told in a tone too stern for a baby. "Your mama needs
your help now. Your playing days is through." That was how a life of
work began for this octogenarian, and for thousands of other African
American women in the early decades of the twentieth century.

My perspectives on African American womanhood in this century
have been permanently altered by these women's resilience, courage,
and fortitude. They saw themselves as going from grace to strength.[1]
They first viewed migration as an opportunity to assist family members,
but very quickly, once they began to work as live-in servants in Washington, something unexpected occurred: migration gave them their first

chance to shed old, demeaning stereotypes and to assume a bold new face. The move brought the women more than increased earnings and fuller employment autonomy. It intensified their abhorrence of the servant role and led them to push back the limits of African American women's work.

The close of the 1990s marks the last decade for many of the voices heard in this book. In fact, some will have already gone on by the time this book reaches print. Therefore, I am ever cognizant that this vital resource will soon be lost forever to the slow, the apathetic, or the careless explorer. It is my hope that historians and others who listen to the past will greet the year 2000 with an alert ear to such voices. I hope that we will continue to listen to the stories of all kinds of people, and listen especially carefully to the frail, sometimes hushed tones of older people whose lives illuminate our own.

You have listened to the "fierce and not melodic" songs of the women in this book. But before you run on, I challenge you to bend this way with me. Examine the foundations of our moment in history. First—dig deep right where you are standing. This is the last time you may find "the old women gathered." This is the last song they may ever sing. I challenge you, historians of tomorrow, to scoop up the baton of their rich heritage and carry it with you as you run. My own dash is guided by two important ancestral spirits—Edward Clark and Jean Chivis Clark. Thank you both for your love and your example of how to love. Daddy, thanks for giving me a loving courage and never giving up on me. Mom, I caught special glimpses of you when I heard the words of the women I interviewed. And I now know why you insisted that I become strong. You gently gave me your love, but you demanded that I learn to wear the pendant of strength you created for me from your own special fortitude. You worked a lifetime to assure its impeccable fit. I understand now that the strength you needed to make this necklace was not yours alone; you used the will you inherited from my grandmother, Katie Johnson Chivis, and my great-grandmother, Eliza

Stewart Johnson, and my great-great-grandmother, the slave "Winnie," and all the capable and courageous African women who preceded them. I accept the mantle each of you decorated so brilliantly and pledge to prepare Abena to wear it well.[2]

NOTES

INTRODUCTION

1. Here and throughout, except in chapter 8, I use pseudonyms to respect the interviewees' expressed concern for privacy. In some cases, the women and their families have achieved prominence in their communities and are uncomfortable identifying themselves as former domestics.

2. The subtle process of women's migration was understood and explained culturally. "Falling out" was a phrase used extensively to describe the differences between male and female migration. One person indicated, for example, that "a man can fall out of North Carolina on their own. No woman could do that." Another respondent stated her uncle "fell out of there in February." When I sought a more complete definition for the term, each person explained it was males who left the rural South with friends and without the direction of kin. For analyses of language appropriation and gender, see Evelyn Brooks Higginbotham, "African-American Women's History and the Metalanguage of Race," *Signs* 17 (Winter 1992): 267; Nancy Grey Osterund and Lu Ann Jones, "If I must say so myself: Oral Histories of Rural Women," *Oral History Review* 17 (Fall 1989): 1–23. For more information, see Linda Nelson, "Begging the Question and Switching Codes: Insider and Outsider Discourse of African-American Women" and Marcyliena Morgan, "Something's in the Water: Women's Talk, Women's Lives" (Papers presented at the Black Women in the Academy: Defending Our Name, 1894–1994 Conference, Boston, 13 January 1994). M. M. Bakhtin, *The Dialogic Imagination: Four Essays,* ed. Michael Holquist and trans. Caryl Emerson and Michael Holquist (Austin: University of Texas Press, 1981). For new analytic methodologies and categories for "ordinary" women the Great Migration period, see Gloria Hull *Color Sex and Poetry: Three Women Writers of the Harlem Renaissance* (Bloomington: Indiana University Press, 1987), 3 and 4. For important general information about women and migration, see Florette Henri, *Black Migration: Movement North, 1900–1920* (Garden City, N.Y.: Anchor Press, 1975); Jacqueline Jones, *Labor of Love, Labor of Sorrow: Black Women, Work, and the Family from Slavery to the Present* (New

York: Basic Books, 1985); Malaika Adero, ed., *Up South: Stories, Studies, and Letters of This Century's Black Migration* (New York: New Press, 1992). Also see Carter Woodson, *A Century of Negro Migration* (New York: Russell and Russell, 1918); Louise Kennedy, *The Negro Peasant Turns Cityward: Effects of Recent Migration to Northern Centers* (New York: Columbia University Press, 1930); Edward Lewis, *The Mobility of the Negro: A Study in the American Labor Supply* (New York: Columbia University Press, 1931); Neil Flingstein, *Going North: Migration of Blacks and Whites from the South, 1900–1950* (New York: Academic Press, 1981); Carole Marks, *Farewell—We're Good and Gone: The Great Black Migration* (Bloomington: Indiana University Press, 1989).

3. One hundred twenty-three in-depth interviews were conducted with persons who were a part of the Great Migration period. All but six of the interviews were recorded on tape. The six not recorded on tape—one due to mechanical failure and five at the request of the speaker—were recorded in notes taken by hand. The interviewing sessions generally ran from one and a quarter to three hours. I also conducted many short follow-up meetings.

After each interview I developed a detailed summary for each tape in longhand. I chose to develop these detailed summaries because I wanted to create a system for quickly retrieving the narrators' feeling and thoughts. As I heard each tape several times, I felt I was better able to convey the words and emotions of the people being interviewed. Twenty-one of the interviews have been transcribed. All will be available for review in the Moorland-Spingarn Research Center of Howard University.

I used a formal questionnaire for the interviews. The questionnaire covered the technical and factual questions—place and date of birth, first jobs, migration data, Washington, D.C., wages, hours worked, size of the household, Social Security, and so on. What I found was that although these facts were important to scholars interested in quantitative detail on women and work, migrants wanted to communicate many of their feelings about the extraordinary transformations they experienced as women and workers central to the Great Migration story. From these interviews I was able to learn, from a participant's point of view, substantial data on this significant facet of U.S. history. These interviews confirmed that for African American women, social progression was not the random result of events thrust upon the individual. It was integral to the process of personal growth, kin interaction, and societal development. For corrective assessments, see Genevieve Fabre and Robert O'Meally, *History and Memory in African-American Culture* (New York: Oxford Press, 1994); Evelyn Brooks Higginbotham, *Righteous Discontent: The Women's Move-*

ment in the Black Baptist Church, 1880-1920 (Cambridge: Harvard University Press, 1993); Gloria Wade-Gales, *Pushed Back to Strength: A Black Woman's Journey Home* (Boston: Beacon Press, 1993); Adrienne Lash Jones, *Jane Edna Hunter: A Case Study of Black Leadership, 1910-1950* (New York: Carlson Publishing, 1990); Dorothy Salem, *To Better Our World: Black Women in Organized Reform, 1890-1920* (New York: Carlson Publishing, 1990), chaps. 7 and 8; Tera Hunter, "Household Workers in the Making: Afro-American Women in Atlanta and the New South, 1861 to 1920" (Ph.D. diss., Yale University, 1990); Dorothy Sterling, ed., *We Are Your Sisters: Black Women in the Nineteenth Century* (New York: W. W. Norton, 1984); Bettina Aptheker, "Black Women's Quest in the Professions," in *Woman's Legacy: Essays on Race, Sex, and Class in American History,* by Aptheker (Amherst: University of Massachusetts Press, 1982), 89-110; and Henri, *Black Migration,* 51.

4. Clark-Lewis, "Duty and 'Fast Living': The Diary of Mary Johnson Sprow Domestic Worker," *Washington History* 5 (Spring/Summer 1993): 51. See also: Judith Rollins, *Between Women: Domestics and Their Employers* (Philadelphia: Temple University Press, 1985); Jo Ann Gibson Robinson, *The Montgomery Bus Boycott and the Women Who Started It* (Knoxville: University of Tennessee Press, 1987); Phyllis Marynick Palmer, "White Women/Black Women: The Dualism of Female Identity and Experience in the U.S.," *Feminist Studies* 9 (Spring 1983): 151-66; Lynda Glennon, *Women and Dualism* (New York: Longman Press, 1982), 220-21; and Herbert Gutman, *The Black Family in Slavery and Freedom, 1750-1925* (New York: Pantheon Books, 1976).

5. Nell Irving Painter, "Forward," in *We Were Always Free,* by T. O. Madden, Jr. (New York: Vintage Books, 1993), x; Deborah Grey White, *Ar'n't I A Woman: Female Slaves in the Plantation South* (New York: W. W. Norton, 1985); Sharon Harley and Rosalyn Terborg-Penn, eds., *The Afro-American Woman* (Port Washington, N.Y.: Kennikat Press, 1978); Patricia Hill Collins, "The Social Construction of Black Feminist Thought," *Signs* 14 (Summer 1989): 745-73; Roslyn Terborg-Penn, "First because We Are Women and Second because We Are Colored Women," *Truth: Newsletter of the Association of Black Women Historians* (April 1985); Carol Turbin, "Beyond Conventional Wisdom," in *To Toil the Livelong Day: America's Women at Work, 1780-1980,* ed. Mary Beth Norton and Carol Groneman (Ithaca, N.Y.: Cornell University Press, 1987), 47-50; Joyce Ladner, *Tomorrow's Tomorrow: The Black Women* (Garden City, N.Y.: Doubleday, 1971); Mary Church Terrell, "The Progress of Colored Women," *Voice of the Negro* (July 1904): 291-94; Addie Hunton, "Negro Womanhood Defended," *Voice of the Negro* (July 1904): 180-82; and Bert James

Lownberg and Ruth Bogin, *Black Women in Nineteenth-Century American Life: Their Words, Their Thoughts, Their Feelings* (University Park: Pennsylvania State University Press, 1976).

6. In the District of Columbia in 1900, there were 44,424 African American women; 26,699 over the age of ten were employed. There were 8,392 working as charwomen, housekeepers, and laundresses; 13,062 were servants. The total number of women working in the servant category is listed as 21,454. In the District of Columbia in 1940, there were 79,284 African American women; 40,912 over the age of fourteen are listed as "in the labor force." There were 11,647 working as charwomen, housekeepers, and laundresses (the separate category for housekeepers working in private homes is not given in 1940); 23,227 are listed as "servants" and "domestic servants." The total number, 34,874 women, are listed in the "service" category; this included cooks, elevator operators, and "other service workers." From 1900 to 1940 more than 80 percent of the African American females employed in Washington, D.C., worked as cleaners, charwomen, laundresses, servants, and domestic servants. For more information, see U.S. Bureau of the Census, *Negro Population in the United States* (Washington, D.C.: GPO, 1915), 521; U.S. Bureau of the Census, *United States Population: Washington, D.C.* (Washington, D.C.: GPO, 1943), 575, 587. Katzman, in *Seven Days a Week,* noted that "problems in the varying qualities of census, especially in regard to statistics of women at work, are notorious. The *constant changes* in census categories makes difficult any comparison of occupational statistics over time. The most serious problems existed in the count of women under the general classification of domestic and personal service. In addition, errors due to inaccurate enumerations and false responses are difficult to estimate. Given the social stigma of domestic service work and the low status of servants among particular ethnic groups, it is possible that some women might not have responded truthfully to being a domestic or working at all." David M. Katzman, *Seven Days a Week: Women and Domestic Service in Industrializing America* (New York: Oxford University Press, 1978), 298-301. Women and census data implications explored in Samuel H. Preston, "African-American Marriage in 1910," *Demography* 29 (February 1992): 1-13; S. Philip Morgan, Antonio McDaniel, Andrew T. Miller, and Samuel H. Preston, "Racial Differences in Household and Family Structure at the Turn of the Century" (Paper presented to the Conference on Demographic Perspectives on the American Family: Patterns and Prospects, State University of New York at Albany, 1990); U.S. Bureau of the Census, *Historical Statistics of the United States: Colonial Times to 1970* (White Plains, N.Y.: Kraus Press, 1989); Alba Edwards, *Sixteenth Census of the*

United States: 1940, Population Comparative Occupation Statistics for the United States, 1870–1940 (Washington, D.C.: GPO, 1943).

7. Anna Julia Cooper, *Voice of the South* (Xenia: Aldine Printing House, 1892). For kin, community, and reform networks, see Cynthia Neverdon-Morton, *Afro-American Women of the South and the Advancement of Race, 1895–1925* (Knoxville: University of Tennessee Press, 1990); Paula Giddings, *When and Where I Enter: The Impact of Black Women on Race and Sex in America* (New York: William Morrow, 1984), 85–131; Jacqueline Rouse, *Lugenia Burns Hope: Black Southern Reformer* (Athens: University of Georgia Press, 1989), 41–85; Hazel V. Carby, *Reconstructing Womanhood: The Emergence of the Afro-American Woman Novelists* (New York: Oxford University Press, 1987), 83–101; Kathleen C. Berkeley, "'Colored Ladies Also Contributed': Black Women's Activities from Benevolence to Social Welfare, 1866–1896," in *The Web of Southern Social Relations: Women, Family, and Education,* ed. Walter Fraser, Jr., Frank Sanders, Jr., and John L. Wakelyn (Athens: University of Georgia Press, 1985), 181–85. The ambiguities inherent in household employment are explored well in Bonnie Dill, *Across the Boundaries of Race and Class: An Exploration of Work and Family Among Black Female Domestic Servants* (New York: Garland Press, 1992); Rollins, *Between Women;* Phyllis Palmer, *Domesticity and Dirt: Housewives and Domestic Servants in the United States, 1920–1945* (Philadelphia: Temple University Press, 1989); Trudier Harris, *From Mammies to Militants* (Philadelphia: Temple University Press, 1982); and Alice Childress, *Like One of the Family: Conversations from A Domestic's Life* (New York: Independent Publishers, 1956). For cross-cultural perspectives, see Mary Romero, *Maid in the U.S.A.* (New York: Routledge, 1992); Roger Sanjek and Shellee Colen, eds., *At Work in Homes: Household Workers in World Perspective* (Washington, D.C.: American Anthropological Association, 1990); Evelyn N. Glenn, *Issei, Niesei, War Bride: Three Generations of Japanese-American Women in Domestic Service* (Philadelphia: Temple University Press, 1986); Ximena Bunster and Elsa Chaney, *Sellers and Servants: Working Women in Lima Peru* (New York: Praeger Press, 1985); Filomina C. Steady, *The Black Woman Cross-Culturally* (Cambridge: Schenkman, 1982); Janet W. Salaff, *Working Daughters of Hong Kong: Filial Piety or Power in the Family?* (Cambridge: Cambridge University Press, 1981); Ester N. Goody, *Parenthood and Social Reproduction: Fostering and Occupational Roles in West Africa* (Cambridge: Cambridge University Press, 1982). For the central issues of African-American women and labor history, see Angela Davis, *Women, Race, and Class* (New York: Random House, 1981) and Jones, *Labor of Love.* For a synthesis and overview of research on feminism, see Nancie Caraway, *Segregated*

Sisterhood: Racism and the Politics of American Feminism (Knoxville: University of Tennessee Press, 1991); Joan Wallach Scott, *Gender and Politics of History* (New York: Columbia University Press, 1988); Anne Firor Scott, "On Seeing and Not Seeing: A Case of Historical Invisibility," *Journal of American History* 71 (June 1984): 7-21; Joan Kelly, "The Doubled Vision of Feminist Theory," in *Sex and Class in Women's History,* ed. Judith Newton, Mary P. Ryan, and Judith R. Waldowitz (New York: Routledge, 1983), 259-70; Gloria Hull, Patricia Bell Scott, and Barbara Smith, *All the Women Are White, All the Blacks Are Men, But Some of Us Are Brave* (New York: Feminist Press, 1982); and bell hooks, *Ain't I A Woman: Black Women and Feminism* (Boston: South End Press, 1981).

1. GOD AND THEY PEOPLE: THE RURAL SOUTH

1. U.S. Bureau of the Census in *Negro Population in the United States, 1790-1915* (New York: Arno Press, 1968), 572 and Henri in *Black Migration,* 26 find that in the 1900-1910 period there were three tenants for every whole or part owner. For the 1920-30 period, more than 75 percent of the African American farmers were tenants or sharecroppers, and the percentage of African American farm owners "continued declining"—John Hope Franklin and Alfred A. Moss, Jr., *From Slavery to Freedom: A History of African Americans* (New York: McGraw-Hill, 1994), 383. By 1940 the decline in African American farm owners continued, as well as "a much lower number of Negro cash and share tenants, and Negro . . . croppers"—Gunnar Myrdal, *An American Dilemma: The Negro Problem and Modern Democracy* (New York: Pantheon Books, 1944), 251-54. Indispensable insight into the plight of sharecroppers in the Report to Earl Peoples, 1939-1940 General Correspondence Files, Lorenzo Greene Papers, Manuscript Collection, Library of Congress, Washington, D.C. (hereafter cited as Lorenzo Greene Papers). See also Susan Mann, "Slavery, Sharecropping and Sexual Inequality," *Signs* 14 (Summer 1989): 774-98; Ralph Shlomowity, "Origins of Southern Sharecropping," *Agriculture History* 53 (July 1979): 557-75; Robert Higgs, *Competition and Coercion: Blacks in the American Economy* (Chicago: University of Chicago Press, 1980), 37-61; Jay Mandle, *The Roots of Black Poverty: The Southern Plantation Economy After the Civil War* (Durham, N.C.: Duke University Press, 1978); Roger L. Ransom and Richard Sutch, *One Kind of Freedom: The Economic Consequences of Emancipation* (New York: Cambridge University Press, 1977), 87-88; Mandle, *Roots of Black Poverty;* Peter Kolchin, *First Freedom: The Responses of Alabama's Blacks to Emancipation and Reconstruction* (Westport, Conn.: Greenwood Press, 1972), 46; U.S. Bureau of the

Census, *Historical Statistics: Of the United States, Colonial Times to 1957* (Washington, D.C.: GPO, 1960), 11–12, 278–79. The Bureau of the Census reported in 1910 that "in the south 3 out of every 4 Negro farmers were tenants"; see U.S. Bureau of the Census in *Negro Population in the United States, 1790–1915, 572.*

2. John Blassingame, *The Slave Community: Plantation Life in the Antebellum South* (New York: Oxford University Press, 1976); Sidney Mintz and Richard Price, *The Birth of African-American Culture: An Anthropological Perspective* (Boston: Beacon, 1992), 84–87; James Oakes, *The Ruling Race: A History of American Slaveholders* (New York: Alfred Knopf, 1982); Paul Escott, *Slavery Remembered: A Record of Twentieth-Century Slave Narratives* (Chapel Hill: University of North Carolina Press, 1979); Social Science Institute, Fisk University, *Unwritten History of Slavery: Autobiographical Accounts of Negro Ex-Slaves* (Nashville: Social Science Institute, 1945); John B. Cade, "Out of the Mouths of Ex-Slaves," *Journal of Negro History* 20 (July 1935): 294–337; and Jones, *Labor of Love,* chap. 1. Compare to Nicholas Lemann, *The Promised Land: The Great Black Migration and How It Changed America* (New York: Knopf, 1991), 9.

3. Joel Williamson, *A Rage for Order: Black/White Relations in the American South Since Emancipation* (New York: Oxford Press, 1986); Jonathan M. Wiener, "Class Structure and Economic Development in the American South, 1865–1955," *American Historical Review* 84 (October 1979): 970–92.

4. Mary F. Berry, "Repression of Blacks in the South, 1890–1945," in *The Age of Segregation: Race Relations in the South, 1890–1945,* ed. Robert Hawks (Jackson: University Press of Mississippi, 1978), 28–45; Harold Woodman, "Sequel to Slavery: The New History Views the Postbellum South," *Journal of Southern History* 43 (November 1977): 523–44; Pete Daniel, "The Metamorphosis of Slavery, 1865–1900," *Journal of American History* 66 (June 1979): 88–99; Edward Ayres, *The Promise of the New South: Life After Reconstruction* (New York: Oxford Press, 1992), vi–vii; Edward L. Ayres, *Vengeance and Justice: Crime and Punishment in the 19th Century American South* (New York: Oxford University Press, 1984); and Morgan Kousser, *The Shaping of Southern Politics: Suffrage Restriction and the Establishment of the One-Party South* (New Haven, Conn.: Yale University Press, 1974).

5. Pete Daniel, *Breaking the Land: The Transformation of Cotton, Tobacco and Rice Cultures Since 1880* (Urbana: University of Illinois Press, 1985), 5–6; William Cohen, "Negro Involuntary Servitude in the South, 1865–1940," *Journal of Southern History* 42 (February 1976): 33–35; and W. E. B. Du Bois, "The Black Codes," in *Justice Denied: The Black Man in White America,* ed. William Chase and Peter Collier (New York: Harcourt, Brace and World, 1970), 166–67.

6. Steven Ruggles, "The Transformation of American Family Structures," *American Historical Review* 99 (February 1994): 118; Andrew Billingsley, *Climbing Jacob's Ladder: The Enduring Legacy of African-American Families* (New York: Simon and Schuster, 1992), chap. 4; and Jones, *Labor of Love,* 46, 59.

7. Lemann, *Promised Land,* 9.

8. Patricia Morton, *Disfigured Images: The Historical Assault On Afro-American Women* (New York: Praeger, 1991), 32–50; Gutman, *Black Family in Slavery and Freedom,* 167–68; Kolchin, *First Freedom,* 62–63; Francis W. Loring and C. F. Atkinson, *Cotton Culture and the South Considered With Reference to Emigration* (Boston: A. Williams, 1869), 4, and Jones, *Labor of Love,* 45.

9. Work as an essential aspect of the lives of African American women receives special attention in Beverly Guy-Sheftall, *Daughters of Sorrow: Attitudes toward Black Women, 1880–1920* (New York: Carlson Publishing, 1990), 93; hooks, *Ain't I A Woman,* chaps. 1 and 2; Jones, *Labor of Love,* 58–61; and Kolchin, *First Freedom,* 62–63.

10. *A Sorrow Beyond Dreams,* a manuscript by Peter Handke at the Schomburg Center for Research in Black Culture, New York Public Library, New York City, extensively discusses the role of women in the South with a number of women domestic servants. For the cultural origins, interpretations, and idealizations of "the Lady," see Morton, *Disfigured Images,* 8–9, 32–35, 71–74, 154; Catherine Clinton, *Plantation Mistress: Women's World in the Old South* (New York: Pantheon, 1982), x–xv; Jacquelyn Dowd Hall, *Revolt Against Chivalry: Jessie Daniel Ames and the Women's Campaign against Lynching* (New York: Columbia University Press, 1979); and Ann Firor Scott, *The Southern Lady: From Pedestal to Politics, 1830–1930* (Chicago: University of Chicago Press, 1970).

11. Cultural priorities of African American women are outlined in Higginbotham, *Righteous Discontent,* 128–37, 143, 180, 192; Rouse, *Lugenia Burns Hope,* 53; Virginia Broughton, *Women's Work as Gleaned from the Women of the Bible, and Bible Women of Modern Times* (Nashville: National Baptist Publishing Board, 1904); Jones, *Labor of Love,* 192–94, 251; Billingsley, *Climbing Jacob's Ladder,* 205–44; Giddings, *When and Where I Enter,* 61–64; Kolchin, *First Freedom,* 62; and Robert Hill, *Research on the African-American Family: A Holistic Perspective* (Boston: University of Massachusetts Press, 1989).

12. Ron Golken and Steven Ruggles, "Race and Multigenerational Family Structure in the United States, 1900–1980," in *The Changing American Family,* ed. Scott J. South and Stewart E. Tolnay (Westport, Conn.: Greenwood Press, 1992); Shepherd Krech III, "Black Family Organization in the Nineteenth Century: An Ethnological Perspective," *Journal of Interdisciplinary History* 12 (Winter 1982): 429–52; Marsha Darling, "The Growth and Decline of the

Afro-American Family Farm" (Ph.D. diss., Duke University, 1982); Ransom and Sutch, *One Kind of Freedom;* Edmond L. Drago, "Sources at the National Archives for Genealogical and Local History Research: The Black Family in Dougherty County, Georgia, 1870-1900;" Escott, *Slavery Remembered,* 170-71; Orville V. Burton, "Ungrateful Servants: Edgefield's Black Reconstruction: Part I of the Total History of Edgefield County, South Carolina" (Ph.D. diss., Princeton University, 1976); Kolchin, *First Freedom,* 69; and Jones, *Labor of Love,* 84.

13. Compare with William A. V. Clark, "Residential Preferences and Residential Choices in a Multiethnic Context," *Demography* 29 (August 1992): 451-54; Miriam L. King and Samuel Preston, "Who Lives with Whom? Individual versus Household Measures," *Journal of Family History* 15 (1990): 117-32; Crandall A. Shifflett, "The Household Composition of Rural Black Families," *Journal of Interdisciplinary History* 6 (Autumn 1975): 241; Tamara K. Hareven, "The Family Process: The Historical Study of the Family Cycle," *Journal of Social History* 7 (Spring 1974): 322-29; and Jones, *Labor of Love,* 85.

14. Barbara Hilkert Andolsen, *Daughters of Jefferson, Daughters of Bootblacks* (Macon, Ga.: Mercer University Press, 1986), and 120; and Leon Litwack, *Been in the Storm So Long* (New York: Knopf, 1979), 434.

15. Jones, *Labor of Love,* 79.

16. Billingsley, *Climbing Jacob's Ladder,* 170-83; Andrew Billingsley, *Black Families in White America* (Englewood Cliffs, N.J.: Prentice-Hall, 1968); Blassingame, *Slave Community;* and Jones, *Labor of Love,* chap. 2.

17. "Unbearable peonage," outlined in an 8 January 1927 report, General Correspondence Files, January-March Folder, Box 36, NAACP Washington, D.C., Branch Records, Manuscript Collection, Library of Congress, Washington, D.C (hereafter cited as NAACP Papers). See also Pete Daniel, *The Shadow of Slavery: Peonage in the South* (Urbana: University of Illinois Press, 1990), x; Mandle, *Roots of Black Poverty;* Nell I. Painter, *Black Migration to Kansas after Reconstruction* (New York: Knopf, 1977), 184-97; Gutman, *Black Family in Slavery and Freedom,* 434-37; and Ray S. Baker, *Following the Colour Line: American Negro Citizenship in the Progressive Era* (New York: Doubleday, Page, 1908), 74-77.

18. Examples of settlement exploitation are seen in the Methyl White/Carl White contract with Isaac Deering and the White/Deering "settlement" receipt. Miscellaneous File, 1938-1939, Lorenzo Greene Papers. Also see Daniels, *Shadow of Slavery,* x-xii; and Arnold Taylor, *Travail and Triumph: Black Life and Culture in the South Since the Civil War* (Westport, Conn.: Greenwood, 1976), 90.

19. Sharecroppers' condition, as late as 1939, reported to be "pitiful. They are hungry, ragged . . . in shacks, and in some cases do not even have water" where they live. See Lorenzo Greene to Frances Danady, 12 June 1939, 1939–1940 General Correspondence Files, Lorenzo Greene Papers. Daniel Novak, *The Wheel of Servitude: Black Forced Labor after Slavery* (Lexington: University Press of Kentucky, 1978); John Cell, *The Highest Stage of White Supremacy: The Origins of Segregation in South Africa and the American South* (New York: Cambridge University Press, 1982); Rossa B. Cooley, *Homes of the Freed* (New York: New Republic, 1926); Giddings, *When and Where I Enter,* 77–80; Gutman, *Black Family in Slavery and Freedom,* 435–37; Lemann, *Promised Land,* 10–21; Jones, *Labor of Love,* 80–87 and Henri, *Black Migration,* 26–27.

20. U.S. Department of Commerce, Bureau of the Census, *Negro Population, 1790–1915* (Washington, D.C.: GPO, 1918), 571.

21. "Work or Fight" manuscript by Walter White outlines the problems of African American women who faced arrest because they refused to work as domestics in the 1917 and 1918 period in six states in the South. Correspondence Clippings Folder, Box C417, NAACP Papers. Mann, "Slavery, Sharecropping and Sexual Inequality," 774–98; Stewart Tolnay and E. M. Beck, "Racial Violence and Black Migration in the American South, 1910 to 1930," *American Sociological Review* 57 (February 1992): 103–16; Giddings, *When and Where I Enter,* chap. 3; Jones, *Labor of Love,* 44–78, 81; Gutman, *Black Family in Slavery and Freedom,* 435–37; Nell I. Painter, *Exodusters: Black Migration to Kansas after Reconstructions* (New York: Alfred Knopf, 1977), 184–97; and Escott, *Slavery Remembered,* 148. A number of these points are discussed in Sylvia R. Frey, *Water from the Rock: Black Resistance in a Revolutionary Age* (Princeton, N.J.: Princeton University Press, 1991); and Painter, *Exodusters,* 184–97.

22. Baker, *Following the Colour Line,* 76. In "Migration and Help," W. E. B. Du Bois calls migration a "self-defense and the most effective protest against Southern lynching, lawlessness, and general deviltry." W. E. B. Du Bois, "Migration and Help," *Crisis* 13 (January 1917): 115. See also Lee E. Williams, *Post War Riots in America: 1919 and 1946* (Lewiston, Maine: Edwin Mellen Press, 1992), 10.

23. Amelia Sullivan to Nannie Helen Burroughs, 27 February 1925, Box 29, Nannie Helen Burroughs Papers, Manuscript Division, Library of Congress, Washington, D.C. (hereafter cited as Nannie Helen Burroughs Papers). See also Krech, "Black Family Organization," 429–52; Gutman, *Black Family in Slavery and Freedom,* 11, 213, 224–29; Billingsley, *Climbing Jacobs Ladder,* 118–27; and Jones, *Labor of Love,* 84–85, 126–27.

24. Krech, "Black Family Organization," 429–52; D. B. Shimkin, Edith M.

Shimkin, and Dennis Frate, eds., *The Extended Family in Black Society* (The Hague: Mouton Press, 1978), 391–405; Bert N. Adams, "Black Families in the United States: An Overview of Ideologies and Research," in Shimkin, Shimkin, and Frate, *Extended Family in Black Society*, 173–80; Elmer P. Martin and Joanne Mitchell Martin, *The Black Extended Family* (Chicago: 1978), 103–14; Elmer P. Martin and Joanne Mitchell Martin, *The Helping Tradition in the Black Family and Community* (Silver Spring, Md.: National Association of Social Workers, 1988); and Harriette Pipes McAdoo, *Black Families* (Newberry Park: Sage Press, 1988).

25. Jones, *Labor of Love*, 64, 87, 101; Mary Frances Berry and John W. Blassingame, *The Long Memory: The Black Experience in American* (New York: Oxford University Press, 1982), 70–86; and Billingsley, *Black Family*, 15–33, 48–71.

26. Shifflett, "Household Composition of Rural Black Families," 241; Hareven, "Family Process," 322–29; and Jones, *Labor of Love*, 85.

27. hooks, *Ain't I A Woman*, 48–49, 62; Joe M. Richardson, *The Negro in Reconstruction in Florida* (Tallahassee: Florida State University Press, 1965), 63; Giddings, *When And Where I Enter*, 60–66, 185; and Litwack, *Been in the Storm*, 244–45. On the Southern idealization of "the white Lady" and femininity, see Kathleen M. Blee, *Women of the Klan: Racism and Gender in the 1920's* (Berkeley and Los Angeles: University of California Press, 1991), 41–48; Glenna Matthews, *Just A Housewife: The Rise and Fall of Domesticity in America* (New York: Oxford University Press, 1987), 193–94; Jane Flax, "Postmodernism and Gender Relations in Feminist Theory," *Signs* 12 (Summer 1987): 621–43; Palmer, "White Women/Black Women," 151–70; Judith Stacey, "The New Conservative Feminism," *Feminist Studies* 9 (Fall 1983): 559–84; Doris Davenport, "The Pathology of Racism: A Conversation with Third World Wimmin," in *This Bridge Called My Back: Writings by Radical Women of Color*, ed. Cherrie Moraga and Gloria Anzaldua (Watertown, Mass.: Persephone Press, 1981), 88; Jacquelyn Dowd Hall, "'The Mind That Burns in Each Body': Women, Rape, and Racial Violence"; Barbara Omolade, "Hearts of Darkness," in *Powers of Desire: The Politics of Sexuality*, ed. Ann Snitow, Christine Stansell, and Sharon Thompson (New York: Monthly Review Press, 1983), 328–49, 350–67; and Sara Ruddick, "Material Thinking," *Feminist Studies* 6 (Summer 1980): 342–67. For nineteenth-century beliefs in leisured ladyhood, Faye Dudden, *Serving Women: Household Service in Nineteenth-Century America* (Middletown, Conn.: Wesleyan University Press, 1983). Dudden shows how the mistress-servant relationship evolved and that servants enabled middle-class women to lead feminists movements. See also Minrose C. Gwin, *Black and White Women of the Old*

South: The Peculiar Sisterhood in American Literature (Knoxville: University of Tennessee Press, 1985), 4-14, 46; Rosemary Daniell, *Fatal Flowers: On Sin, Sex, and Suicide in the Deep South* (New York: Avon Books, 1984), 17; Catherine Clinton, *Plantation Mistress,* x-xv, 6-15, 202-4; and Lawrence N. Powell, *New Masters: Northern Planters During the Civil War and Reconstruction* (New Haven, Conn.: Yale University Press, 1980), 218.

28. This regret was one expressed by many other young women during the Victorian period of the late nineteenth century. But the distance she experienced was in many ways determined by the cultural, economic, and social constraints of her family's situation.

29. Hans A. Baer and Merrill Singer, *African-American Religion in the Twentieth Century: Varieties of Protest and Accommodation* (Knoxville: University of Tennessee Press, 1992), xxii; C. Eric Lincoln and Lawrence H. Mamiya, *The Black Church in the African American Experience* (Durham, N.C.: Duke University Press, 1990); James Cone, *God of the Oppressed* (New York: Seabury Press, 1975); Wallace Charles Smith, *The Church in the Life of the Black Family* (Valley Forge, Pa.: Judson Press, 1985); Benjamin Mays and Joseph W. Nicholson, *The Negro's Church* (New York: Institute of Social and Religious Research, 1933); and E. Franklin Frazier, *The Negro Church* (New York: Schocken Books, 1964).

30. Studies of women in the church include Higginbotham, *Righteous Discontent,* 120-229; Cheryl Townsend Gilkes, "Womanist Ideals and the Sociological Imagination," *Journal of Feminist Studies in Religion* 8 (Fall 1992): 147-51; Harold Dean Trulear, "Reshaping Black Pastoral Theology: The Vision of Bishop Ida B. Robinson," *Journal of Religious Thought* 46 (Summer/Fall 1989): 17-31; Juallyne E. Dodson and Cheryl Townsend Gilkes, "Something Within: Social Change and Collective Endurance in the Sacred World of Black Christian Women," in *Women and Religion in America: Volume Three—The Twentieth Century,* ed. Rosemary Radford Ruether and Rosemary Skinner Keller (San Francisco: Harper and Row, 1986), 80-130; Cheryl Townsend Gilkes, "The Role of Women in the Sanctified Church," *Journal of Religious Thought* (Spring/Summer 1986): 24-41; Jacquelyn Grant, "Black Women and the Church," in Hull, Scott, and Smith, *But Some of Us Are Brave,* 141-52; Eugene Genevese, *Roll, Jordon, Roll: The World The Slaves Made* (New York: Random House, 1974), 232-55; and Jones, *Labor of Love,* 102, 108. See also Albert J. Raboteau, *Slave Religion: The "Invisible Institution" in the Antebellum South* (New York: Oxford University Press, 1978); and Mechal Sobel, *"Trabelin' On: The Slave Journey to an Afro-Baptist Faith* (Westport, Conn.: Greenwood Press, 1979).

31. W. E. B. Du Bois and Augustus Granville Dill, eds. *Morals and Manners among Negro Americans* (Atlanta: Atlanta University Press, 1914); Philip S. Foner,

ed., *W. E. B. Du Bois Speaks, 1890–1919* (New York: Pathfinder Press, 1970), 97; Booker T. Washington, ed., *A New Negro for a New Century: An Accurate and Up-to-Date Record of the Upward Struggles of the Negro Race* (New York: AMS Press, 1973); Elizabeth Botume, *First Days Amongst the Contrabands* (1893; reprint, New York: Arno Press, 1968), 166; Jean Fagan Yellin, "Afro-American Women 1800–1910: Excerpts from a Working Bibliography," in Hull, Scott, and Smith, *But Some of Us Are Brave,* 242–43; and Higginbotham, *Righteous Discontent,* 185–228. For the constructions of African American values and images, see Peter Berger and Richard J. Neuhaus, *To Empower People: The Role of Mediating Structures in Public Policy* (Washington, D.C.: American Enterprise Institute for Public Policy Research, 1977), 26–28; and Henry Louis Gates, Jr., "The Trope of a New Negro and the Reconstruction of the Image of the Black," *Representations* 24 (Fall 1988): 137.

32. These were three of the estimated seventeen thousand who taught in southern states. Ninety percent of these teachers were thirty-four or younger, and 72 percent were unmarried. The educational discrimination patterns of the South are examined by Robert A. Margo, *Race and Schooling in the South, 1880–1950* (Chicago: University of Chicago Press, 1990), 4. He shows how this system perpetuated the existence of a huge supply of low-wage laborers for southerners. Higginbotham notes, as an example of how African American churches resisted this pattern by vehemently supporting schools, that by 1910 no southern black community could claim a single public school offering two years of high school. See Higginbotham, *Righteous Discontent,* 55. Other educational problems are outlined in James D. Anderson, *The Education of Blacks in the South, 1860–1935* (Chapel Hill: University of North Carolina Press, 1988); Henry Allen Bullock, *A History of Negro Education in the South: From 1619 to the Present* (Cambridge: Harvard University Press, 1967); W. E. B. Du Bois, "The Negro in the Black Belt," U.S. Department of Labor Bulletin No. 22 (May 1899): 401–17; Louis Harlan, *Separate and Unequal: Public School Campaigns and Racism in the Southern Seaboard States* (New York: Antheneum, 1968); Jones, *Labor of Love,* 144–45. U.S. Department of Commerce, Bureau of the Census, *Statistics of Women at Work,* 166, 174; and Bureau of the Census, *Negro Population,* 521–22.

33. The southern school is described in detail by Lola Louise Strange Johnson, interview, 18 October 1983, OHP 3-35, Oral History Series of the Washingtoniana Collection, Martin Luther King Memorial Library, Washington, D.C. (hereafter cited as Oral History Series). The descriptions of all the women amplify the difficulties of the African American teacher in the South, who relied on hostile white administrators or poverty-stricken African American par-

ents for their livelihood. The maldistribution of southern county-school funds worked to the detriment of all African American pupils and teachers. Compared to white teachers, African American teachers taught more children (an average of ninety-five for African Americans as opposed to forty-five for whites), taught in smaller schools, had less classroom time, and had fewer books, pencils, and slates. Teachers in the segregated schools, receiving no more than twenty-five to thirty dollars a month, were paid only 45 percent of the salary of white teachers. Jones, *Labor of Love,* 144. See also Margo, *Race and Schooling in the South,* 4, 127; Vincent P. Franklin and James D. Anderson, *New Perspectives on Black Educational History* (Boston: G. K. Hall, 1978); Bullock, *History of Negro Education in the South;* Du Bois, "Negro In The Black Belt," 407; and Harlan, *Separate and Unequal,* 10–13, 245, 257–63.

34. Peculiarly, although the women interviewed for this study each recalled their training, they had difficulty articulating the methodology of training. For a New York grandmother who outlines the "real training" she seeks for her granddaughter, see Ellen Goldstine to Nannie Helen Burroughs, September 1933, General Correspondence, Go File, Box 9, Nannie Helen Burroughs Papers. See also John Langston Gwaltney, *Drylongso: A Self-Portrait of Black America* (New York: Random House, 1980), xxiv–xxvii; Susan Armitage, "Making the Personal Political: Women's History and Oral History," *Oral History Review* 17 (Fall 1989): 107–16; John Van Maanen, *Tales of the Field: On Writing Ethnography* (Chicago: University of Chicago Press, 1988); Charles Briggs, *Learning How to Ask: A Sociolinguistic Appraisal of the Role of the Interview in Social Science Research* (New York: Cambridge Press, 1986); and Harold Garfinkel, *Studies in Ethnomethodology* (Englewood Cliffs, N.J.: Prentice-Hall, 1967), 9, 38.

35. W. E. B. Du Bois, ed., "The Negro American Family," Atlanta University Study No. 13 (Atlanta: Atlanta University Press, 1908), 129; William Pickens, *Bursting Bonds* (Boston: Jordan and More, 1923), 11; Clyde V. Kiser, *Sea Island to City: A Study of St. Helena Islanders in Harlem and Other Urban Centers* (New York: Columbia University Press, 1932), 253–54; and William H. Harris, *The Harder We Run: Black Workers Since the Civil War* (New York: Oxford University Press, 1982), 36, 64, 65.

36. Earl W. Crosby, "Limited Success against Long Odds: The Black County Agent," *Agriculture History* 57 (July 1983): 277–88; Pat Dillingham, "Black Belt Settlement Work," *Southern Workman* 31 (August 1902): 437–44; Michelle Z. Rosaldo, *Women, Culture and Society* (Stanford, Calif.: Stanford University Press, 1974), 12; and Mamie Garvin Fields with Karen Fields, *Lemon Swamp and Other Places: A Carolina Memoir* (New York: Free Press, 1983), 187–97.

37. Geraldine Joncich Clifford, "'Marry, Stitch, Die, or Do Worse': Educat-

ing Women for Work," in *Work, Youth, and Schooling: Historical Perspectives on Vocationalism in American Education*, ed. Harvey Kantor and Divid Tyack (Stanford, Calif.: Stanford University Press, 1982), 223-68; Palmer, *Domesticity and Dirt*, chap. 5; Elizabeth Faue, *Community of Suffering and Struggle: Women, Men, and the Labor Movement in Minneapolis, 1915-1945* (Chapel Hill: University of North Carolina Press, 1991), 15; Maria Steward, *Meditations from the Pen of Mrs. Maria W. Steward Negro* (Washington, D.C.: n.p., 1879); Fannie Jackson Coppin, *Reminiscences of School Life, and Hints on Teaching* (Philadelphia: African Methodist Episcopal Book Concern, 1913); and Louis Daniel Hutchinson, *Anna J. Cooper. A Voice from the South* (Washington, D.C.: Smithsonian Institution Press, 1980).

38. See the "New World A' Coming" radio-series tape C 313 for a program that included the famous Canada Lee in a melodrama showing how African Americans "learn" their servant role. "New World A' Coming" was produced in the studios of YMCA by the City Wide Citizen's Committee on Harlem and is available in the Schomburg Center for Research in Black Culture, New York Public Library, New York City. See also, Pickens, *Bursting Bonds,* 11-12; Kiser, *Sea Island to City,* 253-54; Du Bois, "Negro American Family," 128-29; and Jones, *Labor of Love,* 90-91.

39. "Pick-up" is light dusting, sweeping of floors, and ironing of small clothing items. Compare with classification of Jean Collier Brown, *Household Workers* (Chicago: Science Research Associates, 1940), 24-27. Also see Marc Manganaro, ed., *Modernist Anthropology: From Fieldwork to Text* (Princeton, N.J.: Princeton University Press, 1990), the introduction.

40. Fear of rape was a universal concern to the young women and their families. For examples of the problem in the South, see Mann, "Slavery, Sharecropping and Sexual Inequality," 774-98; Darlene Clark-Hine, "Rape and the Inner Lives of Black Women in the Middle West: Preliminary Thoughts on the Culture of Dissemblance," *Signs* 14 (Summer 1989): 912-20; "More Slavery at the South. By a Negro Nurse," *Independent* 72 (January 1912): 197-98; W. E. B. Du Bois, "The Negroes of Farmville, Virginia: A Social Study," *Bulletin of the Department of Labor* 3 (January 1898): 2, 16; "The Race Problem—An Autobiography. By a Southern Colored Woman," *Independent* 56 (March 1904): 578; Oswald Garrison Villard, "The Negro and the Domestic Problem," *Alexander's Magazine* 1 (November 1905): 11; and Orra Langhorne, "Domestic Service in the South," *Journal of Social Science* 39 (Spring 1901): 170-81. For Washington, D.C., see "Washington, D.C. Rape," *St. Luke Herald* (Richmond, Va.), 24 May 1919, and "Colored Girl Outraged Miscreant Acquitted" in the 1922 August-December File, Box G-34, NAACP Papers.

2. WHO'D HAVE A DREAM? THE MIGRATION EXPERIENCE

1. Walter W. White to Isaiah T. Montgomery, 11 October 1918, Box C 417, NAACP Papers; Emmett J. Scott, *Negro Migration During the War* (New York: Oxford University Press, 1969); Donald Henderson, "Negro Migration of 1916-1918," *Journal of Negro History* 6 (October 1921): 383-498; Robert Higgs, "The Boll Weevil, the Cotton Economy and Black Migration, 1910-1930," *Agriculture History* 50 (April 1976): 335-50; W. O. Scroggs, "The Interstate Migration of Negro Population," *Journal of Political Economy* 25 (December 1917): 1034-43; Thomas J. Woofter, *Negro Migration* (New York: AMS Press, 1971); U.S. Department of Labor, Division of Negro Economics, *Negro Migration in 1916-1917* (Washington, D.C.: GPO, 1919); and Henri, *Black Migration,* 51.

2. During this period, scholars note that "sharecroppers faced choices so constricted as to almost disappear altogether" (Jones, *The Dispossessed: America's Underclasses from the Civil War to the Present* [New York: Basic Books, 1992], 291). Also see Joseph Hill, "Recent Northward Migration of the Negro," *Monthly Labor Review* 18 (March 1924): 475-77.

3. Walter F. White to C. C. Dejoie, 5 October 1918, Box C 417, NAACP Papers, outlines the oppression directed at African American women and girls. "Migration . . . is motivated by an effort to improve their condition of living. Better homes, a better job, a better life for their children . . . and as such, the efforts deserve commendation, not condemnation," U.S. Department of Labor, *Negro Migration in 1916-1917,* 9; W. T. B. Williams was the writer of the report of the Dillard report and the only African American on this team. He insisted that the hope of more respect was the overriding reason for migration from the South. Many studies have shown that this was the hardest motive to assay in spite of the fact that the theme is repeated over and over again. This motivating force for migration "is difficult to express—much harder than simply saying a person wants to earn more money," said Williams in a migration report. A woman migrant pointed out that it was not just a question of wages: "Negroes . . . are tired of being treated as children." See Henri, *Black Migration,* 56. See also Jones, *Dispossessed,* 206; William Cohen, *At Freedom's Edge: Black Mobility and the Southern White Quest for Racial Control, 1861-1915* (Baton Rouge: Louisiana State University Press, 1991), chap. 1; Woodson, *Century of Negro Migration,* 159-62; and W. E. B. Du Bois, "Negro Migration," *Crisis* 14 (March 1917): 65.

4. "Experiences of the Race Problem By A Southern White Woman," *Independent* 56 (March 1904): 593 states the belief that African American women were "the greatest menace possible to the moral life of any community where they live." These ideas are countered in William Trotter, Jr., *The Great Migration*

in Historical Perspective: New Dimensions of Race, Class, and Gender (Blooming-ton: Indiana University Press, 1991); Alferdteen Harrison, *Black Exodus: The Great Migration from the American South* (Jackson: University Press of Missis-sippi, 1991); Marvin Goodwin, *Black Migration in America from 1915 to 1960* (Lewiston, Maine: Mellen Press, 1990); and Adero, *Up South.* Also see Ula Yvette Taylor, "From White Kitchens to White Factories: The Impact of World War I on African-American Working Women in Chicago," *UFA-HAMA-Journal of the African Activist Association* 3 (November 1985): 26–28; Du Bois, "Negro Migration," 65; and U.S. Department of Labor, *Negro Migration in 1916–1917,* 9.

5. Carter G. Woodson claims that a substantial number of educated African American professionals fled the repression of the South before the unskilled and semiskilled African Americans. Woodson, *Century of Negro Migration,* 159–62. Alain Locke strongly disagrees with Woodson. Locke suggests that the "man at the bottom led the migration to the cities, and the professional class simply fol-lowed its clientele." Alain Locke, "The New Negro: An Interpretation," in *The Black American,* ed. Leslie Fishel and Benjamin Quarles (Glenview, Ill.: Scott Foresman, 1970), 437–38.

6. Women stressed that the most powerful "charms" were created by older women for younger women. The spiritual secrets and charms of women were not shared with men; in this area older women were "powerful beings . . . [who] guided them to the other world, the spiritual world." See Wade-Gales, *Pushed Back to Strength,* 248–58.

7. "Contract between Patrick Brogan and freed people: Carter-Dock and family wife Diana and 2 daughters Flora and Bella," Miscellaneous Record Book, 1865–67, Greenville, Alabama. Subassistant Commissioner (vol. 127 in no. 106), Bureau of Refugees, Freemen and Abandoned Lands. Case 29 (30 May 1968, 104–5), Register of Complaints, Cuthbert, Georgia, Agent (no. 238, in no. 859), Bureau of Refugees, Freemen and Abandoned Lands. See Spartan-burg District, Spartanburg, South Carolina, Bureau of Refugees, Freemen and Abandoned Lands for more examples of women with dependents who were given less land than men with similar sized families in 1865–67. See also Jones, *Labor of Love,* 62.

8. Eric Hobsbawm, "Peasants and Politics," *Journal of Peasant Studies* 1 (Oc-tober 1973); Neil R. McMillen, *Dark Journey: Black Mississippis in the Age of Jim Crow* (Urbana: University of Illinois Press, 1989); Giddings, *When and Where I Enter,* 58–63; Davis, *Women, Race, and Class,* 17–18; Ransom and Sutch, *One Kind of Freedom,* 108–31, 147, 161–63; Andolsen, *Daughters of Jefferson,* 94; and Jones, *Labor of Love,* 64.

9. Gutman, *Black Family in Slavery and Freedom,* 213, 224-29. Edward Magdol, *A Right to Land: Essays on the Freedman's Community* (Westport, Conn.: Greenwood Press, 1977), 11; and Jones, *Labor of Love,* 65-66.

10. An additional example of "Negro women more aggressive in asserting their rights" is in a letter from Senator Ben R. Tillman to Mary Bartlett Dixon, 27 November 1914, Box 407, Manuscript Division, Library of Congress, Washington, D.C.

3. NEW DAY'S DAWNING: THE WORLD OF WASHINGTON

1. "Washington The Mecca of Nation's Unemployed Women," *Washington Post,* 10 October 1909, 3-4.

2. Ibid.

3. "Uncle Sam's Girls," n.d., in the "Women in Washington, D.C. 1920-1940" Files, Washingtoniana Collection, Martin Luther King Library, Washington, D.C. (hereafter cited as Washingtoniana Collection).

4. In the 1910 census there was an 8.9 percent increase of African Americans in the District of Columbia. In the 1920 census there was a 16.4 percent increase. U.S. Bureau of the Census, *Negro Population in the United States,* 5. Teresa Barnett, "Analyzing Oral Texts, or, How Does an Oral History Mean?" *Oral History Review* 18 (Fall 1990): 109-13. Also see Hill, "Recent Northward Migration of the Negro," 9; and U.S. Bureau of the Census, *United States Population: Washington, D.C.,* 575, 587.

5. Servants leave their children "in crowded, dirty, hovels. . . . where older children or elderly women" care for small babies "in a half-hearted, ignorant, deadly way." Charles F. Weller, *Neglected Neighbors: Stories of Life in the Alleys, Tenements and Shanties of the National Capital* (Philadelphia: J. C. Winston, 1909), 35-36.

6. Barbara Dodson Walker interview, 10 November 1983, OHP 3-44, Oral History Series. James Borchert, *Alley Life in Washington: Family Community, Religion, and Folklife in the City, 1850-1970* (Urbana: University of Illinois Press, 1980), chaps. 2-3; and W. E. B. Du Bois, ed., "Some Efforts of American Negroes for Their Own Social Betterment," Atlanta University Study No. 13, (Atlanta, Ga.: Atlanta University Press, 1898), 17-18.

7. Housing problems of migrants to Washington discussed in the Mariam D. Butler letter to Nannie Helen Burroughs, 5 June 1927, General Correspondence, But-Byr Folder, Box 3, Nannie Helen Burroughs Papers. See also Borchert, *Alley Life in Washington,* 123-24. George E. Haynes, "Negro Migra-

tion: Its Effect on Family and community Life in the North," *Opportunity* 2 (September–October 1924): 271–74; E. Franklin Frazier, "Occupational Classes Among Negroes in Cities," *American Journal of Sociology* 35 (March 1930): 718–38; T. D. Ackiss and M. C. Hill, "Social Classes, a Frame of Reference for the Study of Negro Society," *Social Forces* 22 October 1943): 92–93; and E. Franklin Frazier, "Family Disorganization Among Negroes," *Opportunity* 9 (July 1931): 206.

8. *North Cacalacky* and *South Cacalacky* are terms for migrants born in North or South Carolina. The twelfth census (1900) shows 5.2 percent of African Americans living in the District of Columbia were "native to the South exclusive of Maryland and Virginia." The fifteenth census (1930) discloses that 20.2 percent of the population were "native to the South exclusive of Maryland and Virginia."

9. For reasons Washington, D.C., was considered North by migrants, see Spencer Crew, "When North Ain't North: A Study of Washington, D. C. Migration, 1900–1950" (Paper delivered at the Center for Washington, D.C. Studies meetings, Washington, D.C., February 1988); and Jones, *Labor of Love,* 152. For a sampling of historical studies of migration, see James R. Grossman, *Land of Hope: Chicago, Black Southerners, and the Great Migration* (Chicago: University of Chicago Press, 1989); Kenneth L. Kusmer, *A Ghetto Takes Shape: Black Cleveland, 1870–1930* (Urbana: University of Illinois Press, 1976); David Katzman, *Before the Ghetto: Black Detroit in the Nineteenth Century* (Urbana: University of Illinois Press, 1973); and Elizabeth Hafkin Pleck, *Black Migration and Poverty, Boston, 1850–1900* (New York: Academic Press, 1979).

10. Ruth Baer interview, OHP 3-32, Oral History Series. Borchert, *Alley Life in Washington,* 13; Letitia Woods Brown, *Free Negroes in the District of Columbia, 1790–1846* (New York: Oxford Press, 1972), 129–42; and Constance McLaughlin Green, *Washington: A History of the Capital, 1897–1950* (Princeton, N.J.: Princeton University Press, 1962), 101–31, 260–72.

11. Boschke's maps confirm the post–Civil War surge in tenant habitations in the alley. Jones's twentieth-century study of the city directory enumerates the names and computes the numbers of new homes built to rent to the alley's African American migrant. Borchert, *Alley Life in Washington,* 17, 19, 28; William Henry Jones, *The Housing of Negroes in Washington, D.C.* (Washington, D.C.: Howard University Press, 1929), 46; Daniel Swinney, "Alley Dwelling and Housing Reform in the District of Columbia" (Master's thesis, University of Chicago, 1938), 94–105, 124–34; Wilber V. Mallalieu, "A Washington Alley," *Survey* 28 (October 1912): 69–71; and Edith Elmer Wood, "Four Washington Alleys," *Survey* 31 (December 1913): 250–52.

12. African Americans in Washington, D.C.'s alleys live in conditions worse than those in the "grimmest slums of New York City," Jacob Riis stressed in House and Senate District Committee testimony. See Green, *Washington,* 152–53. See also Swinney, "Alley Dwelling and Housing Reform," 147.

13. Jones, *Labor of Love,* 185. For an exhaustive description of "rooming houses," see Lola Louise Strange Johnson, OHP 3-35, Oral History Series.

14. Clark-Lewis, "Duty and 'Fast Living,'" 55. For overviews of home-based work, see Eileen Boris, "Black Women and Paid Labor in the Home: Industrial Homework in Chicago in the 1920's," in *Homework: Historical and Contemporary Perspectives on Paid Labor at Home,* ed. Eileen Boris and Cynthia R. Daniels (Urbana: University of Illinois Press, 1989), 33–47; Elizabeth Pleck, "A Mother's Wages: Income Earning Among Married Italian and Black Women, 1896–1911," in *A Heritage of Her Own,* ed. Nancy F. Cott and Elizabeth H. Pleck (New York: Simon and Schuster, 1979), 367–92; Jean Brown, "Household Occupation in the District of Columbia," 8, typescript, circulated by the Washington League of Women Shoppers (1940-41), National Council on Household Employment, as quoted in Palmer, *Domesticity and Dirt,* chap. 6; Myra Hill Colson, "Home Work Among Negro Women in Chicago" *Social Service Review* 11 (September 1928): 385–413; Helen B. Sayre, "Negro Women in Industry," *Opportunity* 2 (August 1924): 242–44; Mary White Ovington, "The Negro Home in New York," *Charities* 15 (October 1905): 25–30.

15. Eliza Johnson to Memphis Johnson, 31 August 1914, author's collection. See also Clark-Lewis, "Duty and 'Fast Living,'" 93.

16. The order of service is posted on boards at the front of many churches. Each week the songs, scriptures, and special notes are placed on this order of service board.

17. The rural South's religious services had rhythmic songs, improvisational communal rites, a centripetal pull of the Holy Ghost, and a mass creativity that people consciously expressed during the worship service. This extemporizing was an aspect of worship the migrants in the large churches said they missed in services in D.C. However, pastors gradually allowed an admixture of the southern styles and influences. See W. E. B. Du Bois, *Souls of Black Folks* (New York: New American Library, 1961), 140–41; Bruno Nettl, *Folk and Traditional Music of the Western Continents* (Englewood Cliffs, N.J.: Prentice-Hall, 1965); Bruno Nettl, "Stylistic Change in Folk Music" *Southern Folklore Quarterly* 17 (September 1953): 216–20; Higginbotham, *Righteous Discontent,* 43; St. Clair Drake and Horace Cayton, *Black Metropolis: A Study of Negro Life in a Northern City* (New York: Harcourt Brace, 1945), 519; and Lawrence Levine, *Black Culture, Black*

Consciousness, 26-28, 138-43. Also see Cone, *God of the Oppressed,* and Mays and Nicholson, *Negro's Church.*

18. The churches the women attended are Asbury United Methodist, John Wesley AME, Metropolitan AME, Nineteenth Street Baptist, and Shiloh Baptist Church.

19. Joan Wallach Scott, *Gender and the Politics of History* (New York: Columbia University Press, 1988), 30; Nancy Fraser, *Unruly Practices: Power, Discourse and Gender in Contemporary Social Theory* (Minneapolis: University of Minnesota Press, 1989); Victor Daly, *Not Only War: A Story of Two Great Conflicts* (Boston: n.p., 1932).

20. Genevese, *Roll, Jordan, Roll,* 218.

21. Weller, *Neglected Neighbors,* 17-22, 97; Mallalieu, "Washington Alley," 71; *Washington Star,* 29 October 1905; Andrew Hilyer, *The Twentieth Century Union League Directory: A Compilation of the Efforts of the Colored People of Washington for Social Betterment and A Historical, Biographical, and Statistical Study of Colored Washington at the Dawn of the Twentieth Century and After a Generation of Freedom* (Washington, D.C.: Union League, 1901), 137, 142; Marion M. Ratigan, *Sociological Survey of Disease in Four Alleys in the National Capital* (Washington, D.C.: Catholic University of America Press, 1946), 114.

22. Weller, *Neglected Neighbors,* 17, 22. Other studies positively depict the migrant's Holy Ghost possessions, analyze rituals, tabulate social events, and record folklore evidence. See Borchert, *Alley Life in Washington,* chap. 6; Genevese, *Roll, Jordan Roll,* 218; Green, *Secret City,* 222-38. See also Higginbotham, *Righteous Discontent,* 42-46. The experiences of women who were active in these small denominations or alley churches can be documented. Written sources do not appreciate or scrutinize the tone and the tincture of "alley" religion in these women's lives. With oral interviews we understand why religion is an indispensable component of any inquiry into migrant women's lives. See Jacquelyn Grant, "Black Women in the Church," 141.

23. *Washington Bee,* 21 April 1888.

24. Frederick Douglass, *Washington Bee,* 24 March 1888. The need for additional discipline and reform work of a "missionary working among our unfortunate and unlearned" is also reexamined in a letter from Chester V. Daniels to Nannie Helen Burroughs, 17 December 1930, Daa-Dau Folder, Box 6, Nannie Helen Burroughs Papers.

25. Woodson and Greene, *Negro Wage Earner,* (New York: Russell and Russell, 1969), 230. Training proposals for the district were part of the information in Record Group 86, Women's Bureau, Household Employment Files, House-

hold Employment—Training. The District of Columbia educational studies show how the city dealt with the problem of education for migrant women and children; however, the lack of contribution from the perspective of the migrant women and the obvious class bias of these government reports make the validity of the data contained therein somewhat dubious. "The Best Club Women's Movement," *African Women's Journal* 6 (Summer 1904): 34–38; *Colored Woman's League of Washington, D.C.: Fifth Annual Report* (Washington, D.C.: Smith Brothers, 1898); *A History of the Phyllis Wheatley Young Women's Christian Association, 1905–1930* (Washington, D.C.: Young Women's Christian Association, 1903); Isabel Burns Lindsay, "The Participation of Negro Women in the Development of Post-Civil War Welfare Services in the District of Columbia," in *Women in the District of Columbia,* ed. International Women's Year Coordinating Committee (Washington, D.C.: International Women's Year Coordinating Committee, 1977); and Debra Newman, *Selected Documents Pertaining to Black Workers Among the Records of the Department of Labor and Its Component Bureaus, 1902–1969* (Washington, D.C.: General Services Administration, 1977).

26. Record Group 351, Records of the Government of the District of Columbia, Records of the Board of Children's Guardians—Children's History, File 787; and Williston Lofton, "Public Education for Negroes," chaps. 1–4.

27. Faue, *Community of Suffering,* 15; Carolyn Steedman, *Landscape for a Good Woman: A Story of Two Lives* (New Brunswick: Rutgers University Press, 1986), 13; Loretta E. Turner, *How Women Earn a Competence* (Oberlin, Ohio: privately printed, 1902), 81; An excellent example of the many letters praising Nannie Helen Burroughs for her occupational and education reform program is Clarence Howard to Nannie Helen Burroughs, 16 March 1917, Bat-Bei General Correspondence Folder, Box 2, Nannie Helen Burroughs Papers. Also see Sharon Harley, "Black Women in a Southern City: Washington, D.C., 1890–1920," in *Sex, Race, and the Role of Women in the South,* eds. Joanne V. Hawks and Sheila L. Skemp (Jackson: University Press of Mississippi, 1983), 59–74; Frances Kellor, *Out of Work* (New York: Putnam and Sons, 1904); Henrietta Roelofs, *The Road to Trained Service in the Household* (New York: Commission on Household Employment—National Board of the Young Women's Christian Associations, 1916), 1; Lucy Maynard Salmon, *Domestic Service* (New York: Macmillan, 1897), 251–60; and Ruth Sergel, *The Women in the House* (New York: Woman's Press, 1938).

28. Lofton, "Public Education for Negroes," 26–30.

29. W. E. B. Du Bois, *The Philadelphia Negro: A Social Study* (New York: Benjamin Blom, 1899), 136–37; American Council on Education, *Thus Be Their Destiny* (Washington, D.C.: American Council on Education, 1941); and

Daniel E. Sutherland, *Americans and Their Servants* (Baton Rouge: Louisiana State University Press), 182-99.

30. Clark-Lewis, "Duty and 'Fast Living,'" 55. Also see Adero, *Up South;* Spencer Crew, *From Field To Factory: Afro-American Migration, 1915-1940* (Washington, D.C.: Smithsonian Institution Press, 1987); and Harrison, *Black Exodus.*

4. A' ENDLESS MIRATION: LIVE-IN SERVICE

1. Compare an analogous use of slavery image in Nannie Helen Burroughs to George Schuyler response, 3 February 1927, Nannie Helen Burroughs Papers, and Clark-Lewis, "Duty and 'Fast Living,'" 55. The matrix of racial discrimination and circumscribed employment opportunities that forced African American women to accept the most unattractive, disagreeable work and paltry wages is examined in Katherine Tillman, "Paying Professions for Colored Girls," *Voice of the Negro* (January/February 1907); Elizabeth Ross Haynes, "Two Million Negro Women at Work," *Southern Workman* 51 (February 1922): 64-72; and Sayre, "Negro Women in Industry," 242-44.

2. From the poem "Turning Other Cheeks," by Carmen Lattimore.

3. Dorothy Dunbar Bromley, "Are Servants People?" *Scribner's* 94 (December 1933): 377-79; Lucy Randolph Mason, "The Perfect Treasure," *Junior League Magazine* (February 1934): 36; Selma Robinson, "Mrs. Spencer's Maid," *Good Housekeeping* (March 1939): 28; Du Bois, *Philadelphia Negro,* 136-37; Lorenzo Greene, *The Negro in Colonial New England* (New York: Atheneum, 1969), 108-9, 290, 350; Edgar J. McManus, *Black Bondage in the North* (New York: Syracuse University Press, 1973), 41-57; Winthrop D. Jordan, *White Over Black: American Attitudes Toward the Negro* (Baltimore: Johns Hopkins University Press, 1969), 80-81, 123; Katzman, *Seven Days a Week,* 159-60; and Sutherland, *Americans and Their Servants,* 3-4.

4. African American servants as "a people apart" is examined by Ruth Baer, Oral History Series. Women did not want to be reminded of their dependence on black, unstylish, hard-to-manage older women—the ideal servant was always a young white woman; however, these "jewels" were impossible to find. For African American women migrants, the relationships "breed hatred and animosity . . . for the superior-inferior role." Alice McDonald, "Do You Know Your Place," *Junior League Magazine* (May 1938): 27-29; Linda Martin and Kerry Segrave, *The Servant Problem: Domestic Workers in North America* (Jackson, Miss.: McFarland Press, 1985), 33. Rollins, *Between Women,* 142, 157-58; "The Sphinx in the Household," *Scribner's Magazine* 49 (September 1911): 379-80;

Katzman, *Seven Days a Week,* 200; and Sutherland, *Americans and Their Servants,* 27, 33-35.

5. Dr. Margaret Morgan, a physician forced to work as a domestic while attending Cornell University, explains the fear, loneliness, and anger of a well-educated woman being forced into the servant role. See Sara Lawrence Lightfoot, *Balm in Gilead: Journey of a Healer* (Reading, Mass.: Addison-Wesley, 1988), 95. For a discussion of Washington, D.C., spatial dictates for servants, see Green, *Secret City,* 42. For earlier periods, see John Vlach, "Evidence of Slave Housing in Washington," *Washington History* 5 (Winter 1994): 66; and Letitia Woods Brown, "Residence Patterns of Negroes in the District of Columbia, 1800-1860," Records of the Columbia Historical Society 47 (1969-70): 72. For an important discussion of why employers wanted servants, as inconspicuously as possible, to use rear portions of house or unseen service areas, see Harris, *From Mammies to Militants,* 15-16; Robert Hamburger, *A Stranger in the House* (New York: Macmillan, 1978); Rollins, *Between Women,* 171 -73; Sutherland, *Americans and Their Servants,* 30.

6. For a discussion of the major problems confronting local servants, see Viola Cotton interview, 30 August 1983, OHP 3-20, Oral History Series. A 1923 national survey found that adult, general-housework maids were paid between $.90 and $1.60 per week. See Elizabeth Ross Haynes, "Negroes in Domestic Service in the United States," *Journal of Negro History* 8 (October 1923): 422-25. Various aspects of household work reform are treated by Alice Stryker Root, "A Word to Employers," a pamphlet issued by the Committee on Household Employment of the National Board of the YWCA, 1917, n.p.; Nancy Woods Walburn, "Elevating Housework to Professional Standing," *Woman's Press* 22 (December 1928): 856-57; *New York Times,* 25 November 1932; Eleanor M. Snyder, "Job Histories of Women Workers at the Summer Schools, 1931-1934 and 1938," U.S. Women's Bureau Bulletin No. 174 (Washington: GPO, 1939), 17; Mary Hornaday, "Want an Ideal Maid? Here's How," *Christian Science Monitor* (March 1940): 5; and Harris, *From Mammies to Militants,* 11. The "elitism" servants savored had little to do with a desire for friendship with wealthy persons, which was an impossibility. And they never indicated a desire to impress people by disclosing their intimacy with rich employers. Special aspects of working for the president, U.S. senators, two Supreme Court justices, and congressman, as well as the Corcoran, Rockefeller, DuPont, and other wealthy families are treated as discussions of employment/survival strategies—not status. Extensive and readily available general accounts are found in the Viola Cotton interview, 30 August 1983, OHP 3-20, and Lola Louise Strange Johnson interview, 18 October 1983, OHP 3-35, both

from the Oral History Series. For general information about the underlying motives, choices, and "somber hues" within which these women worked, see Janet Lane, "Listen, Mrs. Legree," *Colliers Magazine* (December 1939): 27, 43; and Judith McGaw, "'A Good Place to Work': Industrial Workers and Occupational Choice," *Journal of Interdisciplinary History* 10 (Autumn 1979): 227-48. Access to quantitative benefits (such as money or improved future employment opportunities) explained by Eliza Potter, *A Hairdresser's Experience in High Life* (Cincinnati: n.p., 1859), 22, 104, 114. See also Peter Lowenberg, *Decoding the Past: The Psychohistorical Approach* (New York: Knopf Press, 1983); Jeanne Hunnicutt Delgado, ed., "Nettie Kedzie Jones' Advice to Farm Women: Letters from Wisconsin, 1912-1916," *Wisconsin Magazine of History* 57 (Autumn 1973): 3-27; Elizabeth Jordan, "Mrs. Van Nostrands's Night of Triumph," *Harper's Weekly* 52 (7 March 1908): 21; and Sutherland, *Americans and Their Servants*, 144.

7. The solicitous attention employers required is examined by Potter, *Hairdresser's Experience*, 13, 53-55, 60-62; "A Butler's Life Story," *Independent* 69 (July 1910): 82; Edwin Whipple, "Domestic Service," *Forum* 1 (March 1886): 32-33; John B. Guernsey, "Scientific Management in the Home," *Outlook* 100 (April 1912): 821-25; Jones, *Labor of Love*, 127-34, 164-66; Sutherland, *Americans and Their Servants*, 86; and Katzman, *Seven Days a Week*, 184-85, 198-99.

8. For analysis of the live-in household worker's world in reform literature, see Palmer's *Domesticity and Dirt*. For employers' beliefs about leisure corrupting servants, see Mrs. William Parks, *Domestic Duties* (New York: J. and J. Harper, 1828), 110; and Sutherland, *Americans and Their Servants*, 99-102.

9. David R. Roediger in *The Wages of Whiteness: Race and the Making of the American Working Class* (New York: Verso, 1991) investigates the divers social and legal implications of racial prejudice in the United States. Walter L. Fleming recognizes that "old negroes are the best and most willing servants; but they are few in number," in the article "The Servant Problem in a Black Belt Village," *Sewanee Review* 13 (January 1905): 11. A female writer elaborated on "the monotony of stupidity in my servants" in "Experiences of the Race Problem by a Southern White Woman," *Independent* 56 (March 1904): 593; Katzman, *Seven Days a Week*, 158; Sutherland, *Americans and Their Servants*, 5. Compare with Elise Johnson McDougald, "The Task of Negro Womanhood," in *The New Negro: An Interpretation*, ed. Alain Leroy Locke (New York: Boni Press, 1925), 379; Andolsen, *Daughters of Jefferson*, 90.

10. For strategies of resistance, see Robin D. G. Kelly, "'We Are Not What We Seem': Rethinking Black Working Class Opposition in the Jim Crow South," *Journal of American History* 80 (June 1993): 75-112. Forces contributing

to these myths are explored by Evelyn Brooks Barnett, "Nannie Burroughs and the Education of Black Women," in *The Afro-American Woman,* ed. Roslyn Terborg-Penn and Sharon Harley (Port Washington, N.Y.: Kennikat Press, 1978), 97–108. Compare to the racist educational beliefs in "Experiences of the Race Problem by a Southern White Woman," 593–94; Pettengill, *Toilers;* and Katzman, *Seven Days a Week,* 184–95.

11. Palmer, *Domesticity and Dirt,* chap. 2; Hilary Rose, "Hand, Brain and Heart," *Signs* 9 (Autumn 1983): 73–90; To review the "management" suggestions of this period, see Guernsey, "Scientific Management in the Home," 821–25; Ida Bailey Allen, *Home Partners, or Seeing the Family Through* (N.p.: privately printed, 1924), 12–15; Benjamin Andrews, *Economics of the Household* (New York: Macmillian, 1923), 412, 440–48; Mary Hinman Abel, *Successful Family Life on the Moderate Income* (Philadelphia: Lippincott, 1927), 22; Mildred Weigley Woods, Ruth Lindquist, and Lucy Studley, *Managing the Home* (Boston: Houghton Mifflin, 1932), 9; Henrietta Ripperger, *A Home of Your Own and How to Run It* (New York: Simon and Schuster, 1940), xviii; Charlotte Adams, *The Run of the House* (New York: Macmillian, 1942), 15–16; and Bettina Berch, "'The Sphinx in the Household': A New Look at the History of Household Workers," *Review of Radical Political Economics* 16 (Spring 1984): 106–19. See also Matthews, *"Just a Housewife";* Laura Shapiro, *Perfect Salad: Women and Cooking at the Turn of the Century* (New York: Farrar, Straus and Giroux, 1986); Alfred Chandler, Jr., *The Visible Hand: The Managerial Revolution in American Business* (Cambridge: Oxford University Press, 1977), 469–76; and Charles M. Sheldon, "Servant and Mistress," *Independent* 52 (December 1900): 3018–20.

12. Palmer, *Domesticity and Dirt,* 60–61. See also Lois Rita Helmbold, "Beyond the Family Economy: Black and White Working Class Women During the Great Depression," *Feminist Studies* 13 (Fall 1987): 629–55; Julia Kirk Blackwelder, *Women of the Depression: Caste and Culture in San Antonio, 1929–1939* (College Station: Texas A & M University Press, 1984), 43.

13. Exploitation of young women reported on in minutes of the Protective Committee, 13 April 1914, Urban League meeting minutes, National Urban League Records, Manuscript Division, Library of Congress, Washington, D.C. See also Palmer, *Domesticity and Dirt,* 61; Andolsen, *Daughters of Jefferson,* 91.

14. Palmer, *Domesticity and Dirt,* 61.

15. Gail Laughlin, "Domestic Service," *Report of the Industrial Commission on the Relations and Conditions of Capital and Labor . . . And a Special Report on Domestic Service,* vol. 14 (Washington, D.C.: GPO, 1901), 759. See Katzman, *Seven Days a Week,* 150, 325.

16. Lightfoot, *Balm in Gilead*, 96.

17. The popular ideology of the 1920s confirms that mistresses were powerful women who needed an ego-enhancing personal attendant and "who had better things to do than spend all [their] time on housework." Palmer, *Domesticity and Dirt*, 11 and 14; Rollins, *Between Women*, 210; and Erving Goffman, *The Presentation of Self in Everyday Life* (Garden City: Doubleday Anchor, 1959), 151.

18. Jones, *Labor of Love*, 127–34, 164–66; Katzman, *Seven Days a Week*, 202; and Roediger, *Wages of Whiteness*, vii–viii.

19. Interesting "color and comportment" preferences are well revealed in letter of John T. Clark to Nannie Helen Burroughs, 27 April 1917, General Correspondence Files, Cen-Co Folder, Box 4, Nannie Helen Burroughs Papers. See also Robin D. G. Kelley, "'We Are Not What We Seem,': Rethinking Black Working Class Opposition in the Jim Crow South," *Journal of American History* 80 (June 1993): 76–110; Rollins, *Between Women*, 143, 147–48; Katzman, *Seven Days a Week*, 194, 221–22; and Sutherland, *Americans and Their Servants*, 37–38.

20. Charles Dickens, *American Notes for General Circulation*, (Avon: Penguin Press, 1975), 163, 168–69, 177.

21. Kelley, "'We Are Not What We Seem,'" 99. Donald Sutherland says "blacks seemed more willing" to wear uniforms. This research does not support that point. See Sutherland, *Americans and Their Servants*, 128.

22. Berch, "'Sphinx in the Household,'" 106, 115; Villard, "Negro and the Domestic Problem," 6; Katzman, *Seven Days a Week*, 189–92; Kolchin, *First Freedom*, 131–33; and Joel Williamson, *After Slavery* (Chapel Hill: University of North Carolina Press, 1965), 105–8, 159–60.

23. The House of Astor and the House of Vanderbilt were only two of the very rich families that adopted special family liveries to distinguish their servants from those of other millionaires. See Sutherland, *Americans and Their Servants*, 129. Kathryn Allamong Jacob studies both the types of liveries worn and their contextual issues in "Like Moths to a Candle: Washington's 'Nouveau Riche' in the Age of the Robber Barron" (Paper presented at the Urban Odyssey Conference, 18 May 1991, Sumner School, Washington, D.C.) This work gives a detailed treatment of the "family" liveries worn by servants in the homes of the very wealthy of the District of Columbia.

24. To understand "having and being a mind of [their] own," see Alyce Gullattee, "Psychiatric Factors to Consider in Research on the Black Woman," *Journal of Afro-American Issues* 2 (Summer 1974): 199–203; Rollins, *Between Women*, 217; Gwaltney, *Drylongso*, 168; Wade-Gales, *Pushed Back to Strength*, 24; Genevese, *Roll, Jordan, Roll*, 337; G. W. F. Hegel, *The Phenomenology of Mind*,

trans. J. B. Baillie (New York: Harper Colophon, 1967), 238-39; and Suther-land, *Americans and Their Servants,* 29.

25. *Mirate* in southern, low-country dialect describes a situation that is worrisome and bothersome. When you *mirate* you are telling someone about a petty, picky, uncomfortable situation and going on and on about it. A *miration* is similar to a worriment.

26. Social networking is an important process that allows one "to shift . . . attention away from the social structure as a formal system *and to* the way it is seen through the eyes of individual members." Only through an awareness of these networks is it possible to understand the way live-in household workers viewed their social world. See Elizabeth Bott, *Family and Social Network: Roles, Norms, and External Relationships in Ordinary Urban Families* (London: Tavistock Publications, 1971), 3, 248-330.

27. Edmond Blair Bolles, *Remembering and Forgetting: An Inquiry Into the Nature of Memory* (New York: Walker, 1988), 29-92; Osterund and Jones, "If I must say so myself," 2; Gwaltney, *Drylongso,* xxv; and Rollins, *Between Women,* 163.

5. THE TRANSITION PERIOD

1. Childress, *Like One of the Family,* 19-21, 69. See also Dill, *Across the Boundaries.*

2. For oppositional relationships and overlapping publics, see Nancy Fraser, "Rethinking the Public Sphere: A Contribution to the Critique of Actually Existing Democracy," *Social Text* 25/26 (1990): 56-80; Rita Felski, *Beyond Feminist Aesthetics: Literature and Social Change* (Cambridge: Harvard University Press, 1989); John Keane, *Public Life and Late Capitalism: Toward a Socialist Theory of Democracy* (New York: Cambridge University Press, 1984); and Rae L. Needleman, "Domestic Workers in Private Homes," *Social Security Bulletin* 2 (March 1939): 20. See also Peter Berger and Thomas Luckmann, *The Social Construction of Reality: A Treatise in the Sociology of Knowledge* (New York: Anchor Books, 1966), 238.

3. The bifurcation process of women is defined by Sarah Matthews, *The Social World of Old Women* (Beverly Hills, Calif.: Sage Publications, 1979), 90-92. This problem of limited self-image is one all social actors confront when they hold definitions of themselves different from those held by others with whom they interact. See also Hegel, *Phenomenology of Mind,* 237, and Berger and Luckmann, *Social Construction,* 149-56.

4. Harris, *Harder We Run,* quoting Mary V. Robinson, "Domestic Workers and Their Employment Relations," U.S. Department of Labor, *Bulletin of the Women's Bureau,* no. 39 (Washington, D.C.: GPO, 1924), 24, 32-33.

5. Katzman, *Seven Days a Week,* 72; Clark-Lewis, "This Work Had a' End: African-American Domestic Workers in Washington, D.C.," in Norton and Groneman, *To Toil the Livelong Day,* 197-200; Henri, *Black Migration,* 53-60; and "Women and Child Labor," *Monthly Labor Review* 15 (July 1922): 116-17.

6. See Elizabeth A. Meese, *(Ex)tensions: Re-figuring Feminist Criticism* (Urbana: University of Illinois Press, 1990), 130-31 and Carolyn Johnson, *Sexual Power: Feminism and the Family in America* (Tuscaloosa: University of Alabama Press, 1992) for negotiation and self-definition research. Stephanie Coontz, *The Way We Never Were: American Families and the Nostalgia Trap* (New York: Basic Books, 1992), 9 investigates the misconceptions about the multigenerational family's ability to *always* work together. Also see Higginbotham, *Righteous Discontent,* 184-86 and McDougald, "Task of Negro Womanhood," 380, for examples of African American women "exercising their capacity to create a means of comprehending and dealing with . . . social worlds. They were culture creators, as well as receivers and learners." Interdisciplinary Folklore Alliance, *Cultural Rights* (Berkeley: Department of Anthropology, University of California, 1982), 2. Also see Alfred Schultz, *The Phenomenology of the Social World* (Chicago: Northwestern University Press, 1967), 63; Rollins, *Between Women,* 216; and Hegel, *Phenomenology of Mind,* 234.

7. Peter Berger, Brigitte Berger, and Hansfried Keller, *The Homeless Mind* (New York: Random House, 1973), 184.

8. "Colored Girl Outraged Miscreant Acquitted," 1922 August-December File, Box G-34, NAACP Papers. During the interview, this woman went on to relate how she was raped and then required to have an abortion. This happened to her in World War I Washington, D.C. She pointed out that this would not have happened in her rural home, or if she had stayed with family members in D.C. She felt, however, that the choice she had made was a positive one, despite this one terrible incident. "No matter what," she said, "you got chances working out. You had more people to learn from. That's true."

9. Indexical expressions are explained in Garfinkel, *Studies in Ethnomethodology,* 38-40.

10. Tuskegee Institute's Alumni Association's national network and influence in Franklin and Moss, *From Slavery To Freedom,* 270-77. For the importance of clubs to women, see Olivia Goodwin letter, November 1933, General Correspondence Files, Box 9, Nannie Helen Burroughs Papers. Also see Patricia Hill Collins, *Black Feminist Thought: Knowledge, Consciousness, and the Politics of Em-*

powerment (Boston: Unwin Hyman, 1990), 95; Elsa Barkley Brown, "Womanist Consciousness: Maggie Lena Walker and the Independent Order of St. Luke," *Sings* 14 (Spring 1989): 610–33; Anne Firor Scott, "Most Invisible of All: Black Women's Voluntary Associations," *Journal of Southern History* 56 (February 1990): 10; Kelley, "'We Are Not What We Seem,'" 80; and Benedict Anderson, *Imagined Communities: Reflections on the Origin and Spread of Nationalism* (London: Verso, 1983), 14–16.

11. Record Group 351, Records of the Government of the District of Columbia, Records of the Blue Plains Industrial School (Colored), *Minutes,* May–September 1927, National Archives and Records Services, Washington, D.C. For additional information on money raised to assist those hurt by disasters and "unbearable peonage" in Washington, D.C., see 8 January 1927 report, Branch Correspondence Files, April–June 1927 Folder, Box 36, NAACP Papers. The problems citizens were having with the Board of Children's Guardians are outlined in two reports presented to the Washington, D.C., branch of the NAACP. See the Board of Children's Guardians reports—March 1924, January–March Folder, Washington, D.C., Branch Records, Box 35, Manuscript Collection, Library of Congress, Washington, D.C.

12. Ibid. See also S. S. Booker's comments delineating the "importance of colored women to fundraising." S. S. Booker to Nannie Helen Burroughs, 29 January 1917, Nannie Helen Burroughs Papers.

13. Mrs. Barbara Dodson Walker explains how her grandmother, Mrs. Fannie Dodson of Georgetown, helped many other domestic workers while sending her son to Howard University medical school; OHP 3-45, 3-45, Oral History Series. Ruth Baer described African Americans as "a people apart" and recalled in great detail the activities of her Washington, D.C., laundress and the children of the laundress. Ruth Baer interview, Oral History Series. Grace Robinson outlines employers' complaints about their young servants' attitudes. She feels the "unions"—the informal network of women workers—encouraged the women to resist their employers demands. Grace Robinson, "My Maid, Impossible Female: A Search for the Perfect Servant," *Liberty* (March 1930): 52, 54. The affirming aspect of values that conflict with those of the dominant group explored by John W. Roberts, *From Trickster to Badman: The Black Folk Hero in Slavery and Freedom* (Philadelphia: University of Pennsylvania Press, 1989); Matthews, *Social World,* 92.

14. "A Washerwoman," *Independent* 57 (November 1904): 1073–76; Ovington, "Negro Home in New York," 25–30; and Katzman, *Seven Days a Week,* 85–92.

15. For domestic's resentment, see Rollins, *Between Women,* 226–32; Billings-

ley, *Climbing Jacob's Ladder,* 126-27; and Louise A. Tally and Joan Scott, "Woman's Life and Working Nineteenth Century Europe," *Comparative Studies in Society and History* 17 (Spring 1975): 36-64. New attitudes of migrant workers are reflected in the *Washington Bee,* 9 August 1919 and 21 August 1919—editorials noting the "time of cringing over."

6. THIS WORK HAD A' END

1. "What is the matter with the girls?" In 1917 Arabella Cater wrote about the new attitudes of young women. General Correspondence Files, Cart-Cay Folder, Box 4, Nannie Helen Burroughs Papers. Caroline Bird, *The Invisible Scar* (New York: David McKay, 1966), 278-79; Jean L. Noble, "An Exploratory Study of Domestics' View of Their Working World" (mimeographed), 1967, Archives For Black Women's History, Washington, D.C., 1-3; Robinson, "Domestic Workers and Their Employment Relations," 21, 69-71; and Woodson and Greene, *Negro Wage Earner,* 231. For statistical data, see United States Department of Commerce, Bureau of the Census, *Negroes in the United States, 1920-1932* (Washington: Government Printing Office, 1935), 290-99; Katzman, *Seven Days a Week,* 2, 89, 290, 293, 294; and *Negroes in the United States, 1790-1920,* 526.

2. See Erma Magnus, "Social, Economic, and Legal Conditions of Domestic Servants: I and II" (typed report), Washington, D.C., 1934. For perspectives on the hidden transcripts in urban structures for change, see Michael H. Frisch, *A Shared Authority: Essays on the Craft and Meaning of Oral and Public History* (Albany: State University of New York Press, 1990), introduction; Kelley, "'We Are Not What We Seem,'" 112; Ruth Schwartx Cowan, "The Industrial Revolution in the Home: Household Technology and Social Change in the Twentieth Century," *Technology and Culture* 17 (January 1976), 2-4; Patricia Branca, "New Perspective on Woman's Work: Comparative Typology," *Journal of Social History* (Winter): 147; Sutherland, *Americans and Their Servants,* xi, xii, xiii; and Katzman, *Seven Days a Week,* 271-79.

3. Interview with Clara Goldberg Schiffer, a 1930s organizer in Washington, D.C., for the Domestic Workers Union. Her Master's thesis, "Women Domestics in Washington, D.C." (George Washington University, 1939) examines the myriad problems of household workers. Her focus was a comparison of the wage-hour and complaint resolution legislation of the District of Columbia with that of seven states and the federal government. The conclusion proposed wage minimums, maximum employment hours, and benefit compensation

strategies for the District of Columbia. Of special value were her statistics on the 1939 median wage ($7.32), oral interviews with domestic workers, analyses of 414 African American domestics' work orders, notes outlining discussions with Kathryn Fox (District of Columbia Employment Center), and the use of raw data from the Old Age Insurance Bureau. Her research in an unpublished study, "The Wages of Women Domestic Servants" (January 1937), was also very helpful because she details the indignities and working conditions of domestic workers in Washington, D.C. Her interviews, notes, and letters to the New York Women's Trade Union League, dated January to May 1938, reflect local workers' insights into household work's crucible of hardship. Efforts to find solutions to the "domestic-service" problem are described in Mary T. Waggaman, "Efforts to Standardize the Working Day for Domestic Service," *Monthly Labor Review* 9 (August 1919): 512; Genevieve Fox, "Wanted: for General Housework," *Association Monthly* 13 (September 1919): 362; Amey Watson, "Employer-Employee Relationships in the Home," *Annals of the American Academy of Political and Social Science* 143 (May 1929): 49-60; Eleanor Roosevelt, "Servants," *Forum* 83 (January 1930): 24-28; Benjamin R. Andrews, "Household Employment: Its Background and Prospects," *Woman's Press* 25 (July 1931): 2-3; Hazel Kyrk, "The Household Worker," *American Federationists* 39 (January 1932): 36; Bromley, "Are Servants People?" 377-79; "Calls For a Kitchen Code Are Now Heard," *New York Times Magazine*, 14 October 1934; "They Want WPA Jobs," *Toledo (Ohio) News Bee*, 15 July 1937, 3; Evelyn Seeley, "Our Feudal Housewives," *Nation* (May 1938): 613-15; Jean Collier Brown, *The Negro Woman Worker*, U.S. Women's Bureau Bulletin (Washington, D.C.: GPO, 1938), 3; Leila Dorman, "Legislation in the Field of Household Employment," *Journal of Home Economics* 31 (February 1939): 90; Florence Kerr, "Training for Household Employment," *Journal of Home Economics* 32 (September 1940): 437; Jean Collier Brown, "Is a Sixty Hour Week Too Long?" *Woman's Press* 34 (November 1940): 476-77; Susan Ware, *Holding Their Own: American Women in the Thirties* (Boston: Twayne, 1982), chap. 2; and Susan Strasser, "Mistress and Maid, Employer and Employee: Domestic Service Reform in the United States, 1897-1920," *Marxist Perspectives* 1 (Winter 1978): 52-67. For national union organizing efforts, see Van Raaphorst, *Union Maids Not Wanted: Organizing Domestic Workers, 1870-1940* (New York: Praeger, 1988); Clark-Lewis, "This Work Had a' End," 211-12.

4. Christiana Smith to Nannie Helen Burroughs, 14 February 1929, Nannie Helen Burroughs Papers; Grace Fox, "Women Domestic Workers in Washington, D.C.," *Monthly Labor Review* 54 (February 1942): 338-59; Rollins, *Between Women*, 231-32; and Gwaltney, *Drylongso*, 166-69. See also James Spradley and

David McCurdy, *The Cultural Experience* (Palo Alto, Calif.: Science and Research Associates, 1972), 68; Ralph Linton, *The Study of Man* (New York: Appleton-Century-Crofts, 1936), 115.

5. Six women received for a six-day week an average of $.47 per day when they began daily paid household work prior to 1920; sixty-eight women received an average $.70 per day when they began daily paid household work prior to 1930; five women received an average of $.59 per day when they began daily paid household work prior to 1936—the year the last woman of this study moved from live-in service to daily, paid household work. Two women could not recall their first salary. For this study, the highest starting wage was $1.04 per day in 1926, and the lowest wage was $.25 per day in 1930. For studies that compare incomes in other cities for the 1920s and 1930s, see *New York Times,* 25 November 1932; "Westchester Woman Seeking Basis for a voluntary Code for Maids," *New York Sun,* 19 March 1934; Ella Baker and Marvel Cooke, "The Bronx [New York] Slave Market," *Crisis* 42 (November 1935): 330-32; and Sergel, *Women in the House.* The Amey Watson Papers, Labor-Management Documentation Center, Martin P. Catherwood Library, New York State College of Industrial and Labor Relations, Cornell University, Ithaca, New York, has domestic-workers income studies for many urban centers. See the Watson Papers for the following years and towns: 1930 studies of income for Chicago, Indianapolis, Flint, and Peoria, Illinois; 1931-32 for Philadelphia and Omaha, Nebraska; 1934 for Evanston, Illinois; 1936 for Hartford, Waterbury, and Litchfield, Connecticut, and Lynchburg, Virginia; 1939 for Hartford, Ann Arbor, and Brooklyn; and Pittsburgh in 1940. Household employment's main problems arising during the 1920s and 1930s are discussed in "Domestic Service in Philadelphia Homes," *Monthly Labor Review* 35 (July 1932): 33-35; Eleanor Johnson, "Household Employment in Chicago," U.S. Women's Bureau Bulletin 106 (Washington, D.C.: GPO, 1933), 7, 40; "Employment Conditions and Unemployment Relief: Unemployment Among Women in the Early Years of the Depression," *Monthly Labor Review* 38 (April 1934): 790-95; "The Servant Problem," *Fortune* 17 (March 1938): 81-85; Fox, "Women Domestic Workers in Washington, D.C.," 338-45; "Maid Famine," *Milwaukee Sentinel,* 28 September 1941, p. A3; and *Detroit Free Press,* 26 April 1942, 4.

6. Schiffer, "Women Domestics in Washington, D.C.," found that of 414 African American household workers in Washington, D.C., 307 (74.2 percent) earned six, seven, or eight dollars per week; 401 earned ten dollars or less per week. The hours ranged from fifty-five to seventy-two per week; sixty hours work a week was considered "utopian" by the women interviewed by Schiffer. Compare to findings of the National Council on Household Employment,

"Negro Wages in Philadelphia" (Washington: Bureau of Old-Age and Survivors Insurance, 1940), 4; and Erma Magnus, "Negro Domestic Workers in Private Homes in Baltimore," *Social Security Bulletin* 4 (October 1941): 11–12. For strategies for coping with jobs, see Jones, *Dispossessed,* 160-95; Gwaltney, *Drylongso,* 166-67; and Palmer, *Domesticity and Dirt,* 83.

7. Clark-Lewis, "This Work Had a' End," 204-7; "Migration," *Opportunity* 9 (July 1931): 206; and Berger and Luckmann, *Social Construction,* 157. Also see Peter Berger, *Invitation to Sociology* (Garden City, New York: Anchor Books, 1963), chap. 3.

8. "It is an inescapable fact that, like the factory system . . . it was the employer's responsibility to make conditions fit for his workers, so it is now with the employers of domestic help" ("Schedule of Work Hours for Your Maid Of More Importance Than a Uniform," *Washington Herald,* 23 October 1916, 8). Workers quest for freedom is documented in Jones, *Dispossessed,* 137. Identity, status, and clothing meanings are explored in Robin D. G. Kelley, "The Riddle of the Zoot: Malcolm Little and Black Cultural Politics during World War II," in *Malcolm X: In Our Own Image,* ed. Joe Wood (New York: St. Martin's Press, 1992), 155-82; Hunter, "Household Workers in the Making," 151-86; Boris, "Black Women and Paid Labor in the Home," 47; Davis, *Women, Race, and Class,* 231; Woodson and Greene, *Negro Wage Earner* 228-32; Katzman, *Seven Days a Week,* 169, 237; and Berger and Luckmann, *Social Construction,* 89-92.

9. Osterund and Jones, "If I must say so myself," 1-2; Nelson, "Begging the Question"; Morgan, "Something's in the Water"; Mary Anderson, "Plight of the Negro in Domestic Labor," *Journal of Negro Education* (January 1936): 66-72. Joey Lee Dillard in *Black English* notes this marked detachment from personal responsibility may have been caused by time perceptions African Americans use and/or the fact that an average of fifty-nine years had passed since these women had worked as live-in servants. But the narrative distance also appears to reflect a detached and subordinate self-concept in relation to their family members, their live-in employers, and their live-in experience as a whole. See Joey Lee Dillard, *Black English* (New York: Vintage Books, 1972), 62, 102, 282.

10. For examples of the importance of "informal networks" among Washington, D.C., domestic workers, see "Organizing D.C. Housekeepers," *Washington Star,* 10 February 1917; "Why Doesn't the Government Give Protection to Domestic Workers" (pamphlet), Washington, D.C.: Domestic Workers Union, June 1939; Mary T. Waggoman, "Wartime Job Opportunities for Household Workers in Washington, D.C.," *Monthly Labor Review* (March 1945):

575–84; Ruth A. Sykes Report, File 2-366, Records of the National Council of Negro Women, Records of the Government of the District of Columbia, Record Group 351, National Archives, Washington, D.C.; Women's Educational Equity Action Project (WEEAP), "Demonstration Projects Reports" (Washington, D.C.: National Committee on Household Employment, 1970-77) (the series is located in the Mary McLeod Bethune Museum and Archives for Black Women's History); and "Domestic Workers Organizing Project," *Metropolitan Women's Organizing Project Newsletter* (December 1993): 3. Elaborate social networks are the focus of Victoria E. Bynum, *Unruly Women: The Politics of Social and Sexual Control in the Old South* (Chapel Hill: University of North Carolina Press, 1992), chaps. 2 and 3; Berger and Luckmann, *Social Construction,* 72–73, 93–95, 159–80; and Bott, *Family and Social Newtork,* chaps. 3, 4, and 5.

11. Phyllis Palmer, "Housewife and Household Worker: Employer-Employee Relationships in the Home," in Norton and Groneman, *To Toil the Livelong Day,* 184–90. Brown, *Household Workers,* 30–38; Barbara Basler, "Underpaid, Overworked and From the Philippines," *New York Times International,* 28 August 1990, 3; Robin Miller, "A Maid's Tale: Barred From Entering the Front Door," *Baltimore Sun,* 8 October 1990, 6.

12. Nell Irvin Painter, "Foreword," in *The Great Migration in Historical Perspective,* by Joe William Trotter, Jr. (Bloomington: Indiana University Press, 1991), ix.

13. Most studies trace the weakening of these mutual-benefit associations to the widespread unemployment of the Depression. For example, Jessie Blayton stressed that the economic recession of 1926-29 taxed all workers. Gunnar Myrdal suggested that alternative forms of life insurance provided the benefits once available to the migrants solely through mutual-benefit associations. See Jessie Blayton, "Are Negro Banks Safe?" *Opportunity* 15 (May 1937): 139–41; Myrdal, *American Dilemma,* 316–17, 1263. Also see Edward Denison, *Economic Growth in the United States* (Washington, D.C.: Casey Press, 1961), 2–4; Jessie Blayton, "The Negro in Banking," *Bankers Magazine* 4 (December 1936): 511–14; Samuel Rosenberg, *Negro Managed Associations in the United States,* in Berry and Blassingame, *Long Memory,* chap. 6; and Eugene K. Jones, "The Negro in Industry and Urban Life," *Opportunity* 12 (May 1934): 142–44.

14. Cheryl Townsend Gilkes, "Holding Back the Ocean with a Broom: Black Women and Community Work," in *The Black Woman,* ed. LaFrances Rodgers-Rose (Beverly Hills, Calif.: Sage Publications, 1980), 217–32.

15. Toni Morrison, "What the Black Woman Thinks About Women's Lib,"

New York Times Magazine, 22 August 1971, 63. Also see Jean Comaroff, *Body of Power, Spirit of Resistance: The Culture and History of South African People* (Chicago: University of Chicago Press, 1985), 6.

16. "Homage is Paid to Old Servants," *Washington Star,* 24 January 1917, reported the winner of the contest launched by an earlier article, "Domestic Longest in Service of one Family Will Get Ten Dollars," *Washington Star,* 3 November 1916, 2. Also see "Servant in a Family For five Generations," *Washington Times,* 1 November 1916, 7. For an overview of how employers saw African American women as servants first and family members only incidentally, see Jones, *Labor of Love,* 127; Rollins, *Between Women,* 119–122; and Katzman, *Seven Days a Week,* 176.

17. Strategies for survival and empowerment strategies discussed in Hobsbawm, "Peasants and Politics," 12, 16. The "prosaic and constant struggle" as a form of resistance is discussed in James Scott, *Weapons of the Weak: Everyday Forms of Peasant Resistance* (New Haven, Conn.: Yale University Press, 1985). Record Group 351, Records of the Government of the District of Columbia, Records of the Public Welfare Board, Division of Emergency Relief—Subsistence Garden Committee—Annual Report for 1 July 1933 to 30 June 1934, National Archives and Records Service, Washington, D.C. These records have women identified as "domestics" heading community gardens committees in northeast and southwest Washington, D.C.

18. Higginbotham's *Righteous Discontent,* chap. 7, shows how this valorized African American institution created new value systems and mechanisms for women during the "great migration" era. For gender paradoxes, democratic space, and contested space, see August Meier and Elliott Rudwick, "The Boycott Movement against Jim Crow Streetcars in the South, 1900–1906," in *Along the Color Line: Explorations in the Black Experience,* ed. August Meier and Elliott Rudwick (Urbana: University of Illinois Press, 1976), 267–89; Jo Blatti, "Public History and Oral History," *Journal of American History* 77 (September 1990): 615; John Bodnar, "Power and Memory in Oral History: Workers and Managers at Studebaker," *Journal of American History* 75 (March 1989): 1201–21; Barbara Allen, "Oral History and Puerto Rican Women," *Oral History Review* 16 (Fall 1988): 1–93; and Scott, *Gender and the Politics of History.* See also Edward G. Lowry, "Washington Itself Again," *Weekly Review* (24 November 1920): 496–97. Lowry blamed the new wave of segregation in Washington on Woodrow Wilson's pro-South entourage and an influx of public functionaries and civil service employees. Carter G. Woodson wrote that during the 1920s Washington became "southernized"; this factor encouraged the growth of racial animosity. Carter Woodson, *The Negro in Our History* (Washington: Associated

Publishers, 1931), 527-28. See also J. W. Buzzell, "Washington Before, During and After the War," *Stone and Webster Journal* (March 1919): 175-86; Billingsley, *Climbing Jacob's Ladder,* 355-56, 372-74; Andolsen, *Daughters of Jefferson,* 118-20; Jones, *Labor of Love,* 132, 148, 229; Katzman, *Seven Days a Week,* 163.

8. THE SOUND STAYS IN MY EARS

1. McDougald, "Task of Negro Womanhood," 369.
2. Susan L. Taylor, "Passage," *Essence* (October 1991): 51.

INDEX

Page numbers in italics refer to illustrations; names of persons in italics indicate pseudonyms.